the Dancing HAND of GOD

VOLUME 2

*Unveiling the Fullness of God
through Apostolic Signs, Wonders and Miracles*

James Maloney

WESTBOW
PRESS
A DIVISION OF THOMAS NELSON

ISBN: 978-1-4497-3024-6 (e)
ISBN: 978-1-4497-3025-3 (sc)
ISBN: 978-1-4497-3026-0 (hbk)

Library of Congress Control Number: 2011919333

WestBow Press books may be ordered through booksellers or by contacting:

WestBow Press
A Division of Thomas Nelson
1663 Liberty Drive
Bloomington, IN 47403
www.westbowpress.com
1-(866) 928-1240

Printed in the United States of America

WestBow Press rev. date: 11/17/2011

Dedication

To the late Frances Metcalfe and the Golden Candlestick ministry: I pray, by the grace of God, your fifty and more years of intercession and ministry in worshiping our Lord will find the fruit of your sacrifices within these pages.

Acknowledgements

In the course of my life and ministry, there have been many wonderful men and women who have helped shape the person I am today and, therefore, this book. It would take more than space allows mentioning them all, but I could not call this book complete without gratefully acknowledging the following people:

My best friend, confidant, sounding board and "pastor" — my beautiful wife, Joy, for her unwavering support, unconditional love and unending patience; she is unquestionably the most gifted and intelligent woman I have ever met, and I am most grateful for her partnership these past thirty-plus years. My son, Andrew, a man with a spirit of excellence — I recognize the supreme importance of raising up the next generation, and he truly is a person of his mother's and my spiritual DNA. Many of the insights in expounding the teachings of this book come directly from him, and for all of his help in editing the manuscript I thank him. My lovely daughter, Alisa, who I knew would live up to her namesake, "joyful," when I held her in the palm of my hand and told the Lord, "I claim her." I love you all!

My brother-in-law, David Alsobrook, is quite possibly, I consider, the single greatest Bible teacher in modern history. I am most appreciative for his doctrinal insight that helped shape my foundation in the Word. The late Brant Baker and all who were a part of the Shekinah Fellowship team: their love and impartation, encouraging a teenager in the release of the miraculous, left more of an impression on me throughout my

life than they could ever know. Drs. Chuck and Mary Ann Flynn, for all of their timely prophetic wisdom, are two of the finest people I know, and I consider myself most blessed to acknowledge them here. Also, Mario Murillo — simply one of the most dynamic and profound revivalists of our time, in my opinion — his distinct message and release of tremendous power continue to be true inspirations that influence my life to this day.

Table of Contents

Foreword

History has been shaped by people with extraordinary courage. When the courageous ones are friends of God, they impact mindsets and culture for generations. The secret place with God is where friends are made.

In the place of intimacy with God is where eternal victories are won. A true friend prefers the favor of God to the recognition of man. King David was one such individual. He fought the lion and the bear when no one was looking. But David's victory in secret qualified him to beat Goliath when two entire nations were watching. That is a common destiny for a friend of God. God will often trust them with the recognition of man because favor with God is all that matters to them. They earn God's trust, and in turn, God entrusts them with power and authority to do the works of Christ on a very large scale. What is available for everyone is realized by only a few. Dr. James Maloney is such a man: a friend of God, and a chosen vessel of the Lord.

One of the greatest privileges in life is to honor a friend of God. In honoring them, we honor God Himself. He takes it personal. In this case, it is my privilege to honor James for his service to the Lord and for his wonderful book, *The Dancing Hand of God*. I don't know of another book quite like it. It is revelatory, insightful, inspirational, and perhaps most importantly, it is timely. We need this book! Whether it's the report of miracles, the story of his call into ministry, or the insights into church life of the last days, each justifies the careful study of this book. Theories can inspire the imagination. But stories and teachings from authentic biblical experiences release the power for personal transformation. That will no doubt be a byproduct of reading this book.

The story of his call into ministry is one of the most unusual and delightfully supernatural stories I've ever heard. And I never get tired of hearing it. I am fascinated by how God pursued and called James. And while my personal call was so different from his, my understanding of God is expanded through such variety.

James' experiences in the miraculous fascinate me. My heart so longs for the authentic ministry of Jesus to be seen in the earth that each of Dr. Maloney's stories gives me an education. I for one am not satisfied with nice ideas. I must have the real, or at least be in its pursuit. Every time we're together, I get to hear more of the most unusual ways that God uses this man. My faith is strengthened, and my focus becomes more resolved. He has that effect on me.

I need men like James Maloney in my life. The wisdom I gain from them is priceless. And I need books like *The Dancing Hand of God*. There's so much mystery in the life of miracles. Yet Dr. Maloney unravels things that were never meant to remain hidden, as the realm of mystery has become our inheritance.

I pray that as you read this book your heart will burn — burn with new passion for God, burn with hunger for truth, and burn with desire for the authentic gospel that displays miracles, signs and wonders. The ingredients needed for such a fire exist on the pages of *The Dancing Hand of God.*

Bill Johnson
Senior Pastor – Bethel Church, Redding, California
Author – *When Heaven Invades Earth* and
Face to Face with God

1

Unveiling the Holiness of God

THE ALL-NIGHT MEN'S PRAYER MEETING

After being delivered from the demon of rejection and beginning to see my authority over the wall of isolation, the time I spent at CFNI became one of the most powerful eras of my life. I began to sense a call to prophesy over people, and after the school's leadership noticed the gift within me, struggling to come out, they began to cultivate it in my life. A handful of other students and I were given permission, in controlled circumstances, to prophesy over the student body — to practice on them, as it were. I mean, how else are you supposed to learn?

Anyway, the classes were dynamic, my doctrinal knowledge was growing exponentially, my closeness to the Father in prayer and worship had never been stronger. I felt the call of God on my life to keep my covenant with Him and go into ministry, working on behalf of the Golden Candlestick. The anointing was bubbling up from my spirit. It was during this time of growing in Him that He revealed another attribute of Himself to me: His holiness.

A group of about fifty or sixty men, including myself, would meet upstairs in the library for an all-night prayer meeting. It was a perfect opportunity to press through with one's fellow students, calling upon the Lord, interceding as He directed. There was no choice but to stay all night with the guys and pray because the custodian locked the doors at ten o'clock and wouldn't open them up again until six the next morning. "'Night-'night, fellas." Back in the '70s, they were more lax on fire code and the like....

One night, it initially seemed we were warring against something in the spirit. These waves of fervent prayer and war-like tongues would roll through us. Unity was being orchestrated within the group; we were coming into one mind and accord, feeling the movings of the Spirit in unison. It was a really cool sensation to be grouped together and *feeling* what we should pray next.

Then about four in the morning, we finally broke through and reached a heightened realm of the Spirit. The room swooned. Instantaneously all fifty or so of us were slain in the Spirit and lay as dead men for about twenty minutes. Now, when it was all over I asked a couple of the other students if they'd had the same experience as me, to which they replied, yes, they had. I am assuming the rest of the students had the same experience as well, but since I didn't speak to each one of them, I don't know for sure.

As we lay there on the floor, the most intense reverence filled the room. We all fell silent in our prayers and could not open our eyes, no matter how hard we tried. We could not move. The presence of the Lord was in the place, and we all fell out under the power in awe and veneration. Remember we were upstairs in the library, and there was about twenty or twenty-five steps leading up to where we were laying.

Suddenly Someone started walking loudly up the steps. And the strangest thought came to me as I lay there, immobile, my eyes shut tight: *Well, the door's locked. No one can get in.* But nevertheless, I heard Someone trudge up the steps. I recall it was late October or early November, and I was thinking it was rather weird that this Person should be wearing sandals at that time of year, but I remember hearing the clacking *flip-flop* of sandals as He climbed the stairs, one at a time, rather slowly, like He was being deliberate.

The Son of God entered the room. Somehow we knew it was Jesus, and He was wearing sandals and a robe.

I believe He was wearing a robe because He came to stand at my feet for a couple of seconds and then passed by me. As He walked next to me, I could physically feel the hem of His garment cover my entire body from feet to head. If it wasn't a robe, then it possibly might have been a cape or something long like that, trailing over my body as He passed by, but I believe it was a robe. The point is, Jesus walked by me and His train covered over me.

Then I sensed Him walk over to another man laid out on the floor and do the same thing. This went on about twenty minutes, Jesus walking up and down beside people, covering them with His garment (others experienced the same thing, they later told me.) We hardly dared to breathe; no one shuffled or spoke.

After this unique action, Jesus quietly walked back down the stairs. He never said a word.

I suppose He disappeared when He reached the bottom – I doubt He took a stroll across the street, but He might have. He's God so if He wants to walk around that rough section of South Dallas in the middle of the night, He can. I mean, *I* wouldn't, but then I'm not that brave!

After He left, we found we could move and open our eyes, so we stumbled back to our feet and began to discuss what had just happened among ourselves. It was a very singular, strange kind of occurrence obviously, but His walking between us caused us to begin to testify to one another what we'd been set free from, what sin issues we had been struggling with – very personal, private confessions one to another. When His hem covered us, a particular issue or sin was imprinted upon our minds that God wanted to deal with.

Mine was profaneness.

We confessed wrong motives and attitudes, the weights we had been struggling with, our fears and rejections. We asked forgiveness of one another, putting the wrong motives right, returning to a pureness of heart.

The appearance of Christ in that all-night men's prayer meeting gave us an unveiling of what it meant for Him to be holy, and we wanted to be holy as He was holy. Jesus expressed a breaker anointing that unveiled the holiness of God, and we were never the same again.

THE HOLY VERSUS THE PROFANE

I think you would agree that we have many people in the Body, while possibly understanding the Father's heart, they have not met with His holiness. We all need to have an unveiling of His awesome sanctification, and because many of us have not had that unveiling, there is a marked lack of character among His people, a certain lack of integrity. I know that's a strong statement, and it's meant to be corrective in love, but wouldn't you have to agree that we have too much mixture of holiness and unholiness in the Church at large?

Recall from the first chapter of Volume 1 that the purpose of supernatural encounters is so "That I might know Him!" Not just in His love and mercy, but in His holiness and supreme righteousness. See, I think we tend to lack a reverential fear of the Lord sometimes. We let too much sin slide from those who are supposed to be purchased back from sin into the Kingdom of Light. We have too many evangelists falling into habitual sin. Too many pastors getting hooked on illegal or prescription drugs. Too many prophets committing fornication. We have too many members of the congregation still holding on to the old ways of their lives before getting saved. There's too much mixture. Too much profaneness in something that is to be completely holy and set apart: the manifestation of the Kingdom of God.

Again, as always in this book, I'm not trying to bludgeon anyone to death with a stone here. I get the whole "pull out your own plank before pointing out someone else's speck" deal. (Matthew 7:5) The point is not to condemn but to bring to light an issue that must be addressed if we want to see the greater miracles restored to the Church in these end days. I'll say it again, I am not perfect. I have nothing in myself that can compel you to be holy. But the Spirit of God living within me (and I hope within you) compels all of us to separate that which is evil from that which is good, and I am convinced He is mandating me to point out a few of these inconsistencies and then also to share the hope of the restoration of holiness. This book is a book of hope and answers, not doom and gloom.

The Father God is requiring the apostolic ones to teach His people the difference between the holy and the profane, the clean and the unclean. (Ezekiel 44:23) "Holy" is the Greek word *hagios* (Strong's #40) which can be rendered, "to be godlike, to designate sacred and separate that which God designates as sacred and separate." It quite literally means "an awful thing." Not in our modern sense of "awful," but in the old-fashioned sense, "awe-full, serious, severe."

As an example, how many know that the marriage institution is holy? The vows you say are holy before God — you designate them holy because God calls them holy. Therefore, by breaking those vows, for whatever reason, one is guilty of mixing the holy with the profane.

As Iverna Tompkins said in one of her teachings, a profane person says, "I want what I want, when I want it, and I don't care who it hurts, who I've got to walk over to get my selfish way." That was the problem with Esau — he was profane.

"...Lest there be any... profane [godless] person like Esau, who for one morsel of food sold his birthright." (Hebrews 12:16) He minimized the importance of his birthright, the blessing that was rightfully his by his place in his father's house. "...'Look, I am about to die [of hunger]; so what is this birthright to me?'" (Genesis 25:32)

Oh, give me a break, the hairy dude was just hungry — I doubt he would've really died, but it was more important to him to have a full belly; and it made no difference to him how the consequences of his decision would affect the children of Israel by saying, "Here, take it. Here is my birthright. I'll give it away for a bowl of food." Incidentally, the bowl of food was a stew of lentils and some bread. Like, I won't eat that on a diet! If you're gonna mess up a nation for thousands of years because of your stomach, at least demand *filet mignon*, right?

I write facetiously not to patronize but to show just how absurd a profane person can be. Because Esau refused to call holy that which God called holy, his descendants were constantly at odds with his brother's from that point forward. Then afterward, once he was satiated, the poor, foolish man realized what he had given away and sought to have his birthright restored to him. But even then it wasn't in true, godly repentance, because the only thing he was concerned about was what he had lost — not that he had profaned that which was designated holy. (See Genesis 27.)

God is against profaneness as He is completely holy — the two attributes are archenemies and cannot sit beside one another for long. One of the signs and wonders of His apostles is to unveil the profaneness in the Church, calling the people to be holy, thus creating an apostolic company that expresses the holiness of Christ to the world at large. The problem is we have many church leaders and itinerant ministers who exhibit an excessive amount of selfishness and what I term a "Prima Donna" spirit, not to put too fine a point on it. I mean,

I love these preachers in the Lord, but it's hard not to shake my head sometimes and just say, "Oh, please!" when I hear about the latest embarrassment where so-and-so tore into the church custodian because it was three degrees hotter in the auditorium and, therefore, the Holy Spirit couldn't operate. (You think I'm exaggerating.) As if the Holy Spirit cares how hot it is! I'd like to take those kinds of guys to India with me: I'll show you hot!

Yeah, India. Whew. It's 110 degrees, 99% humidity, kids are screaming and crying in the dirt at your feet, two thousand Hindus and Muslims desperately in need of a shower are lined up in front of you waiting for a miracle. It's *not* the fragrance of the Lord you smell in those settings. And yet, somehow, the Holy Spirit still manages to move mightily!

Perhaps He wears a stronger deodorant....

And then to top it all off, you get to eat a bowl of dog meat curry for dinner and sleep on the floor of some poor pastor's hovel with the rats and tomorrow night's meal. Funny how those folks see the mind-blowing miracles, and we don't, isn't it?

Friends, I love you all, but we must stand against this Fresh-Cut Flower Syndrome. I'll explain what I mean. While I recognize no one is perfect, I tire of seeing these leaders, many with powerful ministry expressions, who act caring and unpretentious behind the pulpit, and then the poor soul who has to drive them back to the hotel gets an earful about why the man of God needs fresh-cut flowers delivered daily to his suite. Again, not exaggerating. We need a revelation of the holiness of God, not gardenias! Or was it tulips?

You get the idea.

I recently heard a story of one minister in front of probably two thousand people upbraiding a man for slinking out of the auditorium during the altar call. I mean, he dressed that brother down! I was told the minister spoke to the man as if he was a ten-year-old child, proclaiming that it was his disturbance that would prevent these sick people from getting healed. It was his fault they left the meeting unrestored, thank you very much. Hope you feel good about yourself. Yeah, that won't heap condemnation on the man's head.... Now look, I wasn't there — maybe the man *was* being distracting. OK. Or maybe he was just trying to get to the bathroom. The point is the Holy Spirit is a big enough God to be able to work through the disturbance and touch those people where they're at, noisy toilet-goers aside.

And while you find some stones to toss in my general direction, let me say to that poor man if he happens to read this, "Sir, I apologize on behalf of my minister brethren. Those people would've been healed with or without you needing to use the potty."

This chapter might catch me the most flack out of all, and I actually wrestled with the notion of putting it in... for about five seconds. I hope by this point of the book you know a little of my heart, and you recognize that while I don't censor my convictions, it's from a true desire to see the miraculous prevalent in your life that I write so strongly. I'm not here to call this preacher a jerk, or that pastor a wimp, but I do want to give concrete examples of *why* we aren't seeing the miraculous as we should on a church-wide scale. And perhaps one of those reasons is a veiling of the holiness of God, and a battle between that holiness and the profaneness of mankind.

So let me give an example of just how profane people can get.

THE BLIND GIRL FROM THE ROCKIES

I was ministering at a church service in Colorado, and I had gone over time. It looked like I was going to miss my flight out of there. This happens quite frequently; the life of a traveling minister always seems to be running late to someplace else. Once the service was wrapped up, I was briskly walked to the back of the church in order to hop in a car and try to race over to the local airport just in time to catch my plane.

As I was being escorted down the aisle, a woman seated in one of the chairs had a baby girl asleep on her lap. I later found out she was the sister of the child's mother. She reached out to stop me and said, "Will you please pray for this little girl?"

Honestly, I was feeling extremely rushed and anxious that I would miss my flight, so I didn't really take the time to focus on the child and see what she was in need of. Nevertheless, I bent down to lay my hand on her and prayed, "Lord, just do the creative miracle that she needs." It seemed as if the words just rolled out of my spirit. I smiled at the lady and then left.

The man who drove me to the airport must have been a distant kin to Mario Andretti. I made my flight, the little girl dismissed out of my mind.

It turns out that little girl had been born with no pupils or irises. I mean, there was nothing but white eyeballs. No hole, no color, just white. The pupils and irises had never been created. She was completely blind.

The morning after I prayed for her, the baby was crying in her crib. The mother entered the room, looked down at her child, and screamed. The dad raced in the room in a panic.

The baby was looking up at them with brilliant, sparkling blue eyes!

God had created irises and pupils for her overnight!

I received a letter from the mother's sister — the one who had been at the church — detailing all of this. Sometime later, I was back in the area and was able to meet with the sister. We both rejoiced over so amazing a miracle. After a few minutes' conversation, I looked around and thought to ask:

"So where's the girl? Where are her parents?"

"Oh, they won't come. They aren't walking with the Lord," the sister replied, downcast.

I was crushed. You mean to tell me, after God did that for them, they *still* didn't follow Him? Yep. Turns out they were drug and alcohol users. You would've thought something astounding like that would've been more important than drugs and booze, huh? I mean, if that had happened to *my* daughter, I'd have gone out seeking this God, wondering what He was all about. I would've at least *thanked* Him. Wouldn't you?

It saddens me to say these parents were profane. See, just because someone witnesses a miracle, it doesn't necessarily mean their hearts will be softened toward God. These parents chose their own selfish lifestyle over the benefits of a God who could do something like that for their little girl. That's profane.

I pray that they will change, or at the very least, I hope that little girl will not be profane like her parents....

Partakers of the Divine

When Jesus walked between us that night in the prayer meeting in CFNI's library, I had a startling revelation of just how *HOLY* the Lord is, and He wasn't going to put up with too much of my sniveling pretentiousness or hyper-spiritual arrogance without some worthless mixture of profaneness leaving its mark on my ministry for the next sixty years. Without that unveiling of the holiness of the Father, we can bleed our true intent for miraculous ministry into an imitation of divine power, and we start getting some funky business going on behind the pulpit.

"...As His divine power has given to us all things that pertain to life and godliness through the knowledge of Him who called us by glory and virtue, by which have been given to us exceedingly great and precious promises, that through these you may be partakers of the divine nature, having escaped the corruption [depravity] that is in the world through lust. But also for this very reason, giving all diligence, add to your faith virtue...." (2 Peter 1:2-5)

We as born-again Christians are partakers of the divine nature. That means God Himself lives inside of us, and we have been given life and godliness (that means "God-like-ness," for the record) through the salvation of Jesus Christ provided by the cross. It's not arrogance to acknowledge the "God-like-ness" we possess by being grafted into the Body of Jesus Christ, and in fact, it is error *not* to acknowledge such. But that godliness comes at a price: if God is holy, we must also be holy. To be anything other than holy creates a defilement, and for those of us who stand behind the pulpit, our defilement can be transferred to another person, just as the miraculous power of God residing within us can be conferred upon others.

It's like this, if someone who is defiled comes up to you and gives you a prophetic word, you not only get the word that God intended, it's possible you can get all the other junk behind the prophet, too. It gets all mixed together. So if a word is placed in your spirit that is not of God, and if you accept the word *as from God,* the defilement in the vessel (the prophet) can enter you. You have a choice, and so then you need discernment to make the correct choice. Accept or reject.

Let me give an example.

The "Elder" of the City

I was ministering in a large city and had been asked by some church leaders to attend a ministers' gathering of about seventy or eighty pastors from the local area. They were all rallying around this particular individual.

When I met him, the first thing he said to me after giving his name was, "I am the elder over this city."

Remember that this city is quite large (over a million people.) So when he said that, immediately these warning klaxons went off in my spirit: *Ooo-gah! Ooo-gah!* I knew something wasn't right about this man, but these peers around me, some of them I'd held revivals with before, all believed this man to be tremendously anointed; so I just smiled and nodded.

"That's nice," I said.

"I'd like to give you a prophetic word," this man continued.

Well, sure. I'm always open to hear from the Lord. So he laid his hands on me and proceeded to give me one of the most detailed prophetic words I've ever received. In the many, many years I've been used to give prophetic words and have received them, let me say, I've *never* been given one as detailed and specific as this man's word. He was sharing things that had happened to me when I was six years of age, in my teenage years, things I had shared with my wife the week before, ministry events that had happened to me....

But here's the kicker: the more he shared with me, no matter how specific it was, the worse I felt.... This weight of condemnation came upon me, my stomach ached, my spirit was grieved. I felt *dark*. This word wasn't uplifting me. It was making me feel terrible!

As he continued, I began to sense he was profaned; he had received some sort of defilement and was operating out of a spirit of divination. His *junk* started filtering down to me as he was prophesying.

Finally he finished. And I just stood there, feeling miserable, dirty, defiled myself.

He looked into my eyes, his hands still on my shoulders, and said, "Do you accept this prophetic word?"

When he said that, I saw in his eyes the flash of the demon of defilement — just a little glitter, nothing overt, but it was there! And I knew in that split second of time I had a decision to make. If I saved face in front of these church leaders and said, "Yes," I knew I would enter into everything he was harboring, all his defilement. This is called the Law of Transference.

I think most Charismatics, in order to maintain peace, and probably because the word had been so specific — so it *must* be godly, right? — would have accepted the word.

But I couldn't. Later on, with the help of some minister friends, I was able to just shake it off.

When the ministers of that city heard of my rejection of the word, the majority of those people cut my ministry off. They blackballed my name in that specific area because I'd withstood the "elder of the city."

Sadly to say, several years later, a large majority of those leaders who associated with that man no longer had ministries. Many were ruined. Some no longer had even their families. And I've just recently learned, I'm pained to say, that "elder" died a grievous, painful death just a while back. How sobering is that?

There can be a terrible price for associating with defilement and profaneness, my dear friends. Take care!

Vessels of Vanity

Even if the vessel is sincere in his or her intentions to give you that word, whatever spiritual, emotional or mental baggage they continue to leave unchecked can be attributed to their *vanity*, and eventually the vessel is ultimately lessened in divine unction and left with tarnishing and corruption — an imitation of what was once divine. The key to note here is the vessel's vainness, for it is simply egotism to want to harbor that which spoils one's godly nature.

I can't say it enough: none of us are perfect; we all have issues to work through. But I do mean habitual corruption in a weakened area, consistent or constant defilement over a period of time, *does* lead to an imitation of the divine. It is a simple fact, but maybe not a very popular one. If we continue to deny the sanctifying work of the Holy Spirit, our manifestation of His power will become tarnished. The defilement comes not just from the sin itself, but the *harboring* of the sin. There isn't a blanket "free period" where one can get away with habitual sin — who knows when the defilement enters? We shouldn't be getting to that point in the first place!

So keep balance here, dear readers. There *is* a difference between a single act of sin, which still needs to be confessed, yes; and rather a perpetual state of sin that brings defilement. If a minister lays hands on you, don't be petrified of this principle, for we all have shortcomings, but do be wary of an unremitting area of weakness in the person's life. It takes discernment. You might not inherit the defilement itself, but it is possible to inherit the *oppression* that is associated with the defilement, and that's bad enough as it is!

Back to the main point, it is vanity to assume it's OK to live in a state of persistent contamination with sin. Take a few moments to read Ezekiel 13. I'll spare myself the tedium of writing out the entire passage, and it's good exercise for you to open your Bible while reading this book, since the Bible is what's most important and not what's printed here. Besides, I can't ever say it as nicely as the prophets could! But I will point out a few of the more poignant verses relating to this vanity of imitation men.

"'They have envisioned futility and false divination, saying, "Thus says the Lord!" But the Lord has not sent them; yet they hope that the word may be confirmed.'" (Ezekiel 13:6)

How's that for vanity! "Oh, Lord, I hope this word I'm about to give comes true...." Yuck.

"...'Because you have spoken nonsense and envisioned lies, therefore I am indeed against you,' says the Lord God." (Ezekiel 13:8)

Again, their vanity is not excused. In fact, the Lord God is against them, and trust me when I say that's a *bad thing* to have the Lord God against you.

The bottom line is that the apostolic people must *discern* what is divinely inspired and what an imitation of that divinity is. One of the greatest gifts a church body can incorporate into their culture is the discernment of spirits; and sad to say, in most circles, it is one of the most sorely underused gifts, as made prevalent by the rampant abuse of the supernatural under the guise of being "divinely inspired." That's not to say that every imitation of the divine is demonically motivated, but more often than not it stems from trying to mix the flesh with the godly.

The world is crying out for the divine! Unfortunately, they often are getting an imitation, as seen in the unbridled rise in occult practice being "normalized" in daily life. It takes an apostolic, breaker anointing to unveil the false "supernatural" (the preternatural, actually) from the true supernatural, found only in the realm of the Father's actions.

Kim Clement brings out a great definition of the divine as, "the essence or personality of God manifested." We as apostolic people are supposed to manifest the true essence or personality of the Father as we yield our members to His works. Romans 12:1-2 says, "I beseech you therefore, brethren, by the mercies of God, that you present your bodies a living sacrifice, holy, acceptable to God, which is your reasonable service. And do not be conformed to this world, but be transformed by the renewing of your mind, that you may prove what is that good and acceptable and perfect will of God." There is only one good, acceptable, perfect will of God: that His people be transformed into holy sacrifices. Anything else falls outside His purposes. We are to be *fashioned* into His essence (which is holy.) Being "conformed" to the world is to be united or associated with that which is outside the will of God.

Dear readers, you are what you worship! If you align yourself with this world system that is outside the will of God (meaning a godless age) you cannot be transformed into the likeness of His divine Personage, that which is holy and set apart for a unique work that is against the status quo. Holiness, vanity. Ne'er the twain shall meet.

If we try to express the divine power of God without being transformed into His perfect will, we express a mere imitation, and that can lead people into deception and lust for a world system they have no business following after.

One of the keys to the apostolic is being able to separate that which is divinity from that which is divination. Take Simon the Sorcerer found in Acts 8:9-10. "But there was a certain man called Simon, who previously practiced sorcery [magic] in the city and astonished the people of Samaria, claiming that he was someone great, to whom they all gave heed, from the least to the greatest, saying, 'This man is the great power of God.'"

This warlock (a male witch) operated under a spirit of Balaam (see later in this chapter), which was a familiar spirit that would drift in and out of the soulish realm. Indeed, this spirit does have some power, so much so that Simon was renowned throughout the nation – the people must have seen *something* to laud him so. The chapter in Acts goes on to show that Simon was baptized and believed in the true workings of the Spirit wrought by the apostles, but his great sin was to believe this power could be purchased for a price. See, he didn't fully count himself holy, repenting of his imitation (witchcraft) and turning totally toward the Lord. Simon didn't want the dealings, crushings and humblings of God to transform him into a true vehicle for God's power. He thought he could find a shortcut to the divine. And Peter rebuked him so, saying, "'For I see that you are poisoned by bitterness and bound by iniquity.'" (Acts 8:23)

It pains me to write that I have seen these types of ministers more often than I care to admit. But the good news is the apostles have been sent to discern the intentions of these mixed up people, calling out that which is a familiar spirit and that which is the true Spirit, undiluted and released among the people.

"'And they shall teach My people the difference between the holy and the unholy, and cause them to discern between the unclean and the clean. In controversy they shall stand as judges, and judge it according to My judgments....'" (Ezekiel 44:23-24)

It takes more than an *astonishment* to declare a supernatural act divine. Simon himself "was amazed, seeing the miracles and signs which were done." (Acts 8:13) But it wasn't enough to bring about a true transformation. Even the people of Samaria were astonished at Simon's magic, but the lifestyle of the man did not reflect the conviction, repentance and love of one being transformed into the perfect will of

God. One must have God's *approval* (that is the anointing) in order to display the divine. (Kim Clement)

I want to point out, however, that if you are someone who has been on the brunt end of a defiled minister, don't let it get the best of you. Just shake it off! Remember 1 Thessalonians 5:20 says, "Do not despise prophecies." So often people who get "burned" by a bad prophetic word, inspired by the spirit of Balaam instead of the Spirit of the Lord, turn away from all things supernatural. That's not the proper attitude to have. Just cultivate discernment, seek God's approval on a person, and if you get rubbish, just shrug it off as such. Do not turn away from the supernatural because you've been left with a bad taste in your mouth in the past. Shake it off! Look, even if they're not completely perfect, there are true men and women out there who properly display the approval of God in their ministries — if there is the junk out there, then there must also be the good stuff out there! The question, then, is how do we as apostolic people get that approval?

One key principle in having the approval of God on one's ministry expression can be found in Exodus 30:22-33. This passage is speaking about the holy anointing oil, which you'll recall the *approval* of God is the *anointing* of God manifested in one's life. See how I correlate those two attributes together so nicely and tie in a natural example into a spiritual one?

"'It [speaking of the anointing oil] shall not be poured on man's flesh....'" (Exodus 30:32) That's the principle: the anointing shall not be poured on man's flesh. Flesh is evil. There is nothing good about it, and it must be crucified. No holy anointing will touch the flesh, so quit trying to sanctify your flesh! Sin is in the flesh, and sin will always lead to defilement. The *fleshly* defilement will lead to an imitation, and by trying to make the unholy holy, one inherits a *soulish* defilement. Defilement always, always, always leads to divination (note my repetitive use of "always"?) And divination is the imitation of the divine. And that's bad, remember? In turn, divination leads to further defilement, meaning one inherits something through the defilement — that which we call "iniquity" (being bent toward a particular inclination to sin.)

To simplify, the imitation of the divine leads to defilement, and defilement leads to divination. To be "defiled" is to be "unclean, polluted, soiled, blemished." Iniquity is something that is inherited through defilement. It is the deceitfulness of sin, habitual sins that harden our hearts when they go unconfessed. Remember, we call this the Law of Transference. (A minister friend of mine, Gary Greenwald, has a wonderful book on this principle of transference — I highly recommend you to go out and get it!)

OK, so those are some wordy paragraphs. Make sure you read through them again and understand what I'm trying to convey. There is a vicious cycle that is perpetuated by mixing the holy and the profane. We need the apostolic anointing to lift that veil of deception off of us that says we can have the flesh and the divine operating together. Truly, you can't have your cake and eat it, too. Or something like that.

Hey, let me tell you about this dream I had.

I HAD THIS DREAM

Now, pay attention here, dear readers. This was a *dream* I had. OK? Dreaming. Asleep. Not actually happening in real life. Just wanna make that real clear, folks....

This dream was extremely vivid. Normally I don't remember much of my dreams. I'm usually hiking through a jungle, hear some car horn go off in the trees and wake up to the sound of my alarm clock buzzing. Or maybe I'm a super hero who can fly. Whatever, you get the idea.

The point is this dream was different. And I can tell when I have a prophetic, God-inspired dream because it's always crystal clear, vibrant color and sound, and I wake up immediately after it, remembering every minute detail. I have not had many of these dreams in my life — they're pretty rare. I write all this to show that *this* dream was different than one in which I'm Batman. See the difference?

So anyway in this dream, I enter into this palatial hotel, very posh, and I go up to the front desk to sign in. Whoever was sponsoring the meetings I was going to be preaching at must have been trying to impress me by putting me up in this ritzy, five-star hotel. The entrance was just breathtaking, plants and fountains, marbled tile. Nice. (Incidentally, I've got *no problem* with a pastor putting me up in a swanky hotel, ha ha!)

As I'm signing in, the concierge appears at my left elbow to collect my bags and take me to my room. I turn to look and perceive an extremely attractive woman. She was very beautiful, and she smiled at me and sent off these *vibes*. You know what I mean. Vibes. She certainly wasn't trying to hide her flirtations.

Now remember, everyone, this was a *dream*. It wasn't a literal happening. Can't be too careful emphasizing that....

"I get off at 10 o'clock," she hinted demurely.

Oh, I get it now. She's making a pass at me! I could feel a spirit of sensuality oozing off of her.

And suddenly, in my dream, I realize I'm in a city I've never been in before. I've been away from my family for weeks on end. I find myself missing my wife. I'm tired and weary, and here's this pretty girl flirting with me.

Again... dream. Not really happening.

But in my dream, I'm suddenly hit with this pervasive temptation. I mean, *temptation*. You know, a temptation doesn't just mean a thought that springs up in your mind. A temptation can incite the entirety of your five senses; it can literally consume you. It's not just what you think, it's what you feel, hear, see, taste and smell. And this lady was *not* ugly!

So this temptation floods through me, and thoughts leap into my mind. *Hey, you can do this! You can get away with this! Nobody knows you here in this city. It'll just be one time – this one time in your life, and you can repent later. You know God will forgive you. There's enough grace in Him for this! C'mon....*

See, that's the problem with many people in the Body of Christ: there's always grace. God *has* to forgive you. Go ahead. It's not as bad as we make it out. It's cheap grace, dear friends. I know we can all fall short; I know people have weaknesses, and I'm all for forgiveness. But grace does not come cheaply! This mentality or attitude that says I can go ahead and sin and get forgiveness later must be cut to the quick!

I've got to be honest, as she walked me to my room and this temptation continued to buffet my five senses, I began to feel myself give in. The temptation was lodging in my mind, and I toyed with the idea of giving heed to it.

At that instant, we passed by a ballroom. It was one of those hotels that have fancy meeting rooms with crystal chandeliers and big, round tables. I stopped and stood by the doors and looked in at this huge conference of several hundred people. The girl was stroking my arm, urging me to come up to my room. I could smell her perfume.

Hey, it was a Charismatic meeting. And I recognized the speaker.

In real life, he is a very well known guy. No, I won't tell you his name. Don't ask. In fact, on several occasions in my ministry, I've come to churches where this minister had been just a couple of weeks before. And at the risk of sounding prideful (I trust you know my heart) I was always mopping up after him, so to speak. Whenever I came to a church he'd visited before, there was always havoc left over. Clarity that I would have to bring to this person's unbalanced one-liners and quirky theology. I had discerned some real issues within this man a long time ago, but I had always kept it to myself, praying to the Lord that I was mistaken, or believing that someone close to him would be able to bring some change in his life.

Back to my dream, here's this minister now, and I'm feeling these same iniquities in him again. Except he's moving sometimes very powerfully. Some people are getting blessed, healed, set free, delivered. I want to point out it's not the peoples' fault. They were hungry for the divine, and the Lord was answering them, in spite of this profaned minister.

All the while, this girl's enticing me to follow her to the hotel room.

He preached a powerful message. He moved in word of knowledge, word of wisdom. He went down the prayer line, laying hands on people and they fell under the power.

But it was a fractured, haphazard operation. The anointing was not complete. There were hindrances, gaps in the flow of power; some prophetic words rang true, others sounded off the wall. It was hit and miss. There was no continuity. Some people were getting healed. Some weren't. It was jumbled up. There was a hint of mysticism and carnality. Even though he was saying the right words, I could just tell this man was fractured in iniquity. Part was God operating in spite of the minister, out of mercy, responding to the needs of the crowd. But part was the minister operating out of his own flesh, and when it was of the Holy Spirit, it was sparse. Part was just out and out the enemy causing confusion. It was mixed up and sad.

What made it worse was that the poor people, so desperate to see God move, were unable to discern how mixed this minister's flow was. I felt horrible for them.

How empty *this man is!* I thought to myself with a mixture of compassion and disdain. *What a leanness of soul!* (See Psalm 106:15.)

And as I thought this, instantly Jesus Himself appeared between me and this minister. Oof! I knocked the girl's hand away from mine. Um. Hey. How's it goin'?

The Lord spoke to me audibly in my dream. I mean, I saw His lips move and heard His voice.

He said, "You could get away with *this*." And He pointed to the woman.

I looked down at the pretty girl, feeling embarrassed and ashamed.

"But the consequences would be *that*."

And Jesus pointed to the minister.

I awoke with a start, sweating, hyperventilating. Friends, it is little foxes that spoil the whole vine. (Song of Solomon 2:15) It isn't worth it. Little sins, or what we explain away as "little sins," behind closed doors will eventually affect your ministry in public.

BYPRODUCTS OF INIQUITY

The Book of Joel speaks about how the prophet lamented, crying out in reproof and admonition, to the whole of Israel: elders, children, babies, men and women (that pretty much covers everyone), concerning the priests (we, today, would mean ministers), saying "...Weep between the porch and the altar...." (Joel 2:16-17) In other words, pray and fast, repent, be concerned about what is happening between the altar (that is how one truly acts in privacy) and the porch (how one acts behind the pulpit publicly.) The priests' actions should be the same, on the porch and behind the pulpit.

There should be no discrepancies between how people perceive you and how you really are.

I'm not clubbing anyone to death here. We all have weaknesses that must be overcome; we all struggle with temptation and issues. No one is perfection incarnate. There *is* forgiveness and restoration for those who stumble and fall. But I'm writing about a heart motivation here — deep down, where it counts — what we truly strive for and believe in: the standard of God's holiness. It's a matter of attitude, that we strive for the same level of moral excellence between the porch and the altar.

We should be pressing toward that level of intimacy with Jesus. It should be our one constant endeavor. If we allow seeds of rebellion, or indifference, to be sown and germinate, if we water them with our thought life and harbor their poison, they will spring up into incredibly destructive weeds that choke out the full manifestation of the Father through us.

This is why mutually accountable relationships are vitally important. We must allow people to speak into our lives, and vice versa, perhaps pointing out any blind spots — particular areas in our lives that we cannot see. Not to judge (easier said than done, I know), but to bring a closer level of intimacy with God.

This is especially important of prophetic people, and one of the key reasons why the apostolic must work with the prophetic. An apostle and a prophet in an accountable relationship are much more difficult for the enemy to deceive than lone ministers being tossed willy-nilly out into dark surroundings.

I may write another book that deals with this concept in more detail someday — if I'm not run out of town for *this* book.... (Smile.)

See, prophets can be just as biblically and theologically sound and balanced as any of the other five- (or four-) fold callings. But prophets are more easily susceptible to extremes because they are parabolic; they are the "emotions" of God; they *feel* and are sensitive to the things in the Spirit. Sometimes, if it's just the prophetic in and of itself, the prophet can become so focused on a specific burden of God, he or she can neglect other vital aspects of expression, and they can get off on tangents. Or they can slip into preternatural dealings, especially if there are some dusty skeletons still in the closet (and I'd venture to say, if you're breathing out there, you may still have a skeleton or two.) So the apostolic and the pastoral giftings are to come alongside to bring clarity and definition to what the prophetic is *feeling*. Not to govern, but to provide mutual accountability.

It's unfortunate, but I believe there are too many prophets operating singularly that become unbalanced because they refuse to cultivate mutually accountable relationships with other ministers. (I'm not picking on prophetic people here, 'cause I *am* one, but that's all the more reason for me to write this!)

We *all* need true, Christian friends with whom we cultivate strong, trusting relationships — if anything, just to bounce ideas off each other. To keep us away from mixture or unnecessary extremes. And as with *any* ministry expression, there can be no mixture; it will always lead to iniquity and, then, an imitation of the divine.

So. What is *iniquity*? It can be familiar spirits (I mean demons, if you don't catch my drift), sins, weights (not necessarily habitual sins, but things that are not beneficial to feeding your spirit and thus transforming you into the likeness of God), wrong attitudes ("I despise prophecies") and ulterior motives ("Give me the anointing, Lord, so I can get rich!" — this was Simon's problem.)

What are the byproducts of iniquity? Let's ask the Lord Himself.

Lord, what are the byproducts of iniquity?

"Thus says the Lord concerning the prophets who make my people stray; who chant 'Peace' while they chew with their teeth, but who prepare war against him who puts nothing into their mouths: 'Therefore you shall have night without vision [revelation], and you shall have darkness without divination; the sun shall go down on the prophets, and the day shall be dark for them. So the seers shall be ashamed, and the diviners abashed; indeed they shall all cover their lips; for there is no answer from God.'" (Micah 3:5-7)

Thanks, Lord!

He's saying here that people of mixture will have night, darkness and no vision — that is blindness, veiling, deception, stumbling around with no nightlight and stubbing their toes against the bed frame. You get the idea.

"'But those things which proceed out of the mouth come from the heart, and they defile a man.'" (Matthew 15:18)

Right, Lord, we get it.

Look, I'm trying to lighten the mood here, but don't mistake my use of disarming humor for derisiveness against a very prevalent, sickening misuse of the supernatural at the expense of a lost and hurting world. Stop being profane, ministers! I preach at myself as much as to you. We *cannot* permit any mixture of the unholy to come in contact with that which God demands be kept holy! Cast off your iniquity, do not dilute the anointing of God and try to pass it off as the real deal to some poor soul who wants nothing more than a genuine touch of the Father's power in their lives.

Oh, apostles, come forward with your discernment, teach the people to respect the supernatural, not to despise it! Instruct the people to become enlightened concerning God's holiness, and His perfect will for theirs! The apostolic people of God must discern for themselves if the minister standing before them has defilements in his/her hidden life. They must be able to perceive the Spirit (or spirits) *behind* the minister's operation. (I'm not advocating a judgmental, critical attitude here: always trying to find out something *wrong* with a minister — that's not godly, either! — but, on the other side of the coin, apostolic people cannot be gullible.)

The sixteenth chapter of Acts gives further example of the problem of mixture by recounting the story of a slave girl who was possessed of a spirit of divination. That word for "spirit of divination" (Strong's #4436) is literally "a python" — something that constricts, named after the god worshipped in Pytho. Thankfully Paul was able to see through her python spirit and cast the ugly demon out of her.

How many know what the girl was saying was, indeed, correct? "'These men are the servants of the Most High God, who proclaim to us the way of salvation.'" (Acts 16:17) But the trouble was she tried to use the gift of discernment without the anointing backing it up. She had no right to say what she said, even though it was true. Bottom line, she didn't have the approval of God on her, and so she tried to use *flattery* as a way to insinuate her own mixed-up "gift" into the works of the apostles. It was divination, imitating the divine. Something Paul, "greatly annoyed" (Verse 18), wouldn't stand for. See, Paul's discerning spirit was able to perceive the slave girl was not operating under true anointing. Now calling her on the carpet for it caused him and Silas some trouble (they were beaten and imprisoned), but that was a small price to pay for defending the holiness of God's anointed.

If Paul had continued to permit the demon to speak its flattery through the girl, I am convinced it would have corrupted Paul's and Silas' true anointing. They would have inherited an oppression corresponding to the sin in the slave girl's life. The key to note here is that by permitting a mixture of the holy and the profane, one opens oneself up to inheriting a vexation based on whatever junk the profaned person is carrying; and this oppression stifles the flow of anointing. This is something the apostles are called to set in order. There are yokes that can be placed around a person that bind the manifestation of God. This is one reason why we aren't seeing the healing miracles like we should.

"'Give no regard to mediums and familiar spirits; do not seek after them, to be defiled by them: I am the Lord your God.'" (Leviticus 19:31) We must guard our sanctuaries against these python spirits — it is our responsibility to identify correctly that which may defile the congregation. In Ezekiel 8:9, the Lord commissions the prophet to "...'Go in, and see the wicked abominations which they are doing there.'" Later He says, "...'Son of man, mark well, see with your eyes and hear with your ears, all that I say to you concerning all the ordinances of the house of the Lord and all its laws. Mark well who may enter the house and all who go out from the sanctuary.'" (Ezekiel 44:5) It is vitally important that the apostles, prophets and pastors of the Church *mark well* who is allowed to enter, and who leaves.

Kim Clement taught how apostles discern three attributes of someone who is permitted to enter into the household of the Lord. There are more, no doubt, but I think these three sum up the gist nicely. Firstly, is the person circumcised in their heart and flesh — meaning is he/she set apart for the Lord? Secondly, does the person keep his/her covenant with God and others? Thirdly, is the person not too independent? By properly discerning these attributes in a person, the apostle is able to weed out, so to speak, the profaneness that desperately wants to mix in with the holy. Only by accurately calling out the imitation of the divine can an apostle look upon the Church and say, "For there is no sorcery [enchantment] against Jacob, nor any divination [fortune-telling] against Israel.'" (Numbers 23:23) This is the good report we as the Body are striving for. Otherwise, the people of God will fall away in apostasy.

"Now the Spirit expressly [clearly, explicitly] says that in latter times some will depart from the faith, giving heed to deceiving spirits and doctrines of demons, speaking lies in hypocrisy, having their own conscience seared with a hot iron...." (1 Timothy 4:1-2) Please note that only *some* will depart from the faith — that doesn't mean you! Departing from the faith is not necessarily overtly "back-sliding" and giving away one's salvation (although it *can* be this); but rather, it generally means to turn away from sound, Christian doctrine. This is happening in these latter times, and we must take care to stay on track with what we know the Bible clearly teaches.

The passage of 2 Corinthians 11:4, which was given earlier, speaks of another generation receiving another spirit — one that is anti-Christ. That "different spirit" can be fleshly or demonic, and I could probably rephrase it as, "To strike out with a venomous operation [remember the python?] to bring one under control, to produce a spiritual death, to be consumed for the benefit of another." In short, to attempt to use the gifts without the anointing. This is what the apostles are standing against in these end times. We must be separated wholly unto the true Christ, the real Jesus, that operates in true signs and wonders with true anointing. Again, it takes the approval of God in order to display the divine. There are no shortcuts to the true anointing, for everything else is imitation. We must stand against this mixture in the Spirit. We cannot imitate the anointing when it is not flowing — such operations are only soulish, with no lasting effect. We must stop imitating healings or falling under the power, when the power is not present. You know, it takes an awful lot of Holy Ghost power to knock this ol' boy down! I would strongly admonish you never to let anyone push you down out of some false pretense of "keeping up with the person next to me"! If you don't go down, just stand there and get blessed. If the minister tries to push you down, kindly step back and shake it off.

INHERITING A DEFILEMENT

To share an example of someone inheriting a defilement, when I was a young student at Christ for the Nations, I went to a particular service at a local church where a traveling evangelist was purported as being mightily used by the Lord. Supposedly he had received the mantle of authority from a previously well-known minister, specifically operating in a very distinct word of knowledge. I'll share more about the mentor in a bit.

I arrived roughly an hour before the service started to get a good seat, since this minister was packing the place out every night. I remember the first thing that struck me as I walked through the front door were these people, maybe a dozen, standing around that greeted everyone who entered. Not in and of itself all that uncommon, but beyond just the normal, "Welcome! How are you doing this evening?" they asked some pretty specific questions, for the sake of their "mailing list."

"Hi there! What's your name? Can we get your address? Are there any prayer request needs that you have?"

Well, just let me fill out a piece of paper to drop in the offering bucket for that, right? But, not to be rude, the newcomers would share a lot of their private struggles with these greeters, and then the greeters would escort them to their seats. It struck me as a little odd. I just ducked in and selected my seat, like I wrote, an hour before the service started at 7:00pm.

The minister didn't show up until 9:45!

Now supposedly the minister's flight had been delayed, so in order to kill time, let's just all praise and worship the Lord. I had no problem with that, but in the nearly three hours' interim — and this began to set off those warning klaxons in my spirit: *Ooo-gah! Ooo-gah! Ooo-gah!* — I was slightly perturbed at how often the people on the platform would mention this financial need or that financial need for the ministry. On and on and on. They took up at least three, maybe even *four*, offerings while waiting for the minister's plane to arrive. Yep, I kid you not. It was all very dramatic like: "The man of God is on his way! Are you expecting great things? He'll be here soon... Now, let's take up an offering for—"

This may all sound innocent enough, except for the fact that where I was sitting in the auditorium, I could see the side door of the stage. And on several occasions during that three-hour marathon "giving-session," I saw the minister, who was *supposed* to be on a delayed plane, mind you, peek his wee-little head out the door to see how many people were arriving. Would I josh you?

As the crowds began to swell and another offering was about to be taken, finally at 9:45pm the MC said the man of God had arrived! Now, I'm just fuming at this point, 'cause I've been watching the little rapscallion poke his head out the door a half dozen times the last two and half hours!

And the man of God struts onto the stage with this extremely flamboyant over-extension of his personality. As if to say, "Have you all been expecting me? So *sorry* to have kept you waiting!" (Insert batting eyelashes here.) He sets his Bible down on the podium; doesn't even bother to open it. Doesn't teach one bit out of the Word of God, gives no honor to it whatsoever, and proceeds to call people forward. His mannerisms were *way* over-the-top, so highly exaggerated with every little swish of movement. To me, it was painfully obvious he was trying to impress the crowd with his intense characteristics. The word "melodramatic" comes to mind.

He calls up one person, strikes an Elvis Presley pose and giggles, "Your name is So-and-So... And your address is Such-and-Such... Is this correct?"

"My goodness, why, yes, it is!"

Cheers from the crowd. Yay! Oooh! Ahhh!

Wait a tic, I thought, *wasn't that the same information they were giving those greeters before they sat down?* I may not be the smartest man on the planet, but come on! And I started to piece it together. The game's afoot, my dear Watson! That's why the minister would poke his head out and survey the crowd. Was So-and-So from Such-and-Such still seated over there, in the red shirt and khaki trousers?

This was all bad enough, but what made me wanna gag was when, every few people or so, he'd intentionally *miss* some aspect of their details. Something slightly off. You know, just to show his humility — his humanness — his fallibility. Ah, it's OK, brother, nobody's perfect....

Now before we stone this misguided minister, let me say, he *did* get some revelation, mixed in with his charlatan ways. Specifics about peoples' problems that he could in no way have known without divining it, stuff that wouldn't have been shared to the greeters. Details long ago in peoples' pasts, thoughts and insecurities they were currently dealing with. In spite of his falsities, he *did* have a genuine gift of knowledge from *some* spirit, not necessarily *the* Spirit.

I was sitting there with about 1,000 people, watching this guy bit-bop around with his ostentatious mannerisms and manipulating over-emphasis on finances, just stunned. Not because of the false revelation, not because of the times when he got it right, but because I could actually *feel* this presence as he ministered. It was so very, very close to the true anointing of the Lord; but it was just slightly, ever so slightly, *off*. Something not quite genuine. Just a tad... what's the word I'm looking for? Mystical. That's it. Enchanting. Yeah.

Remember when I wrote that I grew up in a town that was a center for mysticism and Spiritism in So Cal? Well, living under that garbage, thank the Lord, developed within me a sensitivity, I believe, to discerning what's mystical and enchanting and what a true manifestation of the Spirit is. This was *not* a true manifestation; it was too fleshly.

But the people in the auditorium, at least the ones I saw, couldn't tell the difference. They were unable to separate what was holy and what was profaned. It was so sad to me that they couldn't tell this was an imitation of the divine. I didn't feel better than them, I felt so much the worse because I wanted *them* to see he was corrupt. I was mad.

And this thought sprang into my mind: *Rise up! Rebuke the familiar spirit!* I suddenly remembered this verse, "Let two or three prophets speak, and let the others judge." (1 Corinthians 14:29)

I prayed under my breath, "Lord, I believe You've given me discernment and a prophetic spirit, and according to Your Word, I will judge what the prophet speaks. In the name of Jesus, I rebuke that familiar spirit!"

No sooner had I uttered those words than the minister stopped dead in mid-sentence, his hands on one particular victim, and he turned and glared at me. He left the person he was praying for and stalked clear over to my section of the auditorium.

"There are *some* people here who don't think this is a true manifestation of God," he seethed, eyes boring into me. Talk about cold sweat down the back! "Beware," he hissed and pointed his finger *directly at me.* "You will come under the judgment of God!"

Oh, yuck! It still ooks me out to think about it. He stormed off and attempted to continue ministering. But it was fractured, he stumbled over his words, started "missing" it more than he had before. His flow was visibly shaken.

I stomached it for another ten minutes, then I quietly gathered my Bible — which had been sitting unused for nearly four hours now — and slinked out of my chair. A few of my friends from CFNI got up and walked out with me, and as we made our way up the aisle, this minister shooting eye-daggers at my back, people literally *hissed* at me. They started cussing me out. No embellishment. Four-letter words your sailor uncle would've blushed to hear. The curses these people uttered!

I just continued walking, my eyes straight ahead toward the exit sign. They *spit* on my shoes as I passed by them. Yes, actual expectoration. *Ptttooo!* And I liked those shoes....

I've since found out this minister's mentor — the man from whom he had received this "mantle of authority" — was very well known in the '40s and '50s. No, I won't give you his name. Quit asking. But it has since been proven, and is fairly commonly known, that in the latter years of his ministry, the mentor got a little quirky, had some repeated issues with sin and became defiled. So one night, the mentor laid hands on this minister (who was reportedly drunk at the time) — the one that was now glaring at my back — and said, "I give you my anointing, my mantle of authority."

And this minister inherited it. Along with the defilement. And it led to an imitation of the divine. People, we *must* have discernment! Apostles, you *must* be holy! Do not let yourselves become profaned by repeatedly mixing your anointing with the familiarity of the flesh.

Incidentally, I never did receive any judgment from God, as that man said I would. In fact, my life and ministry have been extremely blessed, glory to the Lord!

So there.

THE SEPARATION PRINCIPLE

As shown in the passage previously given in Ezekiel 44:23-24, there is obviously to be a separation of the holy and the unholy. Let's take a look at Samson from Judges 13-16 as an example of one who was separated from the two polar opposites. Samson was a man of supernatural conception; he took the Nazarite — meaning "devoted, consecrated" — vow (no hair cutting, no alcoholic drinks, no touching the dead), and because of this the Spirit would come upon him suddenly, giving an anointing for unusual acts of power.

Every anointed person in ministry has a *key* to their strength and a *Delilah* to their weakness. (Jim Goll) The enemy searches not only for the weakness but for the strength as well. Samson's biggest problem was that he loved the world he lived in, and he wanted both the Spirit and the world (the holy and the profane.)

Really, the man liked his hair played with....

So Delilah gets his hair cut, and the Bible says "...the Lord had departed from him." (Judges 16:20) The Spirit withdrew from his profaneness, only Samson didn't know this so he goes to stand against the Philistines, and they poke out his eyes. How sad!

But Samson was deceived by his profaneness *even though he was anointed.* Yes, one can be deceived by profaneness even though they're still under the anointing, and if they're not careful, they don't recognize when the Spirit's departed. It seemed to Samson that for a season he got away with it; he played with the anointing while Delilah played with his hair (it's an allegorical usage — she might not have actually *played* with his hair, I know.) But he, like so many defiled men and women of God, convince themselves, "I can do anything I want!" I call it the Superman Syndrome. The deception is, they somehow persuade themselves that they are an exception to God's standard. "Well, God must not look too narrowly on my adultery, because the people are still getting healed in my meetings!"

It's also what I call a Messiah Complex. They've exalted or manipulated their position of influence higher than they should. As if they're above the laws of God, and they subscribe to a "cheap grace." "I can do this and just repent tomorrow — God has to forgive me."

And the people are not discerning enough to perceive the profane display of giftedness in the defiled minister's life. "Well, he or she must be a godly person, 'cause, well, look! That guy just got healed...." They don't think that perhaps God healed the person *in spite* of the defiled minister.

Undiscerning people then permit the minister to elevate his/her own personal "revelation" as being equal to scripture, and so we get a "oh, no one's perfect, we forgive you, brother" and the guy's back in the pulpit ninety days later after having partaken in a grievous sin. (That's not so far-fetched of an example — I know it's happened before.) And it breaks my heart! For, now, the people have fallen under the vexation of the minister's defilement themselves!

Don't misunderstand. I'm all for restoration. I believe in forgiveness and grace. I know none are above temptation, and we can all fall into sin if we're not careful. But we cannot lower the standard of God's holiness any longer. There is right and there is wrong. There is profaneness and there is holiness. It's not as gray of an area as you might think! It takes the apostolic to be able to unveil the deception that says grace comes cheap.

Never fear, dear friends! Your protection from deception is not your fear of being deceived — it is your level of intimacy with Jesus! It all goes back to your relationship with Him, and you wouldn't want to hurt Him and cheapen His blood by permitting defilement into your lives and ministries. This chapter is not about fear or beating people up; it's about a call to a deeper level of intimacy with the only One who deserves to be called Messiah. Your discerning ears and eyes are cultivated in a love embrace with the Son of God. Stick with Him, and you won't fail! Be separated unto Him alone, and the Spirit will not flee from you. Allow the Son of God's robe to cover over you, calling out any hidden weights or sins; discard that which is profane! Be separate for the Lord's sake that your anointing will not become polluted.

You must ask yourself this question: have I inherited an imitation of the divine? If so, we must pray for deliverance from the defilement in order to receive the *true riches* of God. The rest of this chapter will deal with seeking out those true riches, and firstly let's share a little on actual riches for, "'Therefore if you have not been faithful in the unrighteous mammon, who will commit to your trust the true riches?'" (Luke 16:11)

THE PROMISE OF PROSPERITY

Poverty can be a curse that comes by refusing instruction, being disobedient and thankless. Proverbs 13:18 says, "Poverty and shame will come to him who disdains [ignores] correction, but he who regards a rebuke will be honored." If you haven't yet, take a few minutes to read Deuteronomy 28, wherein blessings and curses are laid out for the reader.

On the flipside, there are others on this planet that have little of this world's wealth, and it doesn't necessarily come from disobedience or a lack of faith. James 2:5 says, "Listen, my beloved brethren: Has God not chosen the poor of this world to be rich in faith and heirs of the kingdom which He promised to those who love Him?" We are to be a holy company, whether we possess physical riches or not. I believe in prosperity, but my views might hopefully be a little more balanced than the dangerous materialistic values that run rampant in many Western church circles. With that being said, there are clear biblical promises that can give hope, and I do believe having faith can yield material prosperity without the sin of loving money for money's sake.

We have a promise of prosperity. It will be good to define "prosperity" as literally meaning "to have a good journey through life." I'm not necessarily talking about physical wealth, although that can certainly be part of a good journey. The promise of prosperity is for those who are generous, for those who are righteous and holy, for those who meditate on God's laws. For them, there is a promise to be prosperous in this life.

The very first Psalm clearly outlines this promise for those who delight in the law of the Lord. "He shall be like a tree planted by the rivers of water, that brings forth its fruit in its season, whose leaf also shall not wither; and whatever he does shall prosper." (Psalm 1:3) It's not wrong to pray for prosperity.

"Beloved, I pray that you may prosper in all things and be in health, just as your soul prospers." (3 John 2)

"Let them shout for joy and be glad, who favor my righteous cause; and let them say continually, 'Let the Lord be magnified, who has pleasure in the prosperity of His servant.'" (Psalm 35:27)

God takes pleasure in prospering His people so that He might be magnified. "...'The God of heaven Himself will prosper us....'" (Nehemiah 2:20)

We actually are given power from God to obtain wealth. "'And you shall remember the Lord your God, for it is He who gives you power to get wealth....'" (Deuteronomy 8:18)

"Both riches and honor come from You...." (1 Chronicles 29:12)

"As for every man to whom God has given riches and wealth, and given him power to eat of it, to receive his heritage [portion] and rejoice in his labor — this is the gift of God." (Ecclesiastes 5:19)

"Abram was very rich in livestock, in silver, and in gold." (Genesis 13:2)

"There was a man... blameless and upright... who feared God and shunned evil... [who had] a very large household, so that this man was the greatest of all the people of the East." (Job 1:1, 3)

With all of that, it's important to note that the Bible does not always define riches and prosperity in material terms. Prosperity may or may not be related to material wealth.

"Or do you despise the riches of His goodness, forbearance, and longsuffering, not knowing that the goodness of God leads you to repentance?" (Romans 2:4)

"...And that He might make known the riches of His glory on the vessels of mercy, which He prepared beforehand for glory...." (Romans 9:23) "...That He would grant you, according to the riches of His glory, to be strengthened with might through His Spirit in the inner man...." (Ephesians 3:16)

I know I'm quoting a lot of scripture here, but I want to show that to be prosperous is to be found in the riches of His glory, not only in just the bills in your wallet.

"Oh, the depth of the riches both of the wisdom and knowledge of God!" (Romans 11:33)

"In Him we have redemption through His blood, the forgiveness of sins, according to the riches of His grace... that [we] may know what is the hope of His calling, what are the riches of the glory of His inheritance... that in the ages to come He might show the exceeding riches of His grace in His kindness toward us in Christ Jesus... that [we]

should preach among the Gentiles the unsearchable riches of Christ...."
(Ephesians 1:7, 18; 2:7; 3:8)

"To them God willed to make known what are the riches of the glory of this mystery among the Gentiles: which is Christ in you, the hope of glory... that their hearts may be encouraged, being knit together in love, and attaining to all the riches of the full assurance of understanding, to the knowledge of the mystery of God, both of the Father and of Christ...." (Colossians 1:27; 2:2)

These are *true riches* — things worthy of our pursuit; treasures that are for all time and eternity beyond. We seek holiness apart from profaneness and defilement for these kinds of riches. After all, material wealth can fall victim to thieves, moths, rust and corruption, but true riches remain forever!

Before the Messiah brought these riches, Moses had faith even in economic poverty. "By faith Moses, when he became of age, refused to be called the son of Pharaoh's daughter, choosing rather to suffer affliction with the people of God than to enjoy the passing pleasures of sin, esteeming the reproach of Christ greater riches than the treasures in Egypt; for he looked to the reward." (Hebrews 11:24-26)

The true riches didn't consist of the millions in Pharaoh's house. We, too, should choose the reproach of Christ to inherit the greater riches! (Ralph Mahoney) When Jesus came to us in that all-night prayer meeting, we began to desire those true riches, first seeking to cast off defilement, and that singular encounter has stayed with me all these years later.

Knowing Jesus and His power are true riches. "Then Peter said, 'Silver and gold I do not have, but what I do have I give you: In the name of Jesus Christ of Nazareth, rise up and walk.'" (Acts 3:6) "But earnestly desire the best gifts...." (1 Corinthians 12:31)

The church of Laodicea closely models the Church that will exist before the return of Christ — I'm speaking of this age, to be blunt. Jesus was speaking of this type of church in Revelation 3:17-18, "'Because YOU SAY [emphasis added on purpose], "I am rich, have become wealthy, and have need of nothing" — and do not know that you are wretched, miserable, poor, blind, and naked — I counsel you to buy from Me gold refined in the fire, that you may be rich...."'

This type of church is rich in worldly goods but impoverished in the true riches outlined above. The Laodiceans' view of themselves was directly opposed to Christ's divine view of them.

I believe in positive confession. Christ Himself said, "...'Have faith in God. For assuredly, I say to you, whoever says to this mountain, "Be removed and be cast into the sea," and does not doubt in his heart, but believes that those things he says will be done, he will have whatever he says.'" (Mark 11:22-23) But His teaching does not support a "blab it, grab it" mentality.

A mountain does not just speak of material impoverishment, but rather a problem, an insurmountable barrier that must be overcome. Now, keep it in balance, because for some people poverty *is* a mountain in their lives that needs to be cast into the sea; and with correct teaching, they can have faith in God to see that mountain removed. I don't think God intended Christians to starve and go without, but we are called to suffer for the cause of Christ; and the fact of the matter is, most Christians could do with more money. Dare we categorize such poor, suffering saints that make up a significant portion of the worldwide Body as "without faith" because of their geo-economic impoverishment? Tread carefully.

I am a literalist to the Word. I feel that if Christ meant just earthly riches He might have said something to the effect of, "Whoever says to this money, 'Come to me and be cast into my purse....'" Again, I'm being slightly sarcastic here to make the point clear.

There is a thread in current Christianity that some people believe they can directly speak to money itself and command it come to them, and if one's faith is enough, the money must obey. I don't see a whole lot of scriptural basis for that. Perhaps the fish with the money in its mouth, but that money was for a specific *purpose*, not just to obtain wealth. (Matthew 17:24-27)

Our confession cannot be motivated by greed and self-centeredness, otherwise we end up like the Laodiceans, which are spit out of the mouth of Christ. Yes, we can speak prosperity and blessing — of course! Continue to do so. But make sure of your motivation — let it not be profaned, and the earthly wealth will simply be a by-product of your true riches in the mystery of Christ.

To be prosperous does not always involve a life of luxury and comfort. Take a look at Paul, one whom no person of God could argue was lacking in true riches. Peruse Acts 22-28 and see what kind of "prosperous" journey that apostle had! He goes to Jerusalem only to be bound and scourged; he's delivered as a prisoner; he's shipwrecked; a venomous beast attacks him; and finally *three months later* he arrives at his destination. But the treasure he received was that the Maltese were saved! Indeed, true riches!

To be prosperous may mean one faces rejection, false accusations and suffering. Take a look at Joseph. Peruse Genesis 37-47 and see what kind of "prosperous" journey that man had! His brothers knock him into a pit, steal his long-sleeved coat, tell his father a beast ate him and sell the poor soul into slavery. But with all that suffering, Genesis 39:2, 3 says, "The Lord was with Joseph, and he was a successful man... and that the Lord made all he did to prosper in his hand." Was Joseph materially blessed? Why, yes, but not until he had faced rejection, betrayal and false accusations at the hands of iniquitous brothers and an adulterous woman. On top of all that, he faced twelve to thirteen years of imprisonment! He didn't endure the afflictions of Egypt to get rich – his motives remained pure. He maintained a moral standard, integrity and a right relationship with God.

Buying Christ's fire-refined gold may cause you grief, no doubt. The question is will you allow it to make you better or bitter?

So many Christians misrepresent Romans 8:28 by skipping the next verse. The complete thought reads, "And we know that all things work together for good to those who love God, to those who are the called according to His purpose. For whom He foreknew, He also predestined to be conformed to the image of His Son, that He might be the firstborn among many brethren."

The "good" comes out of an *appropriate response* to what seems bad so that you might be conformed to the image of Christ. Only *then* do all things work together for good. How many of you know some Christians that all things are not working together for good? Perhaps their response is mixed with unholiness. To be holy means to respond to the refining fire properly. Having faith may mean being required to use your gift of faith to embrace these sanctifying sufferings that Paul and Joseph endured. It is only by faith that you can hope to have a right response. It is using faith even through poverty and trial – see Hebrews 11:33-40.

Further, giving out of your need can create a rich spirit. By that I mean you are prosperous in your thought life and sentiments. You make more godly decisions on where your money goes and what you desire to obtain. Proverbs 11:24-25 proclaims, "There is one who scatters, yet increases more; and there is one who withholds more than is right, but it leads to poverty. The generous soul will be made rich, and he who waters will also be watered himself."

See, I'm not just making this up!

If you create a giving heart, it is paid back to you in spiritual, true riches. Times of economic difficulty can still generate an inner strength, if you permit it. By giving out of your need, you begin to see the world a little differently. You have a different outlook on life. You become a truly loving giver. It creates a greater sense of compassion for those going through more difficulty than you (and there is *always* someone worse off than you!)

"He who has a generous eye will be blessed, for he gives of his bread to the poor." (Proverbs 22:9)

Create a giving heart; sow into others, and you will begin to inherit a greater discernment of the needs of humanity worldwide. "The rich rules over the poor, and the borrower is servant to the lender." (Proverbs 22:7) A proper attitude of sowing out of need creates blessing and prosperity in your life. It creates a foundation to receive true riches. "When the whirlwind passes by, the wicked is no more, but the righteous has an everlasting foundation." (Proverbs 10:25)

These are very simple, practical principles in laying up true riches. It's not difficult to understand, but it is profound in its applications. The holiness of God, when unveiled in one's life, creates an environment for prosperity — you are blessed because God is blessed by your actions. But if there is a positive, there is also a negative. Next we will consider some pitfalls of prosperity which lead to defilement.

Pitfalls of Prosperity

Believe it or not, times of blessing, success and prosperity will usually test a person more than adversity. "...The prosperity of fools shall destroy them." (Proverbs 1:32, KJV) "'So is he who lays up treasure for himself, and is not rich toward God.'" (Luke 12:21) As simple as it may sound, a key to the apostolic release is merely, "Don't be foolish." Permit me through Paul — since he was smarter than I am — to elaborate.

"Now godliness with contentment is great gain. For we brought nothing into this world, and it is certain we can carry nothing out. And having food and clothing, with these we shall be content. But those who desire to be rich fall into temptation and a snare, and into many foolish and harmful lusts which drown men in destruction and perdition. For the love of money is a root of all kinds of evil, for which some have strayed [erred] from the faith in their greediness, and pierced themselves through with many sorrows." (1 Timothy 6:6-10) Well, it seems like ministers in Paul's day could find themselves in the same predicaments as ministers in our day, huh? That's weird. It's like he was being prophetic or something....

My prosperity theology is pretty basic. I don't think it's wrong to have money, but does money have you? Pretty much I copied it from Jesus, who was even more clever than Paul. "'No servant can serve two masters; for either he will hate the one and love the other, or else he will be loyal to the one and despise the other. You cannot serve God and mammon.'" (Luke 16:13)

This is not a gray area, dear friends. We have a mixture in the Church that stems from many people trying to serve both masters, and it cannot be done. So, then, people are defiled and act unholy when representing Christ to others as "little anointed ones."

More and more often we have error-by-emphasis on material prosperity, and you've heard that money doesn't always bring happiness nor satisfy every want. This is such a well-known topic, even in secular circles, yet we in the Body still struggle with it century after century. It must have been a pretty important concept to Jesus and Paul, because it made it into the Bible.... Our understanding must be enlightened by an apostolic unction. We must deal with this issue of loving material things. We have to cast off this over-emphasis on physical wealth.

"He who loves silver will not be satisfied with silver; nor he who loves abundance, with increase. This also is vanity." (Ecclesiastes 5:10) And remember, vanity is a *bad thing.* "Set your affection [mind] on things above, not on things on the earth." (Colossians 3:2, KJV)

"Do not love the world or the things in the world. If anyone loves the world, the love of the Father is not in him." (1 John 2:15) That's a pretty harsh statement, if you think about it. Does this mean that if a leader is possessed of worldly love, he is not of the Father's love? Considering the apostolic theme of this book and the previous chapters in Volume 1 on the Father's love, ponder this statement for a second. Could this be a hindrance to the true riches of signs, wonders, miracles, healings, deliverances, etc.?

"...If riches increase, do not set your heart on them." (Psalm 62:10) "...'Take heed and beware of covetousness, for one's life does not consist in the abundance of the things he possesses.'" (Luke 12:15) This is the teaching of Christ. From this I would be bold to say that in order to enter into the Kingdom and its apostolic riches, one must be willing to unload one's riches. That is, one must be willing to have the *emotional attachment* to riches broken. I don't begrudge anyone wealth, but I do defy anyone's *connection* to wealth.

If you're unfamiliar with the passage, read Luke 18:18-25. Jesus makes it pretty clear what He thinks about trying to be rich and enter into the Kingdom. I don't believe Jesus thinks it *impossible* for the rich to enter into Kingdom-blessing, but He does require that they remove the bond associated with riches before entering. We must be freed from the love of money before we can receive the true riches of a lifestyle in the Kingdom of God. Our love of Jesus and what He says must take preeminence over any earthly gain we might possess.

Let's tie this all back into the apostles and their determination for a breaker anointing to be released to the people. The acquisition of material wealth deals directly with a person's heart motivation – what the person's focus is centered upon. Since apostles are to release an anointing that sets people free in *all* areas of life, it stands to reason an anointing should be released to unveil these pitfalls of prosperity. The apostolic anointing is not only for the physical, emotional and mental needs of the people; but also for strategies and godly thinking to set people free from impoverishment as well as the love of money.

We have to have a proper motivation and reason for *why* we want to gain material wealth. I don't think God minds His people becoming millionaires as long their hearts are not *set* on the millions. I believe there are going to be many, many apostles that God is going to entrust earthly riches to. Just like Peter and the early church apostles. (Acts 4:34-35) God knew He could trust Peter with great wealth, because the apostle's focus was on the people, and the wealth would be correctly distributed to those who needed it, not hoarded up for the apostle's benefit.

Relating to this subject, I believe the Holy Spirit wants me to make a few statements here that some people may find a bit alarming. But I'm just going to be obedient and trust He bears witness to you my intentions in giving a bit of a warning. Deep breath, here we go.

It is my opinion, after more than thirty years in traveling ministry, that the majority of ministers are not financially remunerated in the level they should be. To be blunt, they're not paid correctly. Of course, there are always exceptions, but it has been my experience that quite a few churches do not give to outside ministers as well as they should.

Come on, people, love me!

But because of this lack, there is a tendency among many apostolic circles to encroach upon God's designated way in how the apostles, prophets and evangelists are to be taken care of financially in the churches they work with. Let me explain.

I believe all true apostles and prophets should advocate and believe in the importance of the local church. People come to church and pay tithes and give offerings in the local setting because the church represents the organism, or vehicle, of expressing Christ's ministry to the community. For them it is their storehouse. Apostles, prophets and traveling ministers need to have accountability and fellowship with the local church. But since there is usually so much money tied up in the tithe, because the church has a budget to make, salaries to pay, its own local outreaches, etc., there is often very little left over for the offering, which is the primary source of income for the roving minister.

So many churches struggle financially to meet their own needs and sometimes neglect the importance of the apostolic, prophetic and evangelistic influence that each local church should have. Nevertheless, as a traveling minister, I am still a huge proponent of operating alongside the local church.

The answer lies in the apostolic breaker anointing for unveiling the Lord's view on gathering material wealth. I am firmly persuaded that God is raising up anointed men and women who are motivated apostolically, prophetically, evangelistically in the workplace, who with the strategies of heaven, are equipped to release wealth into the Kingdom of God... but once again, it should be *alongside* the local church.

Yet, the problem still remains of apostles and traveling ministers struggling financially. You might possess the most dynamic anointing to liberate thousands, but if you don't have money to get down the street to where the needs are, what good is the anointing?

So what does the apostle or the traveling minister do?

Now, some of you are getting what I'm writing here. Look, I believe in apostolic networks, but I think the wineskin of the Church as a whole needs to be changed. By that I mean, the pervading way apostolic associations operate needs to be reworked. We need to see the Church from a more universal perspective.

There are some disquieting trends in apostolic circles to create new venues for finances that sidestep the local church, and while I realize that the Kingdom of God must extend beyond the local church expression, we cannot disregard the church on the street corner. I know there are frustrations and a lack of finances, but apostles must be careful not to tamper with the vehicle that God has set in place (i.e., the local church) in the name of a pseudospiritual prosperity movement.

Some organizations gather key influential people in the workplace — the layperson millionaire, not to put too fine a point on it: doctors, lawyers, entrepreneurs — and compel them to give to the network, over and above, or in many cases, *against* the local church. Apostles cannot belittle or minimize the local church expression! I would say the apostolically motivated workplace person needs to continue tithing to his or her church, if he or she considers it their storehouse, and then give above and beyond to the network, as they are able. Of course, each person must find their own balance in this.

We need a new revelation of what is one person's storehouse — it most certainly *can* be in the framework of an apostolic network, but one should always keep in one's heart the importance and preciousness of the local church. We must be careful about not losing sight of the local church and be led by the Lord in defining our storehouse.

Apostolic networks must take great care not to become greedy in their own financial desires; they run the risk of usurping the authority of God's Word and getting outside of the structure that He created: that is, the local church in a community working to establish the rule of God out there in the world arena. Apostolic networks do, indeed, help in this manner, but it should be in the context of working *alongside* the local church. I'm all for apostolic networks, but they do not replace the church setting. The balance, or safeguard, for apostolic networks is to continue working with the local churches and pastors. For this reason, I think every apostle, every prophet, every evangelist, every family, needs a pastor; not just peers equal to their own calling. Again, each apostle is going to need to find his or her balance in this area. Keep all this in context with the previous chapter (in Volume 1) on church government. One calling does not *rule* over another, but the mutual accountability is not something that can be overlooked. And especially where finances are concerned, a minister cannot be too careful.

I believe God wants His roving ministers to be blessed, to have their financial needs taken care of, but not at the expense of the local church. And yes, some local churches need to have an unveiling of the importance of blessing the traveling ministers accordingly — don't get me wrong. The wineskin change goes both ways, to the church and to the network. But the apostles cannot take away from the importance of the local church; they need to encourage the church to spend its funds in the wisest manner possible. I *believe* in the local church.

I can remember, by way of illustration, being a twenty-three-year-old traveling minister, struggling financially, of course; but in one of those seasons of great open-heavens favor, like in that low desert church (remember Chapter Six in Volume 1?) I'd thought I had arrived at the pinnacle of my ministry.

(I've since been proven so very, very wrong....)

But after one particularly powerful service where it seemed that everyone was healed, everyone was saved, everyone was delivered, a representative of a very well-known minister — if I mentioned his name, you'd know him — approached me.

"I know that Evangelist So-and-So," the representative told me, "will be very open to backing your ministry financially. We've not seen anything like this in someone of such a young age."

Ahh, flattery! How cute! (That's sarcasm....) But I have to admit, my friends, I was tempted. I mean, wow! This evangelist was famous, one of the most well known in the world. They felt he would be interested in totally financing my ministry. Wouldn't you have given it some thought?

The representative went on. "If he desires to support your ministry entirely, you would need to forget about the local church and focus solely on auditorium ministry, where the people come out to you. We'll handle the advertisement; you just show up."

Now, I don't have a problem with auditorium ministry as the Lord directs — I've done so myself on numerous occasions. But to neglect totally the local church just rubbed me the wrong way; how can one simply bypass the pastors? I felt from the Lord at an early age in ministry that I was supposed to support the local church setting, to aid the pastors. How could I do that if I *only* ministered in the arena setting? I felt the Lord say it would take longer to reach the maximum number of people, but it is the way He desired *me* to go. (Again, His way for *me* is not necessarily His way for everyone else.) But if I honored the local pastor, the final outcome of my ministry would be of better quality, and its impact on future generations would be greater.

So I politely declined the representative's gracious offer. And it stung to do so. I really had to die to myself, and it's not always been an easy go in the ministry. I sometimes think (humorously, of course) if I had known, twenty-five years later, I'd still be waiting for that pinnacle of ministry expression.... Well. We'll leave it at that. (Smile.)

Keep a good balance here, friends. Nothing wrong with ministering in conferences, auditoriums, arenas, neutral ground. Not every expression of the Body of Christ is to be within the four walls of a church — I think I wrote something to that effect earlier in Chapter Seven (of Volume 1). We need to look at ministry for the purpose of extending the Kingdom in all areas. I believe we need to get into the workplace, out in the streets, but not at the expense of forgetting the local church setting. God loves the church setting; it's the gathering of His people at the gate of His purpose and anointing, to separate them, equip them, prepare them and send them out.

Apostles and traveling ministers must always be wary of their heart motivations for trying to gather wealth. If they are not, they run the risk of operating in a spirit of Balaam.

THE BALAAM SPIRIT

A great apostle/teacher named Ralph Mahoney had some insights on Balaam that I want to share with you here, mixed in with some of my own thoughts. Balaam was a prophet of the Lord who was not an Israelite. Still, he did receive true revelation from God, except he was a profaned and defiled man. He dipped in and out of legitimate supernatural authority into imitation of the divine. This came about primarily because he loved material gain. In short, he was motivated by money, and he was a very famous man. His name is mentioned some sixty times in fifty-seven verses in no less than eight of the sixty-six books in the Bible. Perhaps we should get to know him? Just a thought. Go ahead and read Numbers 22-25, 31 if you're unfamiliar with this strange man.

Balaam was something of an enigma. He came from unexplained origins — his genealogy is shrouded in mystery (only his father is named as Beor.) All we know is he lived a month's journey, one-way, near the Euphrates River in the land of Pethor (modern day Iraq.)

(Numbers 22:5) His prophecies were one hundred percent accurate; his language was the most eloquent of all the Old Testament prophets; his allegories, the most poetic. In truth, he was second only to Moses in his talents as a prophet, having conversations with God very similarly to the scribe of the Law. Balaam's deception was his love of fame and fortune — this deception was also the most complete of all the prophets, unfortunately…. He ended up being a soothsayer, using enchantments and divinations in an attempt to curse what God had blessed, and he fell on the wrong side of Yahweh. Remember, that's a *bad thing.*

How is it that someone, whom God would have honored if he had stayed true, ended up being slain by an Israelite as a traitor of God and a hater of righteousness as an open advocate for fornication? The promises of riches and honor were too great for him to overcome. He fell into the pitfall of prosperity, and it cost him everything.

Enter Balak, the king of Moab. His kingdom was in the wilderness of Sinai, and he was encamped to the northeast of the Jews. He was shrewd enough to perceive that his monarchy was threatened by these Jews but not shrewd enough to place no faith in the power of sorcery. He figured it was the only way to defeat the Israelites. So Balak sets out to hire the world's most powerful prophet to speak curses over his enemies. This shows the defiled king's value system: "Money can buy anything — everyone has a price!" And unfortunately, in Balaam's case, he was right.

Now, initially, Balaam tried to resist. The first group Balak sent to buy his curses failed to secure the prophet's services. They were unable to subvert his integrity, so the king sent a larger group of more distinguished ambassadors to stroke Balaam's ego. Verses 15-17 in Chapter 22 show the king basically giving the prophet *carte blanche.* "Name your price, man. I'll pay you whatever you want, just come curse these people for me."

The first time around, God tells Balaam, "No way, Jose. They're a blessed people, so don't go." (Verse 12) But the second time 'round, Balaam's now starting to covet those rewards of divination so he brings it up to God again. And God says, "Well, all right, but take care to speak only the word I give you — nothing more, nothing less, OK?" (Verse 20)

The prophet saddles his donkey and hits the road, visions of moolah dance in his head. God's upset over the man's eager attitude toward the financial prospects, and He sends His Angel to snuff the dude out. That seems a little strange when you read it, right? God tells him to go, then seeks to kill him for going. Why would God do that? Because He was sending a dire warning:

"Listen up! You can't mix covetousness with ministry and not suffer consequences for it.... Namely, I plan to kill *you* and let the donkey live...." (Verse 33)

That's funny actually, if you think about it.

Why did God want to kill him? Because Balaam's way was perverse — his desire for material wealth was against God's way. (Verse 32) However, the donkey altered her way and would have been spared. Besides, I'm sure she was a very nice donkey.

Romans 1:27-28 and 2 Thessalonians 2:11-12 says that God sends a strong delusion to evil people and permits the sin itself to punish them. Their actions open the door to deception, but it is God who allows the sin to have its own penalty meted out against unrighteousness. After a fashion, because He permits the sin to punish, it is as if He Himself is sending the punishment. And since He is sending the delusion, one might say He permits Himself to deceive the unrighteous. This is touchy theology among many Christians, and I'm not here to ruffle anyone's feathers, but it would appear in Balaam's case that God did just this. (See Psalm 106, especially Verse 15.)

At any rate, for the sake of proving a point against mixture in the ministry, we'll say that since God told Balaam, "No," the first time, when the prophet pressed Him a second time, God deceived the man and said, "Yes." Then He sent His Angel with a drawn sword to punish him because he was greedy for gain and willing to market his ministry. I am convinced Balaam would have normally seen the Angel, except he was blinded by covetousness.

Samuel the prophet speaks of this blinding. "'Here I am. Witness against me before the Lord and before His anointed... from whose hand have I received any bribe with which to blind my eyes?'" (1 Samuel 12:3) He points out that taking a bribe (money) would have blinded his eyes. Many are blinded in today's Church because of covetousness and the love of riches.

"'...'And the cares of this world, the deceitfulness of riches, and the desires for other things entering in choke the word, and it becomes unfruitful.'" (Mark 4:19)

There's a connection here between deceitfulness of riches and desires [lust] for other things. Deception is blindness, and we cannot see the Angel of the Lord.

"'How the mighty have fallen, and the weapons of war perished!'" (2 Samuel 1:27)

"'...But exhort [encourage] one another daily... lest any of you be hardened through the deceitfulness of sin." (Hebrews 3:13)

We must take care not to be hardened by deceit as Balaam was!

Why do we ignore the pitfalls of prosperity? When Balaam's called to account, he says "...'I have sinned for I did not know You stood in the way against me. Now therefore, if it displeases You, I will turn back.'" (Numbers 22:34) Notice how he still wanted to go, even after the tongue-lashing, sword-waving Angel seeks to kill him. He says, "Well, I've sinned... but *if* You *still* don't want me to go...."

I envision the Angel of the Lord just shaking His head. "Go on then, but only speak what I tell you." (Verse 35)

Colossians 3:5 warns us to, "...put to death... covetousness, which is idolatry." As was in Balaam's case, there is a clear link between covetousness (idolatry) and fornication (immorality.) This is why God called the Israelites' worship of other gods "harlotry." (Jeremiah 3:6, among others)

Balak the king is angry at Balaam because he expected the man to prostitute his prophetic powers to divination and sorcery in order to curse Israel. And even though Balaam tried repeatedly to do so, he found he could only bless it.

Nevertheless, Israel pimps itself out to Moab in Numbers 25. The Moabite women, in cahoots with Balak (and the Midianites), seduce the men of Israel to commit fornication in a "sacred" act of worship to Baal, a god of fertility. This is a *bad thing* that gets God very angry, and 24,000 die in a plague.

See, I told you it was a bad thing....

What Balaam couldn't do by the divination of his prophetic gift was done by lust. Obviously this would bring God's wrath on Israel, and He would have completely destroyed them had not Phinehas, Aaron's grandson, stayed His zeal with his own righteous zealousness.

Pergamos was charged with harboring the spirit of Balaam, as I believe today's modern Church has done in many cases. "...'You have there those who hold the doctrine of Balaam, who taught Balak to put a stumbling block before the children of Israel, to eat things sacrificed to idols, and to commit sexual immorality.'" (Revelation 2:14) To covet material things is to commit immorality. "'You shall not covet your neighbor's house....'" (Exodus 20:17) It goes on to list many material things we are not supposed to covet.

The Church cannot abide the spirit of Balaam any longer — the apostolic anointing must be released to expose the Angel of the Lord so that the people are called to true repentance, turning from their paths, and forgoing the harlotry of divining the gifts!

Just as Paul admonished Timothy, we must also withdraw ourselves from the "useless wranglings of men of corrupt minds and destitute of the truth, who suppose that godliness is a means of gain." (1 Timothy 6:5)

GOLD DUST AND JEWELS FROM HEAVEN

There is a new move in Charismatic circles concerning gold dust and jewels coming down from heaven. There are basically two roads of thought regarding these expressions. Either 1) it is God enticing and romancing people to come to Him by expressing His lavish power on the earthly realm; or 2) it's not of His Spirit, but of conjurers dipping in and out of both the true supernatural, spiritual realm and of the preternatural, soulish realm. For the most part, I lean toward the first road of thought because I have experienced it and believed it to have been a true, godly manifestation. However, in all honesty, I think it might be the second explanation in some occasions.

I believe there are two realms of existence beyond the physical plane we exist in here on earth. I don't want to get into *Star Trek*, quantum physics and the like here, but there is the divine realm in which God exists, and there is a pseudospiritual/soulish realm inhabited by the demonic (familiar spirits.) This is called the preternatural realm. Baalam dipped in and out of both realms. There are false prophets and sorcerers out there on your television who possess some kind of power, divined and profaned though it is, that can produce lying signs and wonders to lead people away from worshipping God. Believe it or not, some psychics can be receiving hidden information, but the Bible speaks against this, saying they are using a familiar spirit. These psychics operate out of the preternatural realm.

True, godly prophets can also dip into that realm, if they are not careful, and such superfluous signs can be produced. I was in a meeting where one prophet actually told me my social security number and how much money was in my billfold. People *ooohed* and *ahhhed*, and I'm thinking, *Now, what on* earth *does that have to do with anything?* What was most strange about that meeting was that the prophet truly did get some anointed words from the Lord that really blessed people. But the flow of anointing was mixed. I believe this prophet operated in both the spiritual and preternatural realms.

It's wrong to think if you're of God, everything you produce or experience has to be of God. We as apostolic people must stay holy and intimate with our Lord Jesus!

My question regarding this current thrust toward gold dust and the like in services is: where does one draw the line? Some Catholics believe *stigmata* to be a true sign and wonder from God. Most Charismatics would disagree. What about the people with oil pouring out of their palms? What about dove feathers floating down? (Turns out in several instances they were just chicken feathers.) Flashing lights, smoke, vapors, thunderous lightning? You get the idea.

Some believe there is a true manifestation of God in the form of gold dust and jewels. But my point is those kinds of manifestations require great discernment to test whether or not they are supernatural or preternatural, and as I've said before, discernment is something that traditionally is sorely lacking in the Body of Christ.

The thing is, if they are true manifestations of God, then they are not an end unto themselves; they must have a purpose that leads people into a greater authority in their day-to-day troubles. I'm tired of hearing about gold dust and jewels appearing in services next to cancer victims and poor people trapped in wheelchairs. That manifested glory must be translated into authority for a person's deliverance. Otherwise we are missing the point.

Let me give an example.

I was ministering at a church wherein one of these brilliant, fifty-carat jewels fell from heaven. Now, I am personally under the persuasion this was a genuine heavenly jewel, a true manifestation of God's power on the earthly plane, because I have one as well.

But while the congregation was flabbergasted by this jewel, passing it back and forth, *oohing* and *ahhing*, I felt someone tug the back of my suit jacket. I turned to look at a woman with cerebral palsy. Tears welled up in her eyes.

"Dr. Maloney," she stammered. "I'm sorry. Can I ask you a question?"

"Sure," I replied, feeling badly for her.

She screwed up her courage; one could see what she was about to say really bothered her. "Well, I'm just wondering. I'm not trying to sound critical, or judgmental, and I think this jewel is wonderful. I appreciate everything I'm hearing and seeing about it." She began crying.

"But I've got to know, if there's so much power and authority here to see this jewel from God manifest, how come it can't be translated into greater faith in my life, and the life of this church, to see me healed of cerebral palsy? I've done everything I know what do to, and I can't seem to get healed. But this jewel sure is amazing...."

And she broke down in sobs, while I just stood there, floored by her humility and anguish.

It was a remarkable moment in my life. I prayed for her, and the Lord did touch her, but I was also shocked into awareness that these jewels just aren't enough!

We've had gold dust and the like for, what, ten or more years now, and I'm still not seeing a deeper level of God's miraculous power being manifested in people's lives on a continuing basis. The apostles must set things in order. If these signs are true manifestations, the same level of authority in Christ to produce these works must also be translated into the same authority creating liberty for people.

Again, Jesus is our great Example. He healed the sick, cleansed the lepers, raised the dead and opened people's eyes. Take the gold dust and find a way to turn it into His works, or let's just do away with it altogether and save ourselves the difficulty in discerning what's holy and what's profane. To me it is those biblical signs and wonders that are so prevalently recorded in Christ's ministry that would validate the gold dust experience. Makes sense right? I want the greater supernatural works, but I also want the Word.

I'm speaking balance here, discernment, not paranoia and fear. Be encouraged. Be admonished in love, and yes, be warned. You don't want the Angel of the Lord coming after you. Because... and let's say it all together, that's a *bad thing!*

I do *not* want to quench the Spirit, but I want the Spirit to use His gifts to heal people. Hey, I'm thankful for gold dust and jewels, if they come; but if they don't, I'm not losing any sleep over it. To be perfectly honest, I don't really care as long as folks are getting healed, delivered and set free in the services. Those are the true riches I'm after. It's those true riches that are going to benefit their personal lives even greater than watching gold dust fall.

Let that apostolic, breaker anointing come upon you so that you might perceive the holiness of God and translate that holiness into miraculous power to change lives! Amen.

Chapter One Outline

"Unveiling the Holiness of God"

THE HOLY VERSUS THE PROFANE

- We all need to have an unveiling of His awesome sanctification, and because many of us have not had that unveiling, there is a marked lack of character among His people, a certain lack of integrity
- There's too much mixture. Too much profaneness in something that is to be completely holy and set apart: the manifestation of the Kingdom of God
- The Father God is requiring the apostolic ones to teach His people the difference between the holy and the profane, the clean and the unclean. (Ezekiel 44)
- "Holy" is the Greek word *hagios* meaning "to be godlike, to designate sacred and separate that which God designates as sacred and separate"
- A profane person says, "I want what I want, when I want it, and I don't care who it hurts, who I've got to walk over to get my selfish way."
- "...Lest there be any... profane [godless] person like Esau, who for one morsel of food sold his birthright." (Hebrews 12:16)
- God is against profaneness as He is completely holy — the two attributes are archenemies and cannot sit beside one another for long

- One of the signs and wonders of His apostles is to unveil the profaneness in the Church, calling the people to be holy, thus creating an apostolic company that expresses the holiness of Christ to the world at large

PARTAKERS OF THE DIVINE

- "...As His divine power has given to us all things that pertain to life and godliness through the knowledge of Him who called us by glory and virtue, by which have been given to us exceedingly great and precious promises, that through these you may be partakers of the divine nature, having escaped the corruption [depravity] that is in the world through lust. But also for this very reason, giving all diligence, add to your faith virtue...." (2 Peter 1:2-5)
- We as born-again Christians are partakers of the divine nature. That means a little bit of God Himself lives inside of us, and we have been given life and godliness ("God-like-ness") through the salvation of Jesus Christ provided by the cross
- That godliness comes at a price: if God is holy, we must also be holy. To be anything other than holy creates a defilement, and for those of us who stand behind the pulpit, our defilement can be transferred to another person, just as the miraculous power of God residing within us can be conferred upon others

VESSELS OF VANITY

- Whatever spiritual, emotional or mental baggage left unchecked can be attributed to *vanity* and ultimately lessens divine unction, leaving tarnishing and corruption — an imitation of what was once divine

- "'They have envisioned futility and false divination, saying, "Thus says the Lord!" But the Lord has not sent them; yet they hope that the word may be confirmed.'" (Ezekiel 13:6)

- "...'Because you have spoken nonsense and envisioned lies, therefore I am indeed against you,' says the Lord God." (Ezekiel 13:8)

- Apostolic people must *discern* what is divinely inspired and what is an imitation of that divinity

- It takes an apostolic, breaker anointing to unveil the false supernatural from the true supernatural, found only in the realm of the Father's actions

- *Divine* is "the essence or personality of God manifested"

- "I beseech you therefore, brethren, by the mercies of God, that you present your bodies a living sacrifice, holy, acceptable to God, which is your reasonable service. And do not be conformed to this world, but be transformed by the renewing of your mind, that you may prove what is that good and acceptable and perfect will of God." (Romans 12:1-2)

- If you align yourself with this world system that is outside the will of God (meaning a godless age) you cannot be transformed into the likeness of His divine Personage, that

which is holy and set apart for a unique work that is against the status quo

- It takes more than an *astonishment* to declare a supernatural act divine

- One must have God's *approval* (that is the anointing) in order to display the divine. (Kim Clement)

- The anointing shall not be poured on man's flesh. Flesh is evil. There is nothing good about it, and it must be crucified

- The imitation of the divine leads to defilement, and defilement leads to divination

- Iniquity is something that is inherited through defilement — the Law of Transference

- By permitting a mixture of the holy and the profane, one opens oneself up to inheriting whatever iniquity the profaned person is carrying

- "'Give no regard to mediums and familiar spirits; do not seek after them, to be defiled by them: I am the Lord your God.'" (Leviticus 19:31)

- "...'Son of man, mark well, see with your eyes and hear with your ears, all that I say to you concerning all the ordinances of the house of the Lord and all its laws. Mark well who may enter the house and all who go out from the sanctuary.'" (Ezekiel 44:5)

- "Now the Spirit expressly [clearly, explicitly] says that in latter times some will depart from the faith, giving heed to deceiving spirits and doctrines of demons, speaking lies in

hypocrisy, having their own conscience seared with a hot iron...." (1 Timothy 4:1-2)

BYPRODUCTS OF INIQUITY

- "...Weep between the porch and the altar...." (Joel 2:16-17)
- There should be no discrepancies between how people perceive you and how you really are
- We must allow people to speak into our lives, and vice versa, perhaps pointing out any blind spots — particular areas in our lives that we cannot see. Not to judge (easier said than done, I know), but to bring a closer level of intimacy with God
- "Thus says the Lord concerning the prophets who make my people stray; who chant 'Peace' while they chew with their teeth, but who prepare war against him who puts nothing into their mouths: 'Therefore you shall have night without vision [revelation], and you shall have darkness without divination; the sun shall go down on the prophets, and the day shall be dark for them. So the seers shall be ashamed, and the diviners abashed; indeed they shall all cover their lips; for there is no answer from God.'" (Micah 3:5-7)
- "'But those things which proceed out of the mouth come from the heart, and they defile a man.'" (Matthew 15:18)
- The apostolic people of God must discern for themselves if the minister standing before them has defilements in his/her hidden life, not in a judgmental, critical way, but also not being gullible

- Apostles discern three attributes of someone who is permitted to enter into the household of the Lord
- Firstly, is the person circumcised in their heart and flesh — meaning is he/she set apart for the Lord?
- Secondly, does the person keep his/her covenant with God and others?
- Thirdly, is the person not too independent?
- By properly discerning these attributes in a person, the apostle is able to weed out, so to speak, the profaneness that desperately wants to mix in with the holy

THE SEPARATION PRINCIPLE

- One can be deceived by the anointing they've had resting on them, and if they're not careful, they don't recognize when the Spirit's departed
- The deception is: one somehow persuades oneself that he or she is an exception to God's standard
- Your protection from deception is not your fear of being deceived — it is your level of intimacy with Jesus
- Be separated unto Him alone, and the Spirit will not flee from you

THE PROMISE OF PROSPERITY

- "'Therefore if you have not been faithful in the unrighteous mammon, who will commit to your trust the true riches?'" (Luke 16:11)

- "Listen, my beloved brethren: Has God not chosen the poor of this world to be rich in faith and heirs of the kingdom which He promised to those who love Him?" (James 2:5)
- *Prosperity*, "to have a good journey through life"
- "He shall be like a tree planted by the rivers of water, that brings forth its fruit in its season, whose leaf also shall not wither; and whatever he does shall prosper." (Psalm 1:3)
- "Beloved, I pray that you may prosper in all things and be in health, just as your soul prospers." (3 John 2)
- "Let them shout for joy and be glad, who favor my righteous cause; and let them say continually, 'Let the Lord be magnified, who has pleasure in the prosperity of His servant.'" (Psalm 35:27)
- "...'The God of heaven Himself will prosper us....'" (Nehemiah 2:20)
- "'And you shall remember the Lord your God, for it is He who gives you power to get wealth....'" (Deuteronomy 8:18)
- "Both riches and honor come from You...." (1 Chronicles 29:12)
- "As for every man to whom God has given riches and wealth, and given him power to eat of it, to receive his heritage [portion] and rejoice in his labor — this is the gift of God." (Ecclesiastes 5:19)
- "Abram was very rich in livestock, in silver, and in gold." (Genesis 13:2)

- "There was a man... blameless and upright... who feared God and shunned evil... [who had] a very large household, so that this man was the greatest of all the people of the East." (Job 1:1, 3)

- "Or do you despise the riches of His goodness, forbearance, and longsuffering, not knowing that the goodness of God leads you to repentance?" (Romans 2:4)

- "...And that He might make known the riches of His glory on the vessels of mercy, which He prepared beforehand for glory...." (Romans 9:23)

- "...That He would grant you, according to the riches of His glory, to be strengthened with might through His Spirit in the inner man...." (Ephesians 3:16)

- "Oh, the depth of the riches both of the wisdom and knowledge of God!" (Romans 11:33)

- "In Him we have redemption through His blood, the forgiveness of sins, according to the riches of His grace... that [we] may know what is the hope of His calling, what are the riches of the glory of His inheritance... that in the ages to come He might show the exceeding riches of His grace in His kindness toward us in Christ Jesus... that [we] should preach among the Gentiles the unsearchable riches of Christ...." (Ephesians 1:7, 18; 2:7; 3:8)

- "To them God willed to make known what are the riches of the glory of this mystery among the Gentiles: which is Christ in you, the hope of glory... that their hearts may be encouraged, being knit together in love, and attaining to all the riches of the full assurance of understanding, to the knowledge of the mystery of God, both of the Father and of Christ...." (Colossians 1:27; 2:2)

- "By faith Moses, when he became of age, refused to be called the son of Pharaoh's daughter, choosing rather to suffer affliction with the people of God than to enjoy the passing pleasures of sin, esteeming the reproach of Christ greater riches than the treasures in Egypt; for he looked to the reward." (Hebrews 11:24-26)

- "Then Peter said, 'Silver and gold I do not have, but what I do have I give you: In the name of Jesus Christ of Nazareth, rise up and walk.'" (Acts 3:6)

- "But earnestly desire the best gifts...." (1 Corinthians 12:31)

- "'Because you say, "I am rich, have become wealthy, and have need of nothing" — and do not know that you are wretched, miserable, poor, blind, and naked — I counsel you to buy from Me gold refined in the fire, that you may be rich....'" (Revelation 3:17-18)

- "...'Have faith in God. For assuredly, I say to you, whoever says to this mountain, "Be removed and be cast into the sea," and does not doubt in his heart, but believes that those things he says will be done, he will have whatever he says.'" (Mark 11:22-23)

- A mountain does not speak of material wealth, but rather a problem, an insurmountable barrier that must be overcome

- "And we know that all things work together for good to those who love God, to those who are the called according to His purpose. For whom He foreknew, He also predestined to be conformed to the image of His Son, that He might be the firstborn among many brethren." (Romans 8:28-29)
- The "good" comes out of an *appropriate response* to what seems bad so that you might be conformed to the image of Christ. Only *then* do all things work together for good
- "There is one who scatters, yet increases more; and there is one who withholds more than is right, but it leads to poverty. The generous soul will be made rich, and he who waters will also be watered himself." (Proverbs 11:24-25)
- "He who has a generous eye will be blessed, for he gives of his bread to the poor." (Proverbs 22:9)

Pitfalls of Prosperity

- "Now godliness with contentment is great gain. For we brought nothing into this world, and it is certain we can carry nothing out. And having food and clothing, with these we shall be content. But those who desire to be rich fall into temptation and a snare, and into many foolish and harmful lusts which drown men in destruction and perdition. For the love of money is a root of all kinds of evil, for which some have strayed [erred] from the faith in their greediness, and pierced themselves through with many sorrows." (1 Timothy 6:6-10)

- "'No servant can serve two masters; for either he will hate the one and love the other, or else he will be loyal to the one and despise the other. You cannot serve God and mammon.'" (Luke 16:13)
- "He who loves silver will not be satisfied with silver; nor he who loves abundance, with increase. This also is vanity." (Ecclesiastes 5:10)
- "Set your affection [mind] on things above, not on things on the earth. (Colossians 3:2, KJV)
- "Do not love the world or the things in the world. If anyone loves the world, the love of the Father is not in him." (1 John 2:25)
- "...If riches increase, do not set your heart on them." (Psalm 62:10)
- "...'Take heed and beware of covetousness, for one's life does not consist in the abundance of the things he possesses.'" (Luke 12:15)

THE BALAAM SPIRIT

- Balaam was a prophet of the Lord who was not an Israelite. He received true revelation from God, except he was profaned and defiled, dipping in and out of legitimate supernatural authority into imitation of the divine
- His prophecies were one hundred percent accurate; his language was the most eloquent of all the Old Testament prophets; his allegories, the most poetic.

- In truth, he was second only to Moses in his talents as a prophet, having conversations with God very similarly to the scribe of the Law
- Balaam's deception was his love of fame and fortune
- "'Here I am. Witness against me before the Lord and before His anointed... from whose hand have I received any bribe with which to blind my eyes?" (1 Samuel 12:3)
- "...'And the cares of this world, the deceitfulness of riches, and the desires for other things entering in choke the word, and it becomes unfruitful.'" (Mark 4:19)
- "'How the mighty have fallen, and the weapons of war perished!'" (2 Samuel 1:27)
- "...But exhort [encourage] one another daily... lest any of you be hardened through the deceitfulness of sin." (Hebrews 3:13)
- "...Put to death... covetousness, which is idolatry." (Colossians 3:5)
- "...'You have there those who hold the doctrine of Balaam, who taught Balak to put a stumbling block before the children of Israel, to eat things sacrificed to idols, and to commit sexual immorality.'" (Revelation 2:14)
- To covet material things is to commit immorality
- "'You shall not covet your neighbor's house....'" (Exodus 20:17)
- Just as Paul admonished Timothy, we must also withdraw ourselves from the, "useless wranglings of men of corrupt minds and destitute of the truth, who suppose that godliness is a means of gain." (1 Timothy 6:5)

2
Unveiling the Faith of God

THE CHICKEN BONE LADY

Part of the curriculum requirements for attending Christ for the Nations Institute was to sign up for a student outreach ministry, so I decided to go out for "Nursing Home Ministry." Sounded pretty simple. Sing to some elderly folks, read them some Bible stories. No biggie. (I'm being sarcastic here, in case you can't tell by the tone of my writing....) Actually, I figured what better place to learn how to minister to the sick, afflicted, oppressed and depressed than in a nursing home! And at that time, way back in the early '70s, the Dallas/Fort Worth area had over one hundred nursing homes just ripe for the pickin'.

So I began to visit some of the nursing homes in and around the school. These visits became amazing times of tremendous experience for me as the Lord began to teach me sensitivity concerning to whom I was to minister. I mean, realistically, just about... *everyone* in a nursing home needs *some* kind of healing, right? There are dozens of rooms, packed with needy people, and just no way to pray for everyone on a Saturday afternoon visit; so what can you do? You begin to recognize the prodding of the Lord. *Pray for this one. Lay hands on that one. That one needs deliverance!*

There were about twelve or fifteen students on the nursing home ministry team, and we'd gather together early in the morning to pray then head out to this place or another, walking from room to room, waiting for the Lord to stop us and say, "Here's one. Pray for this one."

We saw some of the most astounding miracles during these trips. It would take another whole chapter just to highlight each one.

I remember leading a ninety-something-year-old man to the Lord the night before he passed away. There was one elderly woman so tormented by demons, she was strapped down to a bed. As she writhed and screamed, you could watch teeth marks appear on her body as the demons were physically biting her. Dear readers, *that's* demon possessed! So we took authority over the spirits, she was delivered and fell into a peaceful sleep — the first she'd had in weeks. The bite marks (there must have been over a hundred of them) instantly disappeared. There were *those* kinds of miracles.

One in particular, the subject of this recounting, occurred as I was passing by an open door that led into an elderly woman's dormitory. It felt as if the hand of God grabbed hold of my chest and *threw* me into the room. No exaggeration. I was pushed inside to see a daughter panicking over her mother, who was quite obviously choking to death.

It turns out the daughter had been feeding the mother, and the older woman, upon taking a deep, coughing breath, managed to lodge a small chicken bone somewhere in her windpipe. She was not able to breathe and was turning quite a nasty shade of blue.

As I was unceremoniously tossed into the room, the daughter fell to her knees and began to cry out, "God! Oh, God! Don't take my mother from me! I can't live without her!" She suddenly noticed me, tears in her eyes, and blurted, "Is there anything you can do?"

Needless to say I fell to pieces. Every tiny bit of strength, power, faith just ebbed out of my body, leaked out of my shoes and disappeared into that tiled floor. Real dominion man that I am....

I squirmed out of the room, thankfully turning left down the hall, because turning to the right would've put me in a straight line for the elevators, which would've been a completely welcome sight just then. Condemnation replaced the faith that had seeped out. I heard this voice in my head shriek, *You blew it, Jim!* (Please don't call me Jim....)

You'll never be used in ministry again, coward! You had this perfect opportunity to glorify God and you blew it! He won't trust you with anything!

These screams blew through my mind in a nanosecond, and I felt as if I was moving through thick black spiritual mud. I felt so condemned. I shuffled toward the end of the hall where there was a window looking down several stories. The more I walked, the worse I felt.

But I felt in my spirit I was neglecting something that I'd been taught by the instructors at CFNI: one has to learn how to engage one's inner spirit man. So in front of all these nurses that were running into the choking lady's room, I began to pray aloud in warfare-like tongues, whipping my spirit into action. I didn't feel any better, but out of a force of sheer will, I made myself turn back around and wade through that spiritual mud to the woman's room.

I heard someone shouting. "Where's the doctor?"

The nurses were doing CPR, pounding on the poor lady's chest. She was very much blue by now, pallid, deathly. I was still praying fervently out loud in tongues, and this thought jumped into my head, *Great, Jim, what are you gonna do? Now you gotta walk past her room again!*

All of a sudden — I love it! — something leapt up in my spirit, and it felt as if hot oil was poured on the top of my head. It oozed down my hair (yes, I used to have thick, luxurious hair, if you can imagine), ran down my shoulders and covered my entire body in this tingling warmth. Something got a hold of me; it was like liquid confidence, fire burning in my stomach. Again, it was like I changed clothes in a phone booth and became super human.... (Get it now? Like Superman....)

It was faith. Pure, undiluted, raw faith. God's kind of faith — the kind He has in Himself that nothing is impossible to Him 'cause He's

God. When You're God, You can have that kind of faith in Yourself, and You can give a little bit of it away to others. So He gave some of it to me just then.

Before I even fully grasped what was happening, I was caught up in this supernatural experience. I rushed into the room. The four nurses parted like the Red Sea before me, without even looking up; they hadn't even seen me race into the room because their backs were turned to me. They just moved aside, and I bounded up to the woman's bed. She looked dead to me, although I can't state that as medical certainty. She must have at least very nearly expired. At any rate, she was completely without pulse or breath, rigid.

I stuck my hands on her forehead and cried, "I rebuke you, spirit of death!"

Instantly, her eyes fluttered. Color came back into her face. She sat up and took a deep breath.

"What happened?" she croaked, looking around.

You should've seen the nurses' and the daughter's faces. They looked at me like I was wearing a pirate's costume. Or maybe a Superman costume....

I felt the Lord quickly urge me away. I could've stayed and given them my name. You know, hey, tell your pastor to have me at his church! I'm a Bible school student. Something. But they just stared at me, open mouthed, as I calmly walked out of the room and turned right this time, toward the elevators.

Halfway down the elevator, I felt this gift of faith lift off me, and I crumpled to the floor. *What in the world just happened up there?*

THE SPIRIT OF FAITH

"I thank God... as without ceasing I remember you in my prayers night and day, greatly desiring to see you, being mindful of your tears, that I may be filled with joy, when I call to remembrance the genuine [unhypocritical] faith that is in you, which dwelt first in your grandmother Lois and your mother Eunice, and I am persuaded is in you also.

"Therefore I remind you to stir up the gift of God which is in you through the laying on of hands. For God has not given us a spirit of fear, but of power and of love and of a sound mind.

"Therefore do not be ashamed of the testimony of our Lord, nor of me His prisoner, but share with me in the sufferings for the gospel according to the power of God...." (2 Timothy 1:3-8)

We know according to James 5:15 that "...the prayer of faith will save the sick...." But, moreover, it must be a prayer of faith in the Spirit of boldness! The apostolic breaker anointing produces an *unfeigned faith*. A faith with no pretense, no hypocrisy – genuine faith that expects to see *results*. A faith that is simply not just "going through the motions." Genuine faith! Real faith! Indeed, something is to be added to our faith! This is where the apostolic anointing comes in.

According to Hebrews 11:6, we find that, "Now faith is the substance [realization] of things hoped for, the evidence [confidence] of things not seen." It's neat to think of faith as a substance. To quote James again, "The effective, fervent prayer of a righteous man avails much. Elijah was a man with a nature like ours, and he prayed earnestly that it would not rain; and it did not rain on the land for three years and six months. And he prayed again, and the heaven gave rain, and the earth produced its fruit." (James 5:16-18)

It was because of Elijah's energized prayer of faith that even the clouds stopped giving! That's true faith. Faith that works! "For in

Christ Jesus neither circumcision nor uncircumcision avails anything, but faith working through love." (Galatians 5:6) Faith without love avails nothing. It is only the unfeigned faith working by divine love that accomplishes the miraculous.

Second Peter 1:1 speaks of "those who have obtained like precious faith with us by the righteousness of our God and Savior Jesus Christ...." We, too, should obtain "like precious faith" as those of the apostles — faith of the same value, as it means. In other words, faith to see that which the apostles saw. As God is love, God is faith — the substance or material that is faith is just a by-product of His being. He is. And therefore, there is faith.

We are changed into the reflection of Christ as we see Him exhibit and express Himself on this earth — that is faith in action, faith being rewarded. To put a fine point on it, it's the kind of faith that sees miracles. And seeing miracles (putting faith into operation) is one of the ways we are changed into reflections of the Son.

I'm not just talking about overtly supernatural activity here, as important as that is. I also mean faith in action in the day-to-day practicalities of life (i.e., your work, your home, your marriage.) Your faith will turn you into a reflection of Jesus as you see His interventions and His love operating in you as you go about your daily business. Not only do you have the dynamic miraculous, but you have faith to see every challenge or every need met. That is true faith.

The apostolic people must continually be exercising true faith, operating under the Spirit of faith, adding to their faith *more faith* to see Christ revealed in the world through signs, wonders and miracles. This is not just faith that we whip up from our own experiences, but rather a downloaded element of God Himself. As stated in Hebrews 12:2, it is Jesus who is "the author [originator] and finisher [perfecter] of our faith...."

Romans 10:17 shows us where we get faith. "So then faith comes by hearing, and hearing by the word of God." What does this mean? I'm so glad you asked — I've been eager to tell somebody!

We receive faith primarily in three ways: through *instruction*, *inspiration* and *impartation*.

Being taught correctly the Word of God breeds faith — that would be instruction. In the context of this book, it is the apostle's function to instruct properly the saints in the Word of God. And as they do so, believing that they are teaching under the influence of the Holy Ghost sent down from heaven and "...[in] His divine power [that] has given us all things that pertain to life and godliness, through the knowledge of Him who called us by glory and virtue...." (2 Peter 1:3)

That is why it is vitally important for the apostles' lives to be lives of inspiration, preaching and instructing out of their own encounters with the Lord. Not only relating to their peers, but relating as mentors generationally to those the Lord has given them to raise up with "like precious faith." Hearing the wonderful testimonies of faith bringing results in the apostles' lives quickens our faith — that's inspiration. That's why I share all these testimonies in this book: to add *more* faith to your faith.

The spirit of faith can be imparted through the laying on of hands, as shown earlier in 2 Timothy. One of the key expressions of an apostle, in my eyes, is that unction and authority to impart such a spirit of faith. The apostolic anointing is an anointing for reproducing faith in the lives of others.

So how can we sum this up into one definitive statement? Well, how about: so then, faith comes through glory encounters. That's pretty definitive. The more you encounter the authority, love and glory of the Father — the more faith you will receive. Miracles breed miracles. Faith breeds faith. You start with a little one, move on to a bigger one and pretty soon you have this behemoth faith Spirit bounding around your life.

I'll share one of these particular glory encounters with you.

THE MESSENGER ANGEL VISITATION

Let me start here with a word of advice. We should not place undue emphasis on angels. All angelic encounters, if they are true encounters, must point to the authority, holiness and centrality of Jesus Christ alone. We should not seek to initiate communication with angels. I have seen an alarming increase in "angelic" encounters these past few years among Charismatics that I would say border on angel worship, which is deception. (See Revelation 19:10; Hebrews 1, 2.) As important as the ministry of angels is, we are partakers of a higher revelation that even the angels want to look into. (1 Peter 1:12) So please keep this next segment in context with the above admonition. It's not the angel I'm drawing attention to.

It was March 5, 1975, around 2:50pm, when I had a profound encounter with God. What occurred on that day was a commissioning to release an anointing that would increase people's faith. I share this visitation with you now in order to unveil more fully the God-kind of faith that the Father desires His people to possess. As always, I am guarded when I share encounters of these kinds, with a deep desire to present just how humbling it is for the Lord to grace us with His favor. Again, what happened on this day is not for my benefit alone; more so, it is for you in your walk with God, as we all strive and endeavor to release the apostolic spirit in our lives. I give all the glory and honor to the Father alone for permitting me to share this revelation with you. I will have to trust in your discernment and sensitivity to the Holy Spirit that He might convey to you my integrity and brokenness concerning this event. But nevertheless, this occurrence did happen, and I believe I am compelled by God to share it with you for your benefit.

It was during this period of time that I entered into a heightened state of tremendously seeking the Lord in intense prayer and fasting. It was one of those times where I felt the Lord impress upon me that He was dealing with some of the things I have addressed earlier in the book, spiritual and emotional needs that I had concerning my upbringing. Issues that He needed to uproot in order to tear down those walls of isolation that prohibit His divine grace from flowing more fully in one's life. Simply put, just like everyone else, I had junk that needed to be cleaned out. It is always uncomfortable to go through intense dealings of the Lord, but they are always so very, very worth it!

I was praying in my apartment when suddenly I felt a tremendous **heaviness** descend upon my eyes and my flesh. I collapsed on the bed, laying on my stomach, my face turned toward a blank wall as this heaviness grew greater and greater. My eyes were filled with lead, my flesh was that of a dead man's. I could not move a muscle, paralyzed. The weight of God fell upon me, and I shut my eyes, unable to open them.

There was no fear; I felt this tangible presence of the Lord crash down upon me. There was a sense of outstanding divine energy, as well as acceptance, love and peace. But it was a *serious* presence that pressed down upon me, and I caved in, prostrate before the glory of the Lord.

I was pondering why I could not open my eyes under this weightiness of God, when through my eyelids I "saw" a brilliant, bright light fill the room. This light stood right next to me as I lay with my face toward the wall. I came to the shocking realization that if I had the ability to open my eyes, this light would blind me completely. It was almost too much to bear even with my eyes shut tight.

I felt there was someone standing there in this light by my bedside and that he had a message to deliver. When this revelation rose up from my spirit man and illuminated my mind, immediately the angel began to speak to me audibly. He possessed a very commanding voice. (I use "he" in a general sense; angelic "gender" is unimportant here.)

You'd probably like me to tell you exactly what the angel said, right?

Unfortunately, at this time, I'm not completely at liberty to share everything verbatim. A lot of what was said is still coming to pass in my own life. Many of the things the angel shared were extremely personal to me. Some things I have shared with no one else, not even my wife. So don't feel left out.

This visitation went on for twenty minutes — I checked a clock later. In the first part of this visitation, the angel began to quote various keynote verses of scripture that were to convey my expression of life and ministry to mankind. One of the scriptures was Philemon 6. Memorize this verse; it's not long. But it is a powerful portion of scripture in the release of the apostolic spirit of faith. Don't forget this verse; it comes up again later in the chapter... there will be a test.

"...That the sharing of your faith may become effective by the acknowledgment of every good thing which is in you in Christ Jesus." (Philemon 6)

When the angel quoted this verse I was released from the weight that bore me down and I opened my eyes. Instantly I was bodily lifted by the supernatural power of the Spirit and turned around on my back; remember that I had been laying on my stomach. I was then physically moved into a sitting position on the edge of the bed. (Folks, I know what it's like to be *moved* by the Spirit!)

I looked into the realm of the spiritual. It was like clouds in the wall before me. I spoke inwardly, *Holy Spirit, what is it You want to show me?* When I thought this, I was suddenly able to look straight forward, yet I was seeing down, straight down. I don't know how else to describe it. My eyes were up, but I was viewing what was below. I hope that makes sense.

My eyes were opened onto the outer darkness, and I was permitted for a minute or so of time to see the demonic rank and file of hell. I know what it means when the Word says there are principalities, powers, rulers of darkness, spiritual hosts of wickedness in high places. (Ephesians 6:12) It is a caste system of demons, some higher up than others on the evil totem pole.

I will not, nor cannot, begin to convey or describe what these demonic beings look or sound like. I won't dignify them enough to spend any more time on them than necessary to convey my point. The words "revolting" and "disgusting" are too weak.

What I will describe is the total sense of chaos and destruction that permeated the entire place. The demons literally *devoured* one another in a mad, confusing attempt to claw their way toward me. They shrieked and bit and scratched, seething over one another.

And I suddenly felt... *fear.* Paralyzing fear. A sense of desperate alienation in a split second — just one millisecond — a blink of an eye. Fear, cold and clammy, gripped me. It is the most horrifying feeling in the range of human emotions. *They* were out to get me!

And as suddenly as the fear came, I heard the voice of the Lord speak to me:

"My people have **all** authority over **all** the power of the enemy in My name."

Ladies and gentlemen, let me stop right here and declare this simple, undeniable truth: There is *no* demon in hell of which you have to be afraid. I have seen them with my own eyes. You, as a son and daughter of God, in His name have *all*, complete, total authority over the evil one. Period. Fear *no* demon! Yes, exercise wisdom and get the mind of God — don't go picking fights you don't have to, but realize that God has total authority and has given us a right to call on that authority in a time of need.

Instantaneously as the Lord spoke, this *faith* came over me — this energizing, dominion shield of faith rose up over my entire body; it exploded out of my spirit, boldness and warmth flowed through me. I knew I was utterly protected by this shield of faith, and I only had to call upon the name of the Lord and I would be saved.

"I rebuke you in the name of Jesus!" I shouted, pointing my finger at the host of wickedness screaming toward me.

Instantly every demon dissipated. They were there, and then simply weren't. I know this was a vision, so I'm not sure where exactly they went, and I don't really care. The point is, this dominion over the enemy was so complete that I was suddenly found completely safe on my bed, with this angel standing next to me, and I was just *rumbling* with faith.

The angel resumed speaking, and I'll share with you what else was said, in just a little bit. That's what people in the biz call a "cliffhanger"....

FAITH THAT IS ENERGIZED

But meanwhile, back at the ranch, faith must be energized. What I mean by that is there must be a release of virtue (God-like power, or miracles) in our own level of faith. This is what Peter is saying: "But also for this very reason [see verses 1-4], giving all diligence, add to your faith virtue, to virtue..." (2 Peter 1:5) And then he goes on to list all the "good things" that come from faith impregnated by virtue.

The Greek word *arete* (Strong's #703) is translated "virtue" in our modern English, from a Greek word for masculine strength and valor (Strong's #730), even though *arete* itself is a feminine word. We could say it means to have "a good opinion of a person." To be moral, excellent, good, to have some intrinsic, eternal worth. The word later came to mean the "miraculous power," either of God or a person who followed God. Notice how it is similar to *dunamis* and *kabod*. Glory, power, virtue. They are simply attributes of God.

So we could say that miraculous power is to be added to our faith, and from that addition comes forth a greater degree of the knowledge, self-control, perseverance, godliness, brotherly kindness and ultimately love that Peter is so fired up about.

What does this mean to you and me as we strive for an apostolic breaker anointing? If we want a greater release of virtuous knowledge, self-control, etc., etc., we need miracles added to our faith! It, then, becomes exceedingly important to strive for a deep intimacy with God, a love for who He is, an extremely close relationship with Him. And from that intimacy, we enter into such a state of rest, or confidence, in our relationship with Him that it releases the miraculous, adding it to our faith. Therefore, a vibrant closeness to God adds miracles to our faith, then, does it not? Perhaps one of the reasons behind a lack of miraculous power, and consequently the above "good qualities," in a person stems from a lack of profound intimacy with God in their lives.

So, a miracle is an expression of faith, a release of virtue based upon one's relationship with the Father. When faith is properly exercised to see a particular result, a virtue is exhibited, and the desired result is achieved: we see the miracle happen. This is the awesome purpose, responsibility and privilege of apostles that they are used to create a spiritually dynamic atmosphere conducive for people to rise up and express their faith as they see the apostles release their breaker anointing. And the miracles take place. This apostolic dynamic applies to the corporate setting and to one-on-one ministry equally.

FAITH THAT IS EXERCISED

We know that faith is a virtue, an expression of the very existence of God the Father. It is resident in His glory, His character, His charisma. By adding to our faith *more faith* (that is, the God-kind of faith) we increase our own faith's supply of virtue, and miracles are born.

Jesus placed the highest premium on His Father's kind of faith. "…'Have faith in God, for assuredly, I say to you, whoever says to this mountain, "Be removed and be cast into the sea," and does not doubt in his heart, but believes that those things he says will be done, he will have whatever he says.'" (Mark 11:22-23)

Many Christians read this passage of scripture and assume Jesus is giving some kind of "formula" for twisting God's arm to do things for them. That understanding is unenlightened and unbiblical. The whole of Jesus' expression on this earth was tied into a pursuit of God as the Source of faith-virtue; it was tied into His supremely close relationship with the Father. The fig tree withered from the words spoken by Jesus' lips not because Jesus had some ill-concocted notion of the Father as some cosmic gofer, but because Jesus *understood* the Father. He had a deep, unwavering, daily relationship with the Father, and *virtue was added to His faith*. It isn't so much what Jesus said (although what we say *is* important) as what He believed deep in His innermost being. He knew, that He knew, that He knew the Father would honor His words because of His relationship with the Father. His faith was *in* God, not only in what God could *do*. Jesus' entire ministry expression was centralized *in* the Father, not just *for* the Father. See? It's a deeper level.

This is one of the greatest keys to apostolic anointing release: we must learn how not just to minister *unto* the Lord (as in those who say, "I'm doing this ministry work unto the Lord" or "I'm ministering *for* the Lord.") But rather, we must have an understanding that we are ministering in the *Person of Christ* for the Lord. This is where apostles and apostolic people have to comprehend that their focus is always, always centered, or rooted, in the Person of Christ. It's *in* the Person of Christ that we do things *for* the Lord.

Otherwise, many people base their sense of identity in ministry solely on what they're accomplishing for the Lord. They say, "Am I gaining acceptance before Him by doing this or that?" They also constantly strive in their lives to gain acceptance among their peers when they don't seemingly realize that everything they hope to achieve is found in ministering *in* the Person of Christ *for* the Lord Jesus Christ. Take a moment to meditate on this revelation. All apostolic release in ministry is centered in the Person of Jesus, just as Jesus' ministry expression was centered in the Father..

If the apostles and apostolic people would enter into this key revelation, they would cease striving to gain acceptance and approval among peers, or from the Lord, for that matter. Now, I believe there is a place in ministry for acceptance, approval and honor — don't get me wrong. But many people allow it to be a driving force behind their ministries, so they're constantly frustrated because they can never seem to achieve that level of perfection that they envision their ministry expression should be at. And perhaps the initial vision of their ministry expectations was based on a faulty perception to begin with, because they thought it was what they could do *for* Christ, not what they could do *in* Christ.

In other words, the key to apostolic anointing release is in recognizing that all true ministry must be *centered* in Christ, and then doing things *for* Christ. If we would just center our ministries in the Lord and make ourselves available every day, we would leave it up to His measure, His judgment, if we have sufficiently ministered in the level that He intended. This creates a tremendous sense of freedom and release, I daresay even *enjoyment*, in ministering in the Lord, for the Lord. I think it's a great key in releasing the miraculous.

"And whatever you do in word or deed, do all **in** the name of the Lord Jesus, giving thanks to God the Father through Him." (Colossians 3:17, emphasis added)

So let's look at Stephen in the Book of Acts. Here's a person whom the Bible records as "a man full of faith and the Holy Spirit." (Acts 6:5) The apostles laid hands on him (adding to his faith virtue — that's impartation), and the book records that "...Stephen, full of faith and power, did great wonders and signs among the people." (Acts 6:8)

The important thing I want to point out here is that Stephen was *not* an apostle. He was just a "normal" guy (well, what's *normal*, really?) like you and me, but he was full of faith and power. His power stemmed from his faith being energized and exercised — he saw what the apostles did, believed deep down in his spirit that he could do the same, and God honored him for it.

I venture to think that the apostles in the Book of Acts influenced Stephen's life by their examples and impartation, and thus imparted to him a spirit of faith. Today's apostles should operate in like manner, working with "normal" people (I use that term lightly), getting their hands on 'em, and imparting a measure of their *own* faith into the lives of those around them. It is the anointing of the apostle to birth apostolic people into greater faith through imparting a spirit of faith.

Then there's Philip, who was with Stephen when the apostles laid hands on them. Philip was just a "normal" (there it is again!) guy as well. His faith gets energized, he starts to exercise it by evangelizing

Samaria, and "...the multitudes with one accord heeded the things spoken by Philip, hearing and seeing the miracles which he did." (Acts 8:6) Notice, the people *believed* the Christ that Philip was preaching because of the miracles. We as servant evangelists should take note of Stephen and Philip: the miracles of God prove the truth of salvation in Jesus Christ.

These two mighty, "normal" men of God are powerful examples that the virtue of faith can be imparted by the laying on of hands. Let's look at Moses, who was certainly apostolic in his function even before there was such a thing as an apostle. God tells Moses, "...'Take Joshua the son of Nun with you, a man in whom is the Spirit, and lay your hands on him... and you shall give some of your authority to him....'" (Numbers 27:18, 20)

Again, Joshua was a regular dude. He had the Spirit in him, but it took Moses laying his hands on him to *transfer* some of that authority to Joshua. Moses added virtue to Joshua's faith. That this is obvious is without question, seeing all the miraculous exploits that Joshua did in his life after the death of Moses. "Now Joshua the son of Nun was full of the spirit of wisdom, for Moses had laid his hands on him; so the children of Israel heeded him, and did as the Lord had commanded Moses." (Deuteronomy 34:9)

Why did the children of Israel follow Joshua? Because he was a cool guy? Yeah, I'm sure he was, but moreover it was because his faith exhibited a miraculous virtue — the spirit of wisdom resting upon him — that had come to him by the laying on of hands. I'd have followed him, too!

Faith that is Effectual

How, then, does one's faith become effectual? Let's say a person's faith is so full of virtue that it's literally busting out of the seams. That's great! But what good does all that virtue do if it's never exhibited? That's right: *nada*. The big goose egg.

Faith becomes effectual when it is shared or communicated. Without sharing virtuous faith, it can do no good. It is the communication of your faith that makes the signs, wonders and miracles come forth. You've added to your faith virtue, and now you have to let that virtue manifest.

So then, how is faith communicated? Remember the three I's earlier? Inspiration, instruction and impartation. You have it, now give it away to others. Faith is communicated through the generations, as in the case of Timothy receiving his gift of faith from his mother, who got hers through his grandmother. That's the inspiration part.

I'm inspired by people like Smith Wigglesworth, Kathryn Kulhman and Brant Baker. Seeing and hearing what they did made me want to do the same thing. I hope to inspire you, if you've sat under my ministry, or moreover, by reading this book. I want you to do the same things I'm endeavoring to do under the inspiration of the Lord. The problem with this generation is they lack inspiration; they're not inspired to great things. I believe you and I as apostolic people will change that! "See what God did through me — this person has walked out of a wheelchair. Now, you can see that in your own life, too!"

The Philemon Verse

Remember the angelic visitation a little earlier in the chapter? One of the scriptures the angel quoted over me was Philemon 6. Remember when I said it was a powerful portion of scripture in the release of the spirit of faith? Well, here it is:

Philemon (I think it's pronounced "phy-*lee*-mon" depending on what Bible school you went to), a beloved friend of Paul's, received an addition to his faith from the apostle. In Paul's letter to him, he says, "I thank my God... that the sharing of your faith may become effective by the acknowledgement of every good thing which is in you in Christ Jesus." (Verses 4, 6)

Acknowledging every good thing: that's the instruction part. The bottom line is you are what you sit under! Philemon was a blessed person to have sat under so great a virtuous faith as Paul's. Faith that exhibits a virtue can be taught. Faith comes by hearing the Word. If you align yourself with a person who truly exhibits effective faith, you can be taught to operate in a similar fashion.

I use the analogy, having spent so much time in the fine Republic of Texas, of the cowboy who buys a Ford truck just 'cause his daddy always bought a Ford truck. You become like who you know. Republicans tend to vote Republican because their parents voted Republican (not always, I know, but more often than not.) It's the same with active faith: if you spend time with someone who has active faith, you also want to have active faith. So align yourself with the right people!

Effective faith is faith that is divinely energized — we've already said that, but it bears repeating since that's the impartation part. So it goes to show that if faith can be divinely energized, it can also be covered over, smothered and rendered useless. We as apostolic people must avoid this at all costs! The breaker anointing energizes the peoples' faith — it adds to their faith virtue! They become imbued with a spirit of faith! (For further teaching on this, Dr. Roy Hicks, Sr., has some wonderful insights in his book *Faith: Use It or Lose It*.)

My whole ministry has been possessed of an ideal that the peoples' faith can become divinely energized and effective — that they, too, can see miracles that prove the validity of King Jesus. We are the heirs of salvation (Hebrews 1:14), to whom the angels minister. Speaking generationally, I have always endeavored, as an heir of salvation, to link people directly to the miraculous faith that the Golden Candlestick nurtured some fifty years ago. I want to add to your faith virtue, hence the reason this book exists!

"Therefore we also pray always for you that our God would count you worthy of this calling, and fulfill all the good pleasure of His goodness and the work of faith with power...." (2 Thessalonians 1:11) That's why I'm writing this book: I want God to energize your faith so that it works with power! Come, people, now add to your faith virtue!

Now back to the messenger angel visitation, part two. You thought I'd forgotten!

So after the demonic hosts fled at the name of Jesus, I found I was back on the bed with the messenger standing next to me. He continued to speak to me, all the while I felt this dynamic faith bubbling out of my spirit. The angel conveyed to me that there would come a time in my ministry that a particular, special gift of faith impartation would be released, and that I would be able to share this energizing of one's faith with other people.

"But you must wait until the appointed time," the angel said.

So I waited. I waited twenty-five years. Then one day, the angel reappeared and said, "Now is the appointed time." And I remembered Philemon 6.

This anointing flows through me, this powerful, energizing faith. It crawls up my right leg, my right side and flows out of my right hand. At the time, I wasn't exactly sure why it was my right hand only. Since then, I've found a scripture (I always like to find scriptures to support an experience.) You know the one about the right thumb, the right ear and the right great toe? (Leviticus 14:14)

The angel conveyed to me that if I could get the people to believe I had received this visitation from the Lord, the Holy Spirit would release this anointing through my right hand that would break the stronghold, the yoke, around their spirit man that prohibited the flow of faith.

There are many types of strongholds a person may deal with. A stronghold is not necessarily demonic. A stronghold can also be emotional, a soulish bondage, a shell of dullness, an iciness of the heart, a cluttering of one's mind, mental harassment. The word "stronghold" to me simply means "something that is *raised up* that does not permit you to move forward." It is a particular area in one's life that the enemy has a hold on, and he is exerting his strength to hold you down.

A stronghold can be in the body, mind, will or emotions. A thought of doubt lodged in your mind can become a stronghold. A fear of failure. Emotional traumas and wounding, rejection. Physical infirmities that repeatedly beat you down can be strongholds. You get the idea.

This particular stronghold that the angel of the Lord was referring to is a soulish stronghold, in the realm of one's emotions, mind and will. The angel said that as the people received this word and believed in faith, the anointing release would shatter that stronghold around their spirit man. Remember the principle that an apostolic breaker anointing tears off a veiling that smothers over and renders useless a particular manifestation of virtue in a person's life. In this instance, the virtue of dynamic faith.

In other words, through the exhibition or the release of faith — that is, the exercise of faith — one exhibits a virtue. That means the anointing that goes forth from this visitation manifests a virtue out of my hand that goes into the spirit man, breaks off that yoke and energizes one's faith. It's a rush to feel! It literally *bursts* out of my hand, and the responses and reactions from the people are often quite humorous to see. Some become intoxicated in the Spirit; some just feel a serene, strong sense of faith; some have to be carried off, their legs don't work.

They looked shocked; many are physically backed up by the force of it. Just for the record, I'll state it here in print for all to see: this minister doesn't push people down! In fact, when the burst comes out, I have to jerk my hand *back* — sometimes it even hurts a little. I feel the anointing being reciprocated back to me; it rolls back up my arm. I enjoy operating in this expression, because I'm always recharged by it — my faith becomes inspired, and it doesn't make me tired. Sometimes it overwhelms me and I'm blown back! It's shocking. I heard it even stopped some guy's wristwatch once, though I don't know that for a fact. But I think it's quite possible it could! It's tangible and very electric.

I remember sharing this revelation with a group once. As I ministered to the people, I thought one good old country boy described the sensation of this faith virtue being manifested quite well. As it hit him, his eyes opened wide and he said, "Man, that's like gettin' kicked in the chest by a mule!" Well said, brother!

Quite often, after this energizing of faith, we've seen to the glory of God many people healed in their bodies, minds and emotions. The healing anointing then flows out and resonates within them. In some instances, perhaps they had previously been prayed over before and were believing in faith for a healing, and the anointing had, indeed, gone out to them; but because of some discouragement, some issue in their life, a veiling or deception, it caused the process of healing to be thwarted. So the enemy deceived them and said, "Well, God must have removed the healing anointing." But what happens is that soulish yoke raises up and quells the release of virtue. The healing anointing was still there, but in essence, it was merely sitting dormant in their spirits or in the area of their body that needed healing. So once this energizing of their faith takes place, that anointing begins working again, completing the miracle.

The point is this apostolic breaker anointing sets in motion the spirit of faith that is to be resting corporately on the people of God. It is my firm persuasion that as you read this, as your faith becomes inspired, as you have been instructed, and as you believe, an attribute of this anointing can be imparted in your life, and you can begin to see that soulish yoke being broken off your spirit man.

For those ministers out there who desire to be used apostolically, I am convinced that you can teach this particular message, sharing the revelation with others, and expect to see a measure of this manifestation. I believe all supernatural encounters I've had are for your benefit as well as mine. This book should encourage your faith to have encounters like this on your own. However, keep in mind that there is a level of supernatural authority that comes from teaching a message of this kind, and there is another level of authority that comes from having an angelic commissioning to release that anointing.

Why I say this is that in probably a thousand services I've held since this commissioning, there have been maybe a hundred times I've felt the Holy Spirit speak to me that this level of impartation was to be released. This particular anointing is not with me all the time.

I have to wait upon the Lord to release me. Sometimes the people are not prepared or ready to receive it, I believe. Also, I should say that so far, this particular anointing has only been released when people are present at a gathering. They must be physically standing before me.

What's interesting about this manifestation is that, as we know, there is one Holy Spirit with many different types of anointing; and usually, whenever the vessel operates in an anointing – say, the healing anointing or the prophetic anointing – eventually the person, because he or she is still just an earthen vessel, begins to tire and the anointing begins to wane. But with this energizing faith anointing, it has always stayed just as concentrated and strong from the first person I minister to until the last. And then it lifts off. It's very unique.

In the incidents when I've felt the Lord move me in this way, it doesn't matter if it's a large group or a small gathering, the effect is always the same. We've heard many wonderful testimonies from ministers and individuals on how it has activated entire congregations, even whole regional areas, where the gift of faith has been stirred in the people of God, and great moves of His Spirit have followed. Praise the Lord!

A REFINED CHARACTER

I believe it will be these kinds of anointings in these end times that the apostles and apostolic people will flow in to unveil the fullness of God. As I write this, I'm impressed to say one of the reasons I believe God gave me this experience is for all apostles and apostolic people to recognize they have to develop, grow and deepen in their expectations of moving in the signs of an apostle, one of those being a breaker anointing that unveils the faith of the Father. We should all covet the miracles of the apostolic spirit. We must persevere in patience, moving further into the acts of God, setting our root system down in good ground, as it were, so that a great depth and stability are represented to the world. As men and women who are called, we cannot only minister out of our gifts, but out of our characters that have been refined in Christ.

Many people in their early years of ministry are quite aware that the gifts and callings of God are without repentance. (Romans 11:29) They have emotional, mental, spiritual issues that God works through, in spite of them, to touch the world through the gifts of the Holy Spirit. But to grow, to become truly apostolic, they must go beyond the gifts of the Holy Spirit, in that sense, and allow their actual lives to be representative of Christ. Their characters need to minister as much as their gifts, you see.

It takes a lot of contrition on the part of the believer to reach that level. I know I have not yet attained, but I am always pushing for that moment when people see Christ reflected in me, not just Christ's gifts.

A living epistle, known and read of men. (2 Corinthians 3:2) That's what we as apostolic people should be striving for: a word made flesh for the people out there. The spirit of faith upon one's life helps release this kind of growing in character.

Right now, as you're reading this book, I ask you to open up your spirit to receive a measure of this energized faith. Begin to believe that you will see manifestations of the spirit of faith on your own, and I am convinced the Father will honor your intent. There will be struggles and victories, you will be refined, but in the end your very character will manifest the Person of Christ, and the world will see Him through your activities.

Chapter Two Outline

"Unveiling the Faith of God"

THE SPIRIT OF FAITH

- "I thank God... as without ceasing I remember you in my prayers night and day, greatly desiring to see you, being mindful of your tears, that I may be filled with joy, when I call to remembrance the genuine [unhypocritical] faith that is in you, which dwelt first in your grandmother Lois and your mother Eunice, and I am persuaded is in you also. Therefore I remind you to stir up the gift of God which is in you through the laying on of hands. For God has not given us a spirit of fear, but of power and of love and of a sound mind. Therefore do not be ashamed of the testimony of our Lord, nor of me His prisoner, but share with me in the sufferings for the gospel according to the power of God...." (2 Timothy 1:3-8)
- The apostolic breaker anointing produces an *unfeigned faith.* A faith with no pretense, no hypocrisy — genuine faith that expects to see *results*
- "Now faith is the substance [realization] of things hoped for, the evidence [confidence] of things not seen." (Hebrews 11:6)
- "The effective, fervent prayer of a righteous man avails much. Elijah was a man with a nature like ours, and he prayed earnestly that it would not rain; and it did not rain on the land for three years and six months. And he prayed again,

and the heaven gave rain, and the earth produced its fruit." (James 5:16-18)

- "For in Christ Jesus neither circumcision nor uncircumcision avails anything, but faith working through love." (Galatians 5:6)
- It is only the unfeigned faith working by divine love that accomplishes the miraculous
- The apostolic people must continually be exercising true faith, operating under the Spirit of faith, adding to their faith *more faith* to see Christ revealed in the world through signs, wonders and miracles
- "So then faith comes by hearing, and hearing by the word of God." (Romans 10:17)
- We receive faith primarily in three ways: through *instruction, inspiration* and *impartation*
- Being taught correctly the Word of God breeds faith (instruction.) It is the apostle's function to instruct properly the saints in the Word of God, believing that they are teaching under the influence of the Holy Ghost, "...[in] His divine power [that] has given us all things that pertain to life and godliness, through the knowledge of Him who called us by glory and virtue...." (2 Peter 1:3)
- Hearing the wonderful testimonies of faith bringing results in the apostles' lives quickens our faith (inspiration)
- The spirit of faith can be imparted through the laying on of hands — one of the key expressions of an apostle is that

unction and authority to impart such a spirit of faith. The apostolic anointing is an anointing for reproducing faith in the lives of others (impartation)

- Faith comes through glory encounters with the Father, through Jesus, guided by the Holy Spirit

Faith that is Energized

- "But also for this very reason [see verses 1-4], giving all diligence, add to your faith virtue, to virtue..." (2 Peter 1:5)
- *Arete* (Strong's #703) is translated "virtue," from a Greek word for masculine strength and valor. (Strong's #730) We could say it means to have "a good opinion of a person." To be moral, excellent, good, to have some intrinsic, internal worth. The word later came to mean the "miraculous power," either of God or a person who followed God. Notice how it is similar to *dunamis* and *kabod*. Glory, power, virtue. They are simply attributes of God
- So we could say that miraculous power is to be added to our faith, and from that addition comes forth a greater degree of knowledge, self-control, perseverance, godliness, brotherly kindness and ultimately love
- It, then, becomes exceedingly important to strive for a deep intimacy with God, a love for who He is, an extremely close relationship with Him. And from that intimacy, we enter into such a state of rest, or confidence, in our relationship with Him that it releases the miraculous, adding it to our faith

- A miracle is an expression of faith, a release of virtue based upon one's relationship with the Father. When faith is properly exercised to see a particular result, a virtue is exhibited, and the desired result is achieved: we see the miracle happen

- This is the awesome purpose, responsibility and privilege of apostles that they are used to create a spiritually dynamic atmosphere conducive for people to rise up and express their faith as they see the apostles release their breaker anointing

FAITH THAT IS EXERCISED

- "...'Have faith in God, for assuredly, I say to you, whoever says to this mountain, "Be removed and be cast into the sea," and does not doubt in his heart, but believes that those things he says will be done, he will have whatever he says.'" (Mark 11:22-23)

- The whole of Jesus' expression on this earth was tied into a pursuit of God as the Source of faith-virtue; it was tied into His supremely close relationship with the Father

- His faith was *in* God, not only in what God could *do*. Jesus' entire ministry expression was centralized *in* the Father, not just *for* the Father

- This is one of the greatest keys to apostolic anointing release: we must learn how not just to minister *unto* the Lord (as in those who say, "I'm doing this ministry work unto the Lord" or "I'm ministering *for* the Lord.") But rather, we must have

an understanding that we are ministering in the *Person of Christ* for the Lord

- Otherwise, many people base their sense of identity in ministry solely on what they're accomplishing for the Lord. They say, "Am I gaining acceptance before Him by doing this or that?" They also constantly strive in their lives to gain acceptance among their peers when they don't seemingly realize that everything they hope to achieve is found in ministering *in* the Person of Christ *for* the Lord Jesus Christ

- All apostolic release in ministry is centered in the Person of Jesus

- In other words, the key to apostolic anointing release is in recognizing that all ministry is *centered* in Christ, and then doing things *for* Christ. If we would just center our ministries in the Lord and make ourselves available every day, we would leave it up to His measure, His judgment, if we have sufficiently ministered in the level that He intended

- This creates a tremendous sense of freedom and release, even *enjoyment*, in ministering in the Lord, for the Lord. It's a great key in releasing the miraculous

- "And whatever you do in word or deed, do all **in** the name of the Lord Jesus, giving thanks to God the Father through Him." (Colossians 3:17, emphasis added)

Faith that is Effectual

- Faith becomes effectual when it is shared or communicated. Without sharing virtuous faith, it can do no good. It is the communication of your faith that makes the signs, wonders and miracles come forth. You've added to your faith virtue, and now you have to let that virtue manifest

- "...that the sharing of your faith may become effective by the acknowledgment of every good thing which is in you in Christ Jesus." (Philemon 6)

3

Unveiling the Compassion of God

THE DRUNK MAN AT THE BUS DEPOT

I admit I wasn't patient enough to wait around for churches to have me come preach while I was a young whippersnapper attending Christ for the Nations back in the '70s. So I used the nursing home ministry outreach as an avenue to pray for the sick, like I stated in the previous chapter. This period of time was remarkable in the way the Lord began to unveil further aspects of His character to me, teaching me to be sensitive to His guidance in knowing who I should pray for. How I learned who to pray for was to follow this outpouring of love from my spirit to the person in need. Some have called this the divine flow of love.

One afternoon I was ministering with a brother in the Lord under the inspiration of the Holy Spirit, and we'd seen many people saved and touched by God. Afterward, we walked to the Greyhound bus depot. Upon reaching the bus stop, we looked up a flight of about thirty steps to where a restaurant was, up above the waiting area; and about halfway to the top a man was hanging over the railing, getting sick.

We immediately perceived what was wrong with him: he was stone dead *drunk*. A brown paper bag holding a bottle was loosely clasped in one hand as he heaved over the stair railing. His clothes were tattered and filthy. The man quite easily could not have bathed in many months, perhaps years. His eyes were about as bloodshot as eyes could get. He was still getting violently sick, and the position he was in prevented his seeing us gape up at him. He wiped the back of his hand across his mouth, eyes glazed and unfocused. In between his heaves, he bellowed a very strange statement:

"Is there any deliverance from this demon of alcohol?!?"

My friend and I started and exchanged shocked looks. What did he say? We both kind of smirked and immediately knew this had to be some kind of divine set-up, reasonably intelligent people that we were. But at the same time, this flow of compassion rolled out of my spirit toward the man. I knew I was supposed to minister to him. It was that divine flow of love, a deep-seated compassion for his hurts. I felt utterly badly for him, and I desperately wanted to help him.

Instantly my friend and I entered into a vision. This is an extremely rare occurrence for two people to have the same, simultaneous vision. But in front of us, the stairs disappeared from view. They were replaced by what I can only describe as swirling, liquid glory. Fluid light, so thick in front of us that as we began to climb the steps, we had to feel with our toes that they were, indeed, still there. We could not see the ground underneath us. We could only feel the railing. The glory was ankle- to knee-deep, rolling in front of us as we climbed.

It hit the man as we reached him, and for a split second... it consumed him. He disappeared behind this liquid love. Momentarily he returned to our view and stood stock-still straight up.

"I feel God in this place!" he hollered out. And he repented. "God forgive me of my sin! Forgive me for my life! I give it to You!" Obviously, he had known something about salvation before coming into this state of drunkenness.

In an instant, he was sober. His eyes focused; they were unglazed. The brown bag fell from his grip, and he began to shout, "I've been delivered from this demon! Hallelujah! Praise the Lord!"

He took absolutely no notice of us, barreled past us down the steps, whooping and hollering the praises of God. My friend and I hadn't even prayed for him. Now *we* were the ones that clung to the railing, intoxicated by this glory of the Holy Spirit, wondering what had just happened.

THE LOVE WALK

I learned from that singular experience to follow the divine flow of love. Compassion is love that is projected upon a need. I learned that Christ is moved by compassion. (Matthew 14:14, 20:34; Mark 1:41, 5:19, 6:34) He is full of eager yearning to touch the lives of people. We as apostolic men and women must unveil this compassion of God, teaching the saints to follow that divine flow of love, to be free in expressing the power of Christ to a world that is in desperate need of a lot of love. There is a great booklet on the divine flow of love by the late John Osteen.

As was mentioned before, apostolic anointing is released to bring freedom to the Bride of Christ — freedom to express herself to God, freedom to express herself to others and freedom for God to express Himself to her. Why the Father releases this freedom is for the sake of the Bride to understand Him more fully and to understand the Bridegroom (that would be Jesus) completely. Rebekah symbolizes the Bride of Christ in Genesis 24, a chaste woman who left her father, her home, her land and embraced Isaac as her husband. For us to be a Bride worthy of such a Groom, we must *leave* our old lives and begin new ones with Him.

It's a simple concept that is so often overlooked in church circles. We assume once one has been saved, all of the old ways are driven out. This is just not so. As the saying goes, just because you have come out of Egypt (which is a type of sin), doesn't necessarily mean all of Egypt has come out of you in your soulish life. This walk of love into the Groom's arms starts with *leaving* the natural, worldly things behind and focusing all of our attentions upon our new Husband.

Psalm 45:10-11 says to the Bride, "Listen, O daughter, consider and incline your ear; forget your own people also, and your father's house; so the King will greatly desire your beauty; because He is your Lord, worship Him."

Recall John's admonishment, "Do not love the world... for all that is in the world — the lust of the flesh, the lust of the eyes, and the pride of life — is not of the Father but is of the world. And the world is passing away, and the lust of it; but he who does the will of God abides forever.'" (1 John 2:15-17)

Our Husband is fiercely jealous of His Bride and will share her with no other. "'Do not think that I came to bring peace on earth. I did not come to bring peace but a sword. For I have come to "set a man against his father, a daughter against her mother, and a daughter-in-law against her mother-in-law" [see Micah 7:6]; and "a man's enemies will be those of his own household." He who loves father or mother more than Me is not worthy of Me....'" (Matthew 10:34-37)

The apostolic anointing has found us in freedom to express ourselves to our Groom by leaving the old things behind and clinging passionately to Him. After we have left the world behind us, we find ourselves *loving* Him with complete devotion, abandonment and adoration. Just as John was found consistently loving on His Master, so must we.

"Now there was leaning on Jesus' bosom one of His disciples, whom Jesus loved." (John 13:23)

In Jesus' time people ate while laying on their sides against pillows, head-to-feet around a low table, and this is indeed right, for the word "leaning" (*anakeimai*; Strong's #345) also means "reclining." The person reclining closest to Jesus would hold a place of honor, which is why John doesn't name himself as the disciple whom Jesus loved; he was being modest.

I have heard it taught, and I am personally under the opinion that it is correct, that John *repeatedly* leaned on Jesus' bosom; and this is what changed the "Son of Thunder" (Mark 3:17) into the "Beloved." Whether one can be doctrinal about this or not, the point, I think, is to show that being in a love embrace with Jesus changes the person — one is transformed into a true lover of the Groom when one repeatedly avails oneself of laying one's head on the bosom of Christ.

Jesus loved His disciples equally, but it might seem that John made an extra effort to be close to his Lord, and it actually changed his heart. He became possessed of a pure, unadulterated yearning only for Him. Something we must cultivate as well, like the psalm says: "Both the singers and the players on instruments say, 'All my springs are in you.'" (Psalm 87:7)

We must be as Martha's sister, Mary, sitting at the feet of Jesus, listening with complete, rapt attention to His teaching, never averting our gaze, desiring nothing more than to be taught by the Master. (Luke 10:39) We must be constantly *looking* for our Lover, living in a state of satisfied dissatisfaction, as I made mention way back in Volume 1.

"By night on my bed I sought the one I love; I sought him, but I did not find him." (Song of Solomon 3:1)

We are to be constantly searching after Jesus, eagerly anticipating His soon return. We are to be satisfied in knowing we are His beloved Bride, but dissatisfied with our current level, or degree, of intimacy with Him. We are always to be "...looking for the blessed hope and glorious appearing of our great God and Savior Jesus Christ...." (Titus 3:13)

For, "...Christ was offered once to bear the sins of many. To those who eagerly wait for Him He will appear a second time, apart from sin, for salvation." (Hebrews 9:28)

"Finally, there is laid up for me the crown of righteousness, which the Lord, the righteous Judge, will give to me on that Day, and not to me only but also to all who have loved His appearing." (2 Timothy 4:8)

Love must be put in us, first received and then expressed. This love walk is worked out through our *leaving, loving* and *looking* — all for the sake of our Groom. This is the apostolic unveiling of God's great compassion for the Bride and the Groom, giving us the freedom to express ourselves back to the Father what we have received.

Once the apostles have unveiled this compassion of the Father, we are equipped more fully to follow that divine flow of love that is to be the hallmark of our ministry to the world. We do what we do out of a divine love to see their needs met. It is a fruitful lifetime of ministry commemorating this walk of love.

For greater teaching on this, I highly suggest you read *Learning to Love* by David Alsobrook. Some of the thoughts here are extrapolated from that book.

Now let me share with you a couple of particularly dynamic encounters I had that show what happens when one walks in love.

The Dallas State Fair

Dallas, Texas, is particularly known for its annual State Fair. There's a sixty-foot-tall mechanical cowboy that bellows *ad nauseum*, "Howdy, ya'll! Welcome to th' Texas State Fair!" Or something akin to that. And the fair boasts a gigantic Ferris wheel that takes about an hour to go all the way around. Meantime, you rock and sway in the tiny, little compartment held together by two screws after having stood in line hours just to get on the confounded contraption! But they have really good, juicy fried turkey legs....

While ministering with a group of CFNI students at the Fair, I noticed a young lady seated on a bench. I could immediately see she was tormented and vexed by the demonic. I felt the divine flow of love leap out toward her. I perceived this tug of the Holy Spirit, flooded with compassion, and I was drawn to this poor lady. One sister in the Lord came over with me.

"How are you doing?" I asked her. I introduced myself and my friends as students over at Christ for the Nations. She stared back at us blankly. "So, is there anything, you know, we can pray with you about?"

Blunt and to the point. No use beating around the bush. Got a problem? Can we help?

Instead of mocking us, she began to weep. And through her tears, she got out, "I was just fired from my job because I've had this condition for years and years. I can't stop hemorrhaging, and I get so weak. Finally my employer had enough, and he let me go. My husband wants to leave me 'cause he's had it with my problems, and I feel all alone. I'm going to lose my apartment. I don't have enough money for rent. So I don't know. I'm tired of being sick all the time. I'm just thinking about whether or not I want to live anymore...." She continued to sob.

Again, another divine set-up from following the love walk. Even at my young, pliable age while attending CFNI, I began to cultivate this sensitivity to the love that the Lord has for people in need. That flow of compassion — it's always led me right.

Looking back on it now, it's kind of humorous because I recall having just finished a Smith Wigglesworth's book that had a chapter in it entitled "Wilt Thou Be Made Whole?" And he had a tendency to be exceptionally blunt when he went up to pray for people. So I figured if he could do it, why couldn't I?

"Well, let me pray for you," I said. "And when I pray for you, these spirits that are oppressing you are going to lift off your mind, and then when I get done praying for you, I'm going to have you stand up in the name of Jesus, and you're going to be every wit made whole. OK?"

Keep in mind she was a complete stranger, sitting on a bench at the State Fair. Seemed easy enough.

"OK."

But now my mind rationalized, *Oh, boy! You've been presumptuous here, don't you think?* I swallowed that down, feeling this love flow out to the woman, and I shouted back to my mind, *I'm just going to trust in His Word!* And I began to pray for her in the name of Jesus.

Once I'd finished, I had her stand up with me and my friend. For a split second... nothing happened. So I grabbed the woman's hand and my friend's hand and waited. It must've been a funny sight, the three of us in a little circle next to the ice cream stand. Nearby, some Hare Krishnas were chanting, bopping up and down in their robes, handing flowers out to passersby.

Then the power of God fell. I felt it travel down my arm and out my right hand. It jumped into the lady's hand and she collapsed back onto the bench. My friend, she fell out under the Spirit, right there on the concrete, and I was blown back about six or seven feet, staggering under this power. I blanked out for a second, and when I regained myself, I found I could hardly stand at all. From that moment on, something was deposited in my hands, specifically my right. I'll go more into this *dunamis* (remember that word?) anointing release later in the chapter on the power of God.

"I'm healed! I'm healed! Thank You, I'm healed!" The young lady began to cry out. It brought me around, and I have no doubt in my mind she was completely, totally set free from the demonic oppression. My sister in the Lord struggled to her feet, totally drunk in the Holy

Ghost, and we stumbled away from the lady, leaving her to shout and rejoice that God had set her free as she had given her life to Him. Even the Hare Krishnas stood still, gaping, wondering what had just happened.

The Cerebral Palsy Girl

Several years after the above testimony, I was ministering in this one particular home meeting where parents brought their little girl, approximately five years of age, and one could immediately see she was afflicted by cerebral palsy. The parents loved that little girl wholeheartedly, yet understandably, they were devastated by her suffering.

The little dear's equilibrium was off balance and she wobbled when she walked, among all of the other disorders associated with the disease. It was simply terrible to behold this amazing little creature who was forced to struggle with such a pervasive ailment. She would topple over, seemingly always dizzy. My heart seemed rent in two, and I felt this flow of compassion rush out to her. It almost ached.

As I went to lay hands upon her, the Holy Spirit checked me, and I was impressed by Him: *She doesn't need prayer. She needs you to pick her up and just love on her.* So I gathered her in my arms and turned my back on the congregation. I cradled her and just loved on her, my spirit oozing out this burdensome feeling of compassion. Apparently someone in the group was timing this occurrence, for they told me later I had held her in my arms for fifteen minutes. It didn't seem that long to me.

All of this love and compassion poured out of my spirit during that quarter of an hour; it just seemed to cover over her, and the more she soaked it up, the more it continued to build until I felt I would burst. I didn't pray one word over her.

Suddenly I felt the flow of love empty, and I turned to face the parents, my face beaming. I placed the little girl on her feet and said, "You run on to Mommy and Daddy."

And the little girl ran in a perfectly straight line to her parents!

Of course, the whole household fell to rejoicing! I recall a few weeks later returning near the area of that home meeting and encountering the parents in the church parking lot. They said their daughter had been healed of cerebral palsy and could now even climb trees! They gave God all the glory, and I shouted His praise, too! Hallelujah!

Can you see why it pays to follow the divine flow of love?

THE FRIENDSHIP WALK

"Now when he had finished speaking to Saul, the soul of Jonathan was knit to the soul of David, and Jonathan loved him as his own soul. Saul took him that day, and would not let him go home to his father's house anymore. Then Jonathan and David made a covenant, because he loved him as his own soul." (1 Samuel 18:1-3)

"'I am distressed for you, my brother Jonathan; you have been very pleasant to me; your love to me was wonderful, surpassing the love of women.'" (2 Samuel 1:26)

An unveiling of the compassion of God creates a freedom to express ourselves to others — to be friendly, to reciprocate love, to care for one another. The word *soul-tie* does not necessarily connote an evil thing. In fact, everyone has need for friends — it is the human condition, bound in culture, race and society, to relate to others. Friends in their relationships have learned to let walls down. Apostles express their humanity and creativity in their friendships, which in turn expresses love, creating a manifestation of grace. It is because of love that friendships are formed, for love must have an object, and love must be reciprocated. (David Alsobrook)

The Father wanted friendship and fellowship with His creation, mankind. Genesis 1:31 says, "Then God saw everything that He had made, and indeed it was very good...." Jesus also wants friendship and fellowship with His followers — we are a Bride, not a slave.

"'You are My friends if you do whatever I command you. No longer do I call you servants, for a servant does not know what his master is doing; but I have called you friends, for all things that I heard from My Father I have made known to you. You did not choose Me, but I chose you and appointed you that you should go and bear fruit, and that your fruit should remain, that whatever you ask the Father in My name He may give you. These things I command you, that you love one another.'" (John 15:14-17)

Jesus has elevated us from servants to friends, because a servant is given limited information and authority, but He makes known all to His friends.

"A man who has friends must himself be friendly, but there is a friend who sticks closer than a brother." (Proverbs 18:24)

Only hours before His arrest, Jesus was elevating the future apostles from their positions as servants to the higher positions of friends. Indeed, right before He calls them friends, He lays out His greatest commandment.

"'This is My commandment, that you love one another as I have loved you. Greater love has no one that this, than to lay down one's life for his friends." (John 15:12-13)

Christ puts a high premium on friendship, so much so that just a little while later He did just that: laid down His life for His friends. Why? So that we might have "...boldness and access with confidence through faith in Him." (Ephesians 3:12)

In the course of this book, we've shared at great length on that access and boldness, but let's go even a little bit deeper, hopefully shedding some more light on the works of an apostle through a *friendship anointing*.

You and I desire a greater intimacy with the Father, don't we? That in turn means we desire a greater level of fruitfulness in our ministries and our personal relationships. God is speaking to all of us that this is to be a season of time of magnificent fruitfulness. I believe I am hearing the Holy Spirit say that the war with our "wilderness experiences" in our walk with the Lord is coming to an end. So, based on what the Spirit is saying, we could purport that our times of intimacy without fruitfulness are shortly coming to an end! How amazing!

God the Father is entrusting to us a tremendous treasure: His reputation. Yet another definition of His reputation resting upon us might be to say our ability to translate the experiential knowledge we have in Him (that means glory encounters) to others for their benefit. One of the great keys to an apostolic anointing release is the firm desire to bring His reputation into expression, into reality, for other people.

So through our close, intimate friendship with Christ, we have boldness and have access to His reputation, right? Let's look at that word "access." I define it as "freedom to enter into dialogue with Christ's favor and assistance; simply, to have His undivided attention." It is an introduction to the realities of asking the Father for something and having it given to you, no matter how great the need is. It is through this friendship anointing that we have the right to make such a claim, based solely on our relationship status with Jesus Christ: not servants, but friends. And friends can avail themselves of their friends' good graces. We all know that there is no lack in the Father for good graces.

So see, the issue then, when we're not seeing that level of apostolic friendship anointing operating, is *not* a lack of power... but a lack of exercising authority by those that are *under* His authority, those who call themselves His friends. (Remember John 15:14.)

Apostles help people to experience God's love in its highest form. Remember the apostolic unction shows the acceptance of the Father: "I accept you with the same level of fervency that I accepted My own Son." And God *loves* the Son. They're the very best of good Friends, if I might say it that way.

In the context of "laying down one's life for one's friends," we are to offer our lives to people, everything that we have experienced in God, everything that's good in us to give them, to translate those experiences into encounters with the Lord for them. For the purpose of this chapter, it means to work to establish a people that have remarkable revelation in being the friends of God. That's one of the apostle's functions, in light of this revelation.

Even the Holy Spirit desires your companionship. Second Corinthians 13:14 says, "The grace of the Lord Jesus Christ, and the love of God, and the communion [fellowship] of the Holy Spirit be with you all. Amen." The entirety of the Godhead works together for friendship with the creation, for God in all His wisdom knows that we need friends because we are designed to be incomplete without them. That word "communion" (Strong's #2842) is the Greek *koinonia*, and it implies an association, fellowship, mutual sharing, partnership and friendship.

In instigating fellowship with us, it is as if Christ is saying, "I have admitted unto you free, unrestricted access to My Father — keeping back nothing from you which I have received. I will keep nothing back from you! I will lead you into the counsels and plans of My Master. In return, I want you to communicate that fellowship to others."

It is through the friendship of others, tied together in Christ, that He gives the promise, "If two of you shall agree as touching anything..." (Matthew 18:19) That is the open-heavens above the corporate Body. It is directly tied into the level of friendship love you have for your brethren!

In *Learning to Love*, there are four primary purposes for friendship, found in Ecclesiastes 4:9-12. They are for our *work*, our *walk*, our *warmth* and our *warfare*. (Isn't that cleverly homiletic?) Verse 9, "Two are better than one, because they have a good reward for their labor," speaks to our work. Verse 10, "For if they fall, one will lift up his companion, but woe to him who is alone when he falls, for he has no one to help him up," speaks to our walk. Verse 11, "Again, if two lie down together, they will keep warm; but how can one be warm alone?" speaks to our warmth. And lastly, Verse 12, "Though one may be overpowered by another, two can withstand him, and a threefold cord is not quickly broken," speaks to our warfare; for indeed, "'How could one chase a thousand, and two put ten thousand to flight, unless their Rock had sold them, and the Lord had surrendered them?'" (Deuteronomy 32:30)

We are compelled by the revelation of the Father toward friendship, working with others and the Lord to overcome the enemy. We are not meant to go it alone, and so often that is why people fail.

THE HUMANITY OF JESUS

Jesus, of course, was the Firstborn of many brethren. (Romans 8:29) And since He now calls us friends (that's the many brethren part), He makes all things known to us. There is nothing hidden among friends. What He has heard from the Father, He has made known to us; this speaks of union, working together with Christ; the term "co-laborer" is often used. It speaks of shared experiences, shared expressions, encounters with the Father's glory. Heaven's realities are made known to our spirits because there is a joining, a oneness, with our Friend Jesus. We then express that reality to other people.

Apostles are used to bring *humanity* back into their testimonies of Christ's power. Jesus was fully human (and yes, fully God), but apostles manifest the humanity of Jesus Christ as He heard from the Father, had His own glory encounters and translated them to others. Without the breaker anointing to translate these glory experiences, it creates a pseudo-religious expression that seems very surreal and bizarre to the people. In other words, if Christ did not exhibit a breaker anointing as the first Apostle, people would not have understood His miraculous power. "Well, He must just be *only* God, and therefore, we can never accomplish these feats because we are obviously *not* God." His power would remain ethereal, mystic.

But the apostles and apostolic people are called to undo this wrong philosophy. God's power manifested through humanity is not mystical, it is not fantastical. It is very much reality, based upon one's relationship with Jesus Christ and the Father. It is love and friendship that yields such grace and experience with God, boldness and access. Truly, apostles are called to unveil the compassion of the Father. It is the supernatural, yes, but mixed with the humanity — God working alongside His friends. In ultra-religious sects, this smacks of heresy; the apostolic anointing reverses that misconception.

An understanding of one's access as a friend of God yields boldness. Wherever Jesus manifested boldness or confidence to see the Father move, we also can have boldness and confidence to see the same. We have a certainty that God will use us as He used Jesus, and in the sharing of our unique expressions, we can just be *ourselves* — we can simply be human, not super-human, not mystical, not spooky. Jesus, our great Example, was not *weird*. He was human, and He operated in a very human way. He was funny; He was serious; He was normal.

Just like us, the Son of Man had His own unique peculiarities, His own emotional expressiveness, His own personality. He was also anointed with the Holy Spirit. (See Hebrews 1:9 and Acts 2:22.) Here's the deal: the Father is not insecure. He will share His power and authority with mankind, anointing them with the Spirit as they yield to His desires. It is the treasure of His anointing in an earthen vessel (2 Corinthians 4:7), and that pleases the Father greatly. He's excited to dole out Himself into walking, talking bits of dust and dirt because it shows off His greatness in being able to do so. And of course, God can show off if He wants to because, well, He's God....

What happens is the anointing comes upon and into our humanity, and this is what makes us real to people. The problem in the Church is we have too much of a mysticism in being used of God. We're too apprehensive to step out; we're too uptight. We're too timid. That's a lack of boldness and access.

Most people are waiting to come to some ill-notioned level of maturity where they feel they're able to exercise spiritual authority, and really it's an authority that's already theirs based on their position as friends with Christ. Yes, character needs to be developed. I'm not minimizing the importance of maturation in our walk with the Lord. We should all be increasing in depth and knowledge and intimacy with our Friend. But what better way to develop godly character than by operating as God did? And the truth of the matter is we're called His friends *now*, not later.

The enemy has used this wrong notion as a form of condemnation, that one is not mature enough in God to be used. He convinces the people they're not worthy, and it's nothing more than a veiling of deception — something the apostolic breaker anointing casts off.

See, when I first started ministering at nineteen years of age, I was seeing the same level of grace and favor in the miraculous as I am now at... well... I'm not going to tell you my age.... Suffice to say it's over the half-century mark....

Alas....

Of course, hopefully, I've grown and deepened in my walk with the Lord, maturing to a point where these kinds of signs and wonders are operating, with more consistency, out of a *godly character* instead of just positional relationship with Jesus. (Remember the refined character bit and ministering in the Person of Jesus from the previous chapter.)

I'm not underrating character here, but in stressing this friendship anointing, there is freedom to be ourselves, to be natural. Yes, sanctified expressions. Dignity is something I highly esteem from anyone who stands behind the pulpit. Be righteous in all things. But we should have a confidence to exercise a boldness based upon our acceptance and access to the Lord, in spite of human frailty.

The problem with many people in the Church is they're trying to be *someone else*, but acceptance says that access is granted to ask favor of the Lord with all of our human characteristics and human limitations. He accepts that we are merely humans — note, I'm not conveying that *sin* is excused; I'm showing that *humanity* is understood by the Father. It is an acceptance and an identification in the healing ministry of the Lord. Keep it in balance in light of the unveiling of the holiness of God.

The apostolic breaker anointing, through the character and lives of the apostles, must unveil the love God has for humanity, and even further, the undeniable grace and favor that comes along with such a compassion for mankind.

Let me share an example of the friendliness and compassion of Jesus, along with His understanding of humanity.

A Dinner Meeting in Kentucky

I believe it was springtime, 1977, when I was speaking at a banqueting dinner of about a hundred people in the great commonwealth of Kentucky. We had just gotten through chowing down on a good meal; everyone was belching and sleepy, checking their watches. Wasn't it time for a *siesta?*

Altogether not a very conducive atmosphere for a miracle service, but the barbeque spare ribs were *mmm!, mmm!* good....

It was getting very late by the time they turned the service over to me — dessert took a while, and I admit I was a little frustrated at the time constraint. I've repented of irritation since then....

But finally I got up to share my testimony, and I didn't feel any anointing at all. I mean, nothing. People were glancing around, coughing in napkins, laying their heads down on the tables. I shook my head and decided to close my Bible.

"You know," I basically quipped, after relating just a small portion of my salvation experience. "There's not a real strong anointing here. I think we ought to close the service down. I mean, if anyone wants prayer they can come up later. I'll be sitting over there with my pie and ice cream...." Might not have been word for word, but something to that extent.

I proceeded to return to my seat, much to the shock of the conference leaders.

As I was walking off the platform, a mother and her daughter (approximately fifteen-years-old) were sitting in the congregation. And I guess the mother thought her daughter's opportunity was escaping, so she grabbed the girl and slowly made her way up front. By this time, I'd already sat down, waiting for the MC to close the service. Maybe it was cobbler, not pie....

It was obvious to see the daughter was in excruciating pain. She sported a back brace from her neck to the base of her spine, bent over almost double. We found out later her spinal column was bent in a half circle. Folks, that's a crooked spine!

She'd had all kinds of medical attention. Nothing could fix the problem. The condition was debilitating, getting worse and worse. The pain must've been unimaginable! I could see it in her eyes and my heart went out to her. So I stood and went over to her and the mother. Immediately I felt this flow of compassion spill out of my spirit toward the young girl, in spite of the BBQ burps, and I reached out my hand to place it on her forehead.

All of sudden (goodness, that happens a lot!), I heard a powerful voice from behind me say, "Stop! Don't minister to her."

I don't hear these kinds of voices all the time, so I can be a little dense, I suppose. I assumed it was the enemy, so I raised my hand a second time to place on her forehead. I heard the voice again, more emphatically this time.

"I said stop.... Do not minister to her!"

I rebuked the enemy under my breath (I know, I know, duh, right?) and reached out a finger to touch the top of her head a third time. Now the voice was authoritative, and maybe even a little put out.

"Stop! Do *not* minister to her!"

So I figured this was probably the voice of the Lord, smart man that I am, and I turned toward the right side of the auditorium to stare at the white wall where this voice was coming from. It's like I went into slow motion. I entered into a transcendent, trance-like experience. (Acts 22:17) The whole wall seemed to become transparent and I was looking *through* it where I saw a flickering light moving briskly toward me.

I remember thinking the light was kind of unusual because it was trotting very quickly, bouncing up and down quite high. It was skip-skip-skip-to-my-lou*ing its way into the room. I got the distinct impression it was very jovial, having a whole lot of fun, like someone might hop from rain puddle to rain puddle, I guess. I'm not making this up, dear friends.... I saw this light with my naked eye. A few individuals, after the experience, told me they had seen the light too.

The moment the voice had spoken to me the entire room had become saturated with the anointing of God. Instantly, people began to sob; some fell down on their knees, crying out to the Lord. Others were mute and somber. When the light entered, those that saw it cried out and began to worship, for there was Someone in the light.

I saw His similitude as I looked into this dancing light, the outline of Jesus in His glorified state. (Numbers 12:8) I'm so sorry, my friends, I am not able to describe just how powerful He looks, even just His side profile. I have no words. He is absolutely mind-boggling to behold. There is no comprehension in the English language. My flesh became extremely heavy, and I feared I would collapse. For a brief second I thought my heart was going to stop, there was so much *power* emanating off Him. And yet, it was that same power that was sustaining me as Jesus came and stood by my side.

Now, the Lord help me if I embellish an experience of this nature. You are just going to have to settle it in your mind and spirit that I am too afraid of that power I saw in the Lord to lie about what I saw here.

The Lord Jesus pulled up alongside of me, turned and smiled. Yes, He smiled. It was so obvious He found all of this quite humorous, not in a snide, sneering way, but in a very innocent, funny way. I can put it like this: I felt He was in a playful mood.

"Excuse Me," the Lord said. "I will minister to this one."

Ladies and gentlemen, believe me when I write I took a *h-u-g-e* step backward. Jesus turned to face the teenage girl. Now, mark carefully, because I mean this with the utmost humility before Jesus Christ, but the point I must convey in all of this is that He was being... well, humorous. To Him this was a great source of mirth, being able to minister to this girl. His sense of humor, at least in this instance, was almost... I guess I would use the word "feisty," but that's not quite right. His demeanor was playful, not sarcastic in the slightest; but kind of like when two brothers wrestle around on the floor, giggling but not in a stupid way.

The young lady was having an open vision of Him approaching her (Luke 1:11), she later conveyed to us. As He faced her, Jesus looked over His shoulder at me with a little bit of a good-natured grin and a sparkle of excitement in His eye. It seemed as if He was thinking, "Watch this!"

He raised His right index finger, and in a very exaggerated, slo-mo way lightly, ever so lightly, just — boop! — touched the top of her forehead.

That was it. He said nothing. Did not pray. Just boop! and walked back over to me, chuckling. I heard Him laugh. He sidled up next to me — remember I had backed up — and grabbed me in a side hug around my waist. He actually bumped into me, knocking me as He came up. God is my witness; it was one of the greatest experiences in my life. The Lord Jesus Christ put His arm around me and hugged me. All still in a very playful manner, but it was a tight, manly hug. I mean, a bear hug. Instantly the Holy Spirit brought into my mind the scripture, "...There is a friend who sticks closer than a brother." (Proverbs 18:24)

After s-q-u-e-e-z-i-n-g me, He stepped back a foot or so to look me in the eye. I will stupidly try to describe what His eyes looked like. It was like looking into liquid love. I saw eternity, fire, pools of infinite glory; they glittered with authority. I guess that's not too bad.

He spoke to me. "You can go ahead and finish your healing service now...."

Oh, well, thanks.

"Remember I call you My friend." And He gave the biggest, heartiest laugh and then walked back through the wall.

It goes without saying that we had no problem with people coming up and getting healed, saved, delivered; the dessert course totally forgotten. And obviously the young lady was totally set free! That should go without mentioning.

The Faith Walk

Hebrews 11:6 declares, "But without faith it is impossible to please Him, for he who comes to God must believe that He is, and that He is a rewarder of those who diligently seek Him." We must experience the God of love! An unveiling of His compassion yields a freedom for God to express Himself to us, and He rewards us with the supernatural, but since the carnal mind is enmity against God (Romans 8:7) we must pursue faith in Him who can instill love within us, for love must be put *in* us before we can express it. Man is not the source of love; he is merely the recipient and expresser of it. To the extent one receives and expresses love, it can be said that one knows God.

"He who does not love does not know God, for God is love." (1 John 4:8)

Christ warned, "'But I know you, that you do not have the love of God in you.'" (John 5:42) He was showing that everyone needed love experiences in the Father, that which has been termed the "hug therapy" of the Creator — love encounters with Him who holds you tightly in His embrace, and you are renewed in your understanding of just what Love is.

When Jesus was relating the Father's love toward His people in regaling us with the parable of the prodigal son, He said, "'And he arose and came to his father. But when he was still a great way off, his father saw him and had compassion, and ran and fell on his neck and kissed him.'" (Luke 15:20)

That word "fell" is the Greek *epipipto*, meaning "to seize, embrace, fall upon, press upon" (Strong's #1968), and is similarly found in Acts 10:44 where it says, "While Peter was still speaking these words, the Holy Spirit fell upon all those who heard the word."

Quite literally, the expression of the Holy Spirit is a hug around the neck.

The point is that once you have received a hug around the neck from God, you can become a love messenger, expressing that hug therapy to others. Apostolic people must become sensitive to the unmet love needs of others and desire to fulfill them — spiritually, to hug some necks out there in the world.

When John is speaking of love, he says, "This is love, that we walk according to his commandments. This is the commandment, that as you have heard from the beginning, you should walk in it." (2 John 6) But he is speaking about more than just an obscure concept — it is *projected love* that is commanded. Love that is focused, directed, on the needs of another. God is sending forth His love messengers, moved to focus that love they have received on the needs of the people He causes them to come into contact with. Remember this: when love is projected, that is when grace is manifested! We end up coming full circle, complete in Christ, through the manifestation of the glorious! (Colossians 2:10)

THE UNITY FACTOR

"Behold, how good and how pleasant it is for brethren to dwell together in unity! It is like the precious oil upon the head, running down on the beard, the beard of Aaron, running down on the edge of his garments. It is like the dew of Hermon, descending upon the mountains of Zion; for there the Lord commanded the blessing — life forevermore." (Psalm 133)

The purpose of the apostolic anointing is to convey further the blessing of life forevermore — that abundant life found in the heart of the Father. A principle of this life is found in the unity of the brethren.

Back to the keys of binding and loosing based upon the revelation of the anointing given to us by the Christ, I want to bring out another concept from that passage of scripture (Matthew 16:17-19) by comparing it to Matthew 18:18-20. Here Jesus says, "'Assuredly, I say to you, whatever you bind on earth will be bound in heaven, and whatever you loose on earth will be loosed in heaven. Again I say to you that if two of you agree on earth concerning anything that they ask, it will be done for them by My Father in heaven. For where two or three are gathered together in My name, I am there in the midst of them.'"

To recap, and to save you the trouble of flipping back through a hundred pages, I'll remind you that the anointing revelation of the Person of Christ is in the truth of binding and loosing, meaning that whatever is already bound in heaven, we bind down on earth, based on the unveiling of that anointing revelation. In other words, heaven will back your binding. Further, whatever is already loosed in heaven, we loose down here on earth, again based on the unveiling of that anointing revelation. So to say, heaven will back your loosing.

To further that revelation, I want to show that the key to binding and loosing is found in the unity of the brethren, from Verses 19-20 of Matthew 18.

The flow of oneness is *agreeing* together on the will of God — to be of a single vision and purpose. To be in unity. "To agree," I can define as "to harmonize with another, to make a symphony of sound together." I'm talking about synergy, to utilize a popular business term. I'm talking about the Body moving together as a single unit, a flowing river, functioning in total synchronization toward a common goal — that is, the release of the anointing.

When an individual church is in proper order, flowing in the apostolic, prophetic, pastoral, teaching, evangelistic graces, it means that true unity can be found within that group of brethren (and sistren, although that's not a word....) An anointing is released when all the pistons are firing correctly, so to speak. When one attribute or expression lacks, the fullness of unity is not obtained, and the anointing release can be hampered. This book speaks to the apostolic expression specifically, but this truth in unity holds constant with any of the gifts the Lord has given to the Church. As the apostles and prophets release their anointing upon the pastoral, teaching and evangelistic expressions, a unity or *cohesiveness* is formed among the saints.

It takes all expressions working together for unity to come off. I think we could all agree that in the Church as a whole, we lack unity. This, I am convinced, stems from the Church being out of order with regards to the expressions of the apostle and the prophet. When there is disorder, there is not as powerful of a release of anointing to set the saints free from all of their life issues, and even possibly demonic scenarios that steal our unity in the Body.

"There is one body and one Spirit, just as you were called in one hope of your calling; one Lord, one faith, one baptism; one God and Father of all, who is above all, and through all, and in you all." (Ephesians 4:4-6)

Goodness, Paul was the man when it came to eloquence in writing!

"Can two walk together, unless they are agreed?" (Amos 3:3)

That's a good point, Amos!

I'll make a statement that one of Jesus' greatest burdens in His ministry to His disciples on earth was to convey to them the need for unity and agreement. "'Now I am no longer in the world, but these are in the world [speaking of the disciples], and I come to You. Holy Father, keep through Your name those whom You have given Me, that they may be one as We are... that they all may be one, as You, Father, are in Me, and I in You; that they also may be one in Us, that the world may believe that You sent Me.... I in them, and You in Me; that they may be made perfect in one, and that the world may know that You have sent Me, and have loved them as you have loved Me." (John 17:22, 21, 23)

"'...Every kingdom divided against itself is brought to desolation, and every city or house divided against itself will not stand.'" (Matthew 12:25)

Apparently the Anointed One was adamant about unity and togetherness. The revelation of the Father's love for the world is manifested through the oneness of Christ's people — that's you and I, fellow members! Without it, His Kingdom is brought to desolation. By "desolation," I mean "laid to waste, to be of no usefulness." It is incumbent upon us *not* to render the works of Christ's Kingdom to no avail. See the importance of unity in the Body?

Ever notice how "Trinity" and "unity" are very similar words? That's because the Trinity of the Father, the Son and the Holy Spirit operate in perfect unity and accord — not one disconcordant thought or action has ever passed between Them in all of eternity. So great is Their Oneness that to separate One from Another destroys the very fabric of existence. The Kingdom comes crashing down and is made to no usefulness should They operate out of sync even for a split second. That's the difference between Their Kingdom and Satan's "kingdom" (I mean, "world system.") The enemy's sole purpose is to divide, to separate, to bring into discord.

Think of it this way; each Member of the Trinity serves the Other. It's awesome to think of the Father *serving* the Son, the Son *serving* the Father, the Spirit *serving* the Son, and so on and so forth. But that is exactly what unity is: "preferring one another." I'll be bold to say I don't see the Body preferring one another as often as it should. The apostolic, breaker anointing comes to set this disunity aright. The key to Church life, to releasing the power of Christ in the Body, is found in just how unified we are.

"And through the hands of the apostles many signs and wonders were done among the people. And they were all with one accord in Solomon's Porch. Yet none of the rest dared join them, but the people esteemed them highly. And believers were increasingly added to the Lord, multitudes of both men and women, so that they brought the sick out into the streets and laid them on beds and couches, that at least the shadow of Peter passing by might fall on some of them. Also a multitude gathered from the surrounding cities to Jerusalem, bringing sick people and those who were tormented by unclean spirits, and they were all healed." (Acts 5:12-16)

I believe that for the life of the Church to flourish, we must focus on the *cell life* of the churches. It is in the relationship of the two or the three operating in one accord together that the wholeness of life is found. Like the human body, so many drastic deficiencies can be tied to the breakdown of just one or two cells operating out of whack. If the cells break down, the entire church becomes unhealthy. Cell groups are an important function in a church.

Paul, again the wordsmith, in his letter to the Colossians itemized the characteristics of the born-again person. "But above all these things put on love, which is the bond of perfection." (Colossians 3:14)

Kindness, mercy, meekness, humility, longsuffering, bearing with one another, forgiveness, etc. and etc. All of these are wonderful attributes of a healthy church, but they can be summed up in *love*. Love is the perfect glue to make a church stick together.

The apostle makes similar mention of good attributes for the new man in his letter to the Ephesians, admonishing them, "...endeavoring to keep the unity of the Spirit in the bond of peace... [Christ] from whom the whole body, joined and knit together by what every joint supplies, according to the effective working by which every part does its share, causes growth of the body for the edifying of itself in love." (Ephesians 4:3, 16)

"...And not holding fast to the Head, from whom all the body, nourished and knit together by joints and ligaments, grows with the increase that is from God." (Colossians 2:19)

What a way with words! Wish *I* was that good!

Let me try.

For the Body to function in tip-top condition all the joints and ligaments must be well nourished, working together. How can the foot tread if the hip aches? How can the hand grasp if the elbow throbs? Metaphorically, I speak of proper "joints" as relationships with one another, and proper "ligaments" as attitudes held among the brethren. Take a moment to search yourself — do you have failing joints, loose ligaments?

That was pretty good....

The breaker anointing of the apostle "cells" working in the Body bestows freedom from grudges, hurts, reservations. The measure of life in the Body is the measure of absence of reservation and restriction. Freedom, liberty, to move about, to run a marathon, as it were. To bend over to pick up the morning paper. To work in the garden. I can go on and on, but I won't. You get the idea.

Holiness comes before unity – I mean holiness based on conviction, not compromising the truth. "...'But on this one will I look: on him who is poor and of a contrite spirit, and who trembles at My word.'" (Isaiah 66:2) "...Till we all come to the unity of the faith and of the knowledge of the Son of God, to a perfect man, to the measure of the stature of the fullness of Christ...." (Ephesians 4:13) "...That He might present her to Himself a glorious church, not having spot or wrinkle or any such thing, but that she should be holy and without blemish." (Ephesians 5:27)

When the cells of the Body are sick, they manifest as spots, wrinkles, blemishes — let's just say it: spiritual zits! I'm tired of pizza-faced churches; we need some Clearasil! All hail acne-free living!

That was *really* good....

Clearasil in the form of an intense *hatred of sin* and an intense *fear of the Lord*.

JUDGING RIGHTEOUSLY

Indeed, beware of "...A false witness who speaks lies, and one who sows discord among brethren." (Proverbs 6:19) Let me throw light on two sins that cut off the flow of life in the Body:

- The Evil Eye of Suspicion — hate it!
- The Evil Tongue of Iniquity — hate it!

These two sins are some important fleshly issues that the apostles have to deal with constantly. They must discern them when they occur and war against them, breaking their power over the people. It takes an apostolic anointing working with all of the four-fold to root these evils out, cut them to the quick and dispose of them among the group. We as apostolic people must *always* be vigilant in stamping out these sins when they are found, and we must take great care to overcome these sins in our own lives. If we are ignorant of our calling as apostolic people, if we choose to ignore these evils, the devil will eat our lunches, so to speak, and we are hampered in our expression of the Father in our lives.

"...Lest Satan should take advantage of us; for we are not ignorant of his devices." (2 Corinthians 2:11)

Concerning these sins and the operations of Satan, don't be uninformed. He is a tempter. (Matthew 4:3) That word "tempter" is allegorically synonymous with "serpent." (1 Thessalonians 3:5) We as apostolic people must overcome temptation through confession of the written Word!

He is a "deceiver," allegorically synonymous with a "scorpion." (Luke 10:17-22) When Jesus said, "I saw Satan fall like lightning from heaven," (Verse 18) it's not just that He was specifically referencing his fall from the grace of God (which the eternal, pre-incarnate Word would certainly have witnessed); but also, or rather, his fall at the hands of the seventy who cast out demons in the name of Jesus.

We as apostolic people must overcome his deceptions by studying the counsel of the Lord — do *not* accept falsities for the truth! No matter what the devil might say, you are given "authority to trample on serpents and scorpions." (Verse 19)

So trample him!

Notice that, "In that hour, Jesus rejoiced in the Spirit...." (Verse 21) The Greek suggests that He was quite literally leaping and dancing, shouting with excessive joy. Gives a whole new meaning to the verse, huh?

So dance on the scorpion!

The devil is an "accuser," a "slanderer," allegorically synonymous with a "dragon." (Revelation 12:7) The word for "accuser, slanderer" is used to describe one who prosecutes as in a courtroom, one who points the finger, "*J'accuse!*" Satan accuses the believer before God; he accuses God to the believer; he accuses a believer to himself; he accuses other Christians to the believer. He's a busy dragon! As seen in Job 1, Satan accuses us before God. But we have an Advocate in Jesus, who delights in placing a muzzle on the snapping beast. As Jesus overcomes the accuser in heaven, we must overcome him here on earth!

So muzzle the dragon!

Concerning accusing the brethren to the brethren, so often Satan uses our mouths to sow discord and discontent, placing a spirit of condemnation on the accused. Mark 7:20-23 is speaking to the evil eye of suspicion I mentioned earlier. An "evil eye" is to look at people and immediately think evil, or to look at them in order to discover something wrong, having no merit for judgment, just looking upon the outward appearance.

"For we do not commend ourselves again to you, but give you opportunity to boast on our behalf, that you may have an answer for those who boast in appearance and not in heart. Therefore, from now on, we regard no one according to the flesh. Even though we have known Christ according to the flesh, yet now we know Him thus no longer." (2 Corinthians 5:12, 16) That phrase "according to the flesh" means after the "outward, natural order of things."

"'Do not judge according to appearance, but judge with righteous judgment.'" (John 7:24) God always judges with a righteous judgment; our judgment is often filtered through outward appearances. We must reverse this action and judge righteously, not after the flesh, but after the Spirit.

"Now when He was in Jerusalem... many believed in His name when they saw the signs which He did. But Jesus did not commit Himself to them, because He knew all men, and had no need that anyone should testify of man, for He knew what was in man." (John 2:23-25) What this passage means is Jesus didn't need anyone to tell Him what another person was like. He perceived what was *inside* the man, not just what His physical eyes could show Him.

"And be kind to one another, tenderhearted, forgiving one another, even as God in Christ forgave you." (Ephesians 4:32)

That phrase "be kind" could also read "be easy-going." How often are members of the Body *not* easy-going! But remember God is going to let you be judged by the same measure of judgment that you use on others, so it's in your best interest to be "easy-going," if I might hazard an admonition.

It's the old *beam versus sliver* notion in Matthew 7:1-5 all over again. "'Judge not, that you be not judged. For with what judgment you judge, you will be judged; and with the measure you use, it will be measured back to you.'" (Verses 1-2)

"But why do you judge your brother? Or why do you show contempt for your brother? For we shall all stand before the judgment seat of Christ. Therefore let us not judge one another anymore, but rather resolve this, not to put a stumbling block or a cause to fall in our brother's way." (Romans 14:10, 13)

Criticism and slander bind your brother from being used to bless others. They put a stumbling block in the way of young Christians, and even some more mature Christians! A "stumbling block" causes one to "back away" — you don't want to be responsible for causing a person to back away from the blessings of God toward the lusts of the flesh. Preach the truth, but preach it in love. Always.

The word "judge" has a dual meaning. One connotation is bad — judging someone in a poor light, passing a sentence upon them. The other connotation is righteous, "to deliver," as those found in the book of Judges. Get it?

It is possible to identify a fault without heaping up condemnation. We are to judge, not by condemning, but by seeing a need and reaching out to minister to it, to deliver a person, not sentence them to incarceration in a jail cell of self-denunciation (ahhh, I waxed eloquent!)

Please note we *are* to judge spiritual matters. "But he who is spiritual judges all things, yet he himself is rightly judged by no one." (1 Corinthians 2:15) But the reason behind judging spiritual matters is to restore the judged in the Spirit, not condemn but parole. "Brethren, if a man is overtaken in any trespass, you who are spiritual restore such a one in a spirit of gentleness, considering yourself lest you also be tempted. Bear one another's burdens, and so fulfill the law of Christ." (Galatians 6:1-2)

This answers the question, "Am I my brother's keeper?" (Genesis 4:9) with a resounding, "Well, yes, you are!" By keeping our brothers, instead of hanging them out to dry, we restore them to the Spirit, crying out, "Just where are your accusers now?" (See John 8:10.)

"'Moreover if your brother sins against you, go and tell him his fault between you and him alone. If he hears you, you have gained your brother. But if he will not hear, take with you one or two more, that "by the mouth of two or three witnesses every word may be established." And if he refuses to hear them, tell it to the church. But if he refuses even to hear the church, let him be to you like a heathen and a tax collector.'" (Matthew 18:15-17)

Here Christ is providing a standard operating procedure for dealing with faults in the Church. We all know this passage, but how often do we *not* follow it! First, go to the person alone, *then* take two or three, *then* bring it before the Body. In that order. We would do well to take the word of Jesus as law, not polite suggestion, as such above contestation, and in doing so, save ourselves a lot of heartache and misery, I am convinced.

Concerning the tongue of iniquity (hate it!), reference James 3:6, 8. "And the tongue is a fire, a world of iniquity [unrighteousness]. The tongue is so set among our members that it defiles the whole body, and sets on fire the course of nature [existence]; and it is set on fire by hell. But no man can tame the tongue. It is an unruly evil, full of deadly poison."

Question: Has your tongue been a blessing or a curse?

Question: Has the tongue of another been used as a blessing or a curse to you?

Perhaps it requires an unveiling of apostolic unction to answer these questions fully. Perhaps we must cultivate a sensitivity — no, a **hatred** — toward suspicion and iniquity. Perhaps we have need to repent to another for allowing our tongues and eyes to be instruments of sinful judgment and action. Perhaps.

Note God's judgment on Egypt for their sin. "The Lord has mingled a perverse spirit in her midst; and they have caused Egypt to err in all her work, as a drunken man staggers in his vomit." (Isaiah 19:14) Wow, that's a strong visual, isn't it? What is it about vomit that just really crystallizes a concept in one's mind? It's just full of chunky grossness.

"Perverse" we might say means "to say something in order to cast to the ground." And "a wholesome [healing] tongue is a tree of life, but perverseness in it breaks the spirit." (Proverbs 15:4) See, in order to bring down the humanistic strength of Egypt, God mingled a perverse spirit with them — a spirit that would cause them to cast each other down to the ground by the *things they said with their mouths.*

They criticized, condemned and verbally attacked one another with projectile vomitings of an iniquitous tongue. (I can't really say I waxed eloquent *there*!)

But the point is: don't be like Egypt! Instead, let us war against the evil eye and the evil tongue, let us judge rightly, let us come together in unity and make Jesus' words truth in action. "'And the glory which You gave Me I have given them, that they may be one just as We are one....'" (John 17:22)

Apostles must develop discernment in their spheres of influence concerning the evil eye of suspicion and the evil tongue of iniquity. We must cultivate sensitivity toward judging righteously! Apostolic people must seek out that breaker anointing that demonstrates the power of God to overcome the perverse spirit, to undo the works of suspicion and iniquity. It is in this vein that the fullness of the compassion of the Father is found. Love one another!

Chapter Three Outline

"Unveiling the Compassion of God"

THE LOVE WALK

- Compassion is love that is projected upon a need
- We as apostolic men and women must unveil this compassion of God, teaching the saints to follow that divine flow of love, to be free in expressing the power of Christ to a world that is in desperate need of a lot of love
- Rebekah symbolizes the Bride of Christ in Genesis 24, a chaste woman who left her father, her home, her land and embraced Isaac as her husband. For us to be a Bride worthy of such a Groom, we must *leave* our old lives and begin new ones with Him. This walk of love into the Groom's arms starts with *leaving* the natural, worldly things behind and focusing all of our attentions upon our new Husband
- "Listen, O daughter, consider and incline your ear; forget your own people also, and your father's house; so the King will greatly desire your beauty; because He is your Lord, worship Him." (Psalm 45:10-11)
- "Do not love the world... for all that is in the world — the lust of the flesh, the lust of the eyes, and the pride of life — is not of the Father but is of the world. And the world is passing away, and the lust of it; but he who does the will of God abides forever.'" (1 John 2:15-17)

- "'Do not think that I came to bring peace on earth. I did not come to bring peace but a sword. For I have come to "set a man against his father, a daughter against her mother, and a daughter-in-law against her mother-in-law" [see Micah 7:6]; and "a man's enemies will be those of his own household." He who loves father or mother more than Me is not worthy of Me....'" (Matthew 10:34-37)

- After we have left the world behind us, we find ourselves *loving* Him with complete devotion, abandonment and adoration

- "Both the singers and the players on instruments say, 'All my springs are in you.'" (Psalm 87:7)

- We must be constantly *looking* for our Lover

- "By night on my bed I sought the one I love; I sought him, but I did not find him." (Song of Solomon 3:1)

- Love must be put in us, first received and then expressed. This love walk is worked out through our *leaving, loving* and *looking* — all for the sake of our Groom. This is the apostolic unveiling of God's great compassion for the Bride and the Groom, giving us the freedom to express ourselves back to the Father what we have received

THE FRIENDSHIP WALK

- "Now when he had finished speaking to Saul, the soul of Jonathan was knit to the soul of David, and Jonathan loved him as his own soul. Saul took him that day, and would not let him go home to his father's house anymore. Then

Jonathan and David made a covenant, because he loved him as his own soul." (1 Samuel 18:1-3)

- "I am distressed for you, my brother Jonathan; you have been very pleasant to me; your love to me was wonderful, surpassing the love of women.'" (2 Samuel 1:26)

- An unveiling of the compassion of God creates a freedom to express ourselves to others — to be friendly, to reciprocate love, to care for one another

- "You are My friends if you do whatever I command you. No longer do I call you servants, for a servant does not know what his master is doing; but I have called you friends, for all things that I heard from My Father I have made known to you. You did not choose Me, but I chose you and appointed you that you should go and bear fruit, and that your fruit should remain, that whatever you ask the Father in My name He may give you. These things I command you, that you love one another.'" (John 15:14-17)

- "This is My commandment, that you love one another as I have loved you. Greater love has no one that this, than to lay down one's life for his friends." (John 15:12-13)

- Through our close, intimate friendship with Christ, we have boldness and have access to His reputation (His favor)

- Apostles help people to experience God's love in its highest form: "I accept you with the same level of fervency that I accepted My own Son."

- "If two of you shall agree as touching anything in heaven..." (Matthew 18:19)
- That is the open-heavens above the corporate Body. It is directly tied into the level of friendship love you have for your brethren

The Humanity of Jesus

- Apostles are used to bring *humanity* back into their testimonies of Christ's power. Jesus was fully human (and yes, fully God), but apostles manifest the humanity of Jesus Christ as He heard from the Father, had His own glory encounters and translated them to others
- Without the breaker anointing to translate these glory experiences, it creates a pseudo-religious expression that seems very surreal and bizarre to the people
- If Christ did not exhibit a breaker anointing as the first Apostle, people would not have understood His miraculous power
- God's power manifested through humanity is not mystical, it is not fantastical. It is very much reality, based upon one's relationship with Jesus Christ and the Father. It is love and friendship that yields such grace and experience with God, boldness and access
- What happens is the anointing comes upon and into our humanity, and this is what makes us real to people

- God accepts that we are merely humans — note, *sin* is not excused, but *humanity* is understood by the Father. It is an acceptance and an identification in the ministry of the Lord
- The apostolic breaker anointing, through the character and lives of the apostles, must unveil the love God has for humanity, and even further, the undeniable grace and favor that comes along with such a compassion for mankind

The Faith Walk

- "But without faith it is impossible to please Him, for he who comes to God must believe that He is, and that He is a rewarder of those who diligently seek Him." (Hebrews 11:6)
- An unveiling of His compassion yields a freedom for God to express Himself to us, and He rewards us with the supernatural
- Man is not the source of love; he is merely the recipient and expresser of it. To the extent one receives and expresses love, it can be said that one knows God
- "He who does not love does not know God, for God is love." (1 John 4:8)
- "This is love, that we walk according to his commandments. This is the commandment, that as you have heard from the beginning, you should walk in it." (2 John 6)
- It is *projected love* that is commanded. Love that is focused, directed, on the needs of another. God is sending forth His love messengers, moved to focus that love they have received

on the needs of the people He causes them to come into contact with

- When love is projected, that is when grace is manifested

THE UNITY FACTOR

- "Behold, how good and how pleasant it is for brethren to dwell together in unity! It is like the precious oil upon the head, running down on the beard, the beard of Aaron, running down on the edge of his garments. It is like the dew of Hermon, descending upon the mountains of Zion; for there the Lord commanded the blessing — life forevermore." (Psalm 133)

- "'Assuredly, I say to you, whatever you bind on earth will be bound in heaven, and whatever you loose on earth will be loosed in heaven. Again I say to you that if two of you agree on earth concerning anything that they ask, it will be done for them by My Father in heaven. For where two or three are gathered together in My name, I am there in the midst of them.'" (Matthew 18:18-20)

- "There is one body and one Spirit, just as you were called in one hope of your calling; one Lord, one faith, one baptism; one God and Father of all, who is above all, and through all, and in you all." (Ephesians 4:4-6)

- "'Now I am no longer in the world, but these are in the world [speaking of the disciples], and I come to You. Holy Father, keep through Your name those whom You have given Me,

that they may be one as We are... that they all may be one, as You, Father, are in Me, and I in You; that they also may be one in Us, that the world may believe that You sent Me.... I in them, and You in Me; that they may be made perfect in one, and that the world may know that You have sent Me, and have loved them as you have loved Me.'" (John 17:22, 21, 23)

Judging Righteously

- Satan accuses the believer before God; he accuses God to the believer; he accuses a believer to himself; he accuses other Christians to the believer
- Concerning accusing the brethren to the brethren, so often Satan uses our mouths to sow discord and discontent, placing a spirit of condemnation on the accused — looking at people and immediately thinking evil, or looking at them in order to discover something wrong, having no merit for judgment, just looking upon the outward appearance
- "Do not judge according to appearance, but judge with righteous judgment.'" (John 7:24)
- "'Judge not, that you be not judged. For with what judgment you judge, you will be judged; and with the measure you use, it will be measured back to you.'" (Verses 1-2)
- "But why do you judge your brother? Or why do you show contempt for your brother? For we shall all stand before the judgment seat of Christ. Therefore let us not judge

one another anymore, but rather resolve this, not to put a stumbling block or a cause to fall in our brother's way." (Romans 14:10, 13)

- We are to judge, not by condemning, but by seeing a need and reaching out to minister to it, to deliver a person, not sentence them to incarceration in a jail cell of self-denunciation
- We *are* to judge spiritual matters
- "But he who is spiritual judges all things, yet he himself is rightly judged by no one." (1 Corinthians 2:15)
- "Brethren, if a man is overtaken in any trespass, you who are spiritual restore such a one in a spirit of gentleness, considering yourself lest you also be tempted. Bear one another's burdens, and so fulfill the law of Christ." (Galatians 6:1-2)
- "'Moreover if your brother sins against you, go and tell him his fault between you and him alone. If he hears you, you have gained your brother. But if he will not hear, take with you one or two more, that "by the mouth of two or three witnesses every word may be established." And if he refuses to hear them, tell it to the church. But if he refuses even to hear the church, let him be to you like a heathen and a tax collector.'" (Matthew 18:15-17)

4

Unveiling the Confidence of God

ANOTHER BUS DEPOT TESTIMONY

I don't know what it was about that bus depot in downtown Dallas, but the Lord really used it while I was attending Christ for the Nations to unveil certain attributes of His nature. From the previous chapter, I've already shared that He started at that time to teach me sensitivity to the divine flow of love, to operate out of compassion. But there was another remarkable occurrence at that depot that taught me a level of boldness to reach out to people in need. I was learning to step out in confidence, free from intimidation, free from the circumstances that surrounded my life: my upbringing, my youth, my fears of rejection. I can see now the Lord was developing within me attributes of His own confidence, and I'd like to share a little with you on how that confidence relates to the release of the apostolic anointing.

So I found myself once again at the bus station, waiting around for the Lord to lead me to a person who needed some ministry. It's funny, but I recall having just finished another powerful Smith Wigglesworth book that outlined how one should make themselves available for ministry, and the Lord would answer their obedience. To be bold as a lion! To step out with confidence and meet the people where they're at!

Here at the bus station....

But the Lord honored my zeal.

Feeling as excited and emboldened as Smith Wigglesworth must have felt, I eagerly watched a bus pull into the depot, thinking to myself, *Well, here's an opportunity, Lord!* I felt I could take on the whole world. Lemme at 'em!

The bus stop had a whole group of people there, maybe two hundred or so, comprised solely of African Americans, which seemed strange to me at that moment. Like they were one big group coming from somewhere together.

As I was pondering where all these men and women came from, a bus pulled up, and a gentleman disembarked sporting a small suitcase in one hand and a cane in the other. It was obvious, as he gingerly stepped off the bus, that he was unable to bend one of his legs. He grimaced, leaning on the cane for support.

I stood in front of the man, stopping the people behind him trying to get off the bus, and in my most Wigglesworth-iest voice, I boldly asked, "Do you desire to be made whole?"

Everybody stopped and looked at me.

I think I might have even adopted a James Earl Jones accent. Wigglesworth would've been proud! The man's eyes narrowed on me, and I thought he was going to burst out laughing. But instead he said, "Are you talkin' about that healin' stuff? Y'know my sister was just at a Kathryn Kulhman miracle service and got healed of cancer. I'm scheduled this week to have this bum leg amputated. I got dozens of tumors in this leg that the doctors can't do nothin' about. It's why I'm here in the city."

Talk about a divine setup!

"Well, let me pray for you in the name of Jesus, and we'll believe you'll get healed."

Sounded simple enough to him, so he nodded. I invoked the name of Jesus and rebuked the tumors. That was it.

"Well, son...." He tottered for a second, and then dropped his suitcase and cane. "Here goes...."

And he took a hard step forward on his bad leg. As it came down to strike the concrete, I heard a *snap! crackle! pop!* and amazingly, he took a step forward. The tumors in his leg had disappeared entirely! He was instantly made whole!

You can imagine how he and I began to rejoice. The man was twirling around, *singing* praises, his cane and suitcase forgotten. We were having our own private revival meeting. It was just phenomenal.

But what was most funny was what the group of some two hundred Black men and women were doing. I mean, they were going *nuts!* Leaping, twirling, screaming, whooping and hollering — right there in front of the bus terminal, causing a tremendous scene. Everybody was just having a good ol' fashioned Holy Ghost shoutin' party.

I was dumbfounded as to why all these people would be shouting and rejoicing.

It took several minutes for me to discover the whole lot was coming back from a Pentecostal revival conference....

The Parrhesia Principle

See, the issue we have in the Body of Christ is that we all know God is *capable* of healing, because in order to be God, He must be all-powerful. And some Christians take it a step further, maintaining that God is not only capable of healing, but that it is actually His *will and desire* to make people whole. Now, it's one thing to believe God wants to heal; it's quite another thing to believe that God wants to heal *through* His people. There's where an intimidation can arise. What needs to happen is for His people to have an unveiling of the boldness they are to possess.

Remember way back I mentioned that I would share more in depth on the boldness the apostles displayed in Acts 4:31?

I'm glad you do....

Well, as a man of my word, let's take a few moments and discuss this *parrhesia* of the Holy Spirit, seeing as how it ties so nicely into the theme for this chapter.

The Greek word *parrhesia* (Strong's #3954) means "boldness" in our familiar English tongue. It means "confidence, freedom of speech, to be outspoken, the opposite of fear, cowardice and intimidation." Once the people were filled with the Holy Ghost, *parrhesia* came upon them.

The apostles of today, like the apostles of the early Church, are called to equip the apostolic people with boldness, through the power of the Holy Spirit. It is part of their breaker anointing — and a pretty major part at that! Where are the people of God without boldness? Confined to a shackling of intimidation and fear, two things which God the Father never intended His children to have.

We are to have freedom from intimidation, for we have a brand new, open policy from God, backed by the authority of His throne. We have immediate, unrestricted access to everything He possesses, which is... everything.... He is a God of justice, mercy and freedom; whatever we do and say, it is to be done to the glory of God (1 Corinthians 10:31) — and we are to have boldness in working on His behalf; of course, always, always by His wisdom and direction.

But this boldness only comes from relationship with the Holy Spirit. Boldness, to me, is one of the greatest pieces of evidence that one is baptized in the Holy Spirit, not just the evidence of speaking in tongues — although that's vitally important in my book, too! See, it takes confidence to be able to speak in tongues; it takes *parrhesia*.

There is a religious spirit warring against us as an apostolic people. It endeavors to bring a sense of intimidation. It desperately desires to limit the expression of our authority in the Lord. It seeks to bring us down to a level of mediocrity and nominalism. It is the enemy called "Average." (I'm not sure where I heard that phrase from; I believe it was Bob Mason. Anyway, he had an excellent point: our enemy is "Average.") It wants us to be maintained in the *status quo* of mere existence. It wants us to remain in our comfort zone of indifference toward the moves of God.

The apostles and apostolic people must war against this spirit of lethargy. It's a big problem in the Body of Christ. To understate, there is great importance to be placed on the expression of God as a rushing, mighty Wind, and it is the calling of the apostolic to restore that expression! I feel alarmed that we as the Church are being sedated by this religious spirit into accepting the nominalism of the "Almost Experience" — you recall that expression from earlier, right? I see it is creating an entire generation of younger people who have not learned to engage their spirit man with the *Parakletos* (Strong's #3875), who is the Comforter, the Holy Spirit. (John 14:26)

The breaker anointing casts off the dullness of Average, showing the people the aggressive side of the Holy Spirit (yes, there is an aggressive side of the Spirit; we'll go into that later.) He is not just passive, walking alongside to encourage and uplift us in the time of need. In the *parrhesia* of the Spirit, we see He is bold in nature as He walks alongside us, helping us by increasing *our* level of boldness and activity. He helps us be less lethargic toward the moves of God, see?

The apostles have a great quest in seeking the boldness of the Holy Spirit to invade peoples' lives. They recognize that the things in the realm of the spiritual have to be expressed here on earth to counteract the expressions of the world and its power. And the world certainly has its own expressions. The world lures and seduces people in complacency and acceptance of circumstances. Their eyes fall on the natural and ignore or fear the supernatural power of God which supersedes any circumstances they might be going through.

The Spirit must be allowed to move in a powerful, aggressive way to break off the spirit of intimidation and unbelief that says if a person gets engaged in the acts of God, he or she will only be disappointed again and again. My dear friends, this is a lie of the enemy! It is a curse of limitation!

The Curse of Limitation

In my eyes, one of the greatest callings of the apostles is **to reverse the curse that limits the expression of God through His Holy Spirit.** The apostles are filled with a boldness to act with authority in signs, wonders and miracles to establish the Kingdom of God in the hearts of people here on earth. The dominion and authority that is already established in heaven is to be released here on earth.

"'Your kingdom come. Your will be done on earth as it is in heaven.'" (Matthew 6:10) It *is* in heaven, already. His will is done. What we have to do is make His will that is *already* in action in heaven be in action here on earth. What we hear taking place in the supernatural realm is to be heard taking place in this realm, too.

We've highlighted him briefly before, but let's take another look at Philip in Acts 8. Specifically Verses 7 and 8. Here's Philip down in Samaria, preaching Christ to the people, and "...the multitudes with one accord heeded the things spoken by Philip, hearing and seeing the miracles which he did."

Now I'm blessed to say I've *seen* a lot of miracles. But *hearing* miracles? How does one *hear* a miracle? The next verse tells us, "For unclean spirits, crying out with a loud voice, came out of many who were possessed; and many who were paralyzed and lame were healed. And there was great joy in that city."

Deliverance from a demon is *hearing* a miracle take place. Because demons mute, that is to say "bind," the true sound of God. And when the demon is released, the true sound of the Kingdom is heard: rejoicing... as in "great joy" being established in Samaria.

The devil wants us quieted, muted, sitting still, having no freedom, liberty or confidence. But hearing in the miraculous realm releases the miraculous on *this* realm, and after the release of every miracle there is to be great joy, because we are seeing His will be done on earth as it is in heaven. The breaker anointing brings about the rejoicing sounds of deliverance from the spirits of limitation.

I've taken teams into some pretty remote places of the earth, some jungles in India for example. And where we've gone into these various isolated areas way out in the sticks we've encountered demonic powers that have gone uncontested for generations: superstitions, vexations, occult activity, paganism, animism. And inside of two hours, no joking, it is so astounding to watch these strongholds thrown down because of God's miraculous intervention. It creates an entire atmosphere of jubilation.

It's not just the miracles themselves, see. It's the expression of freedom and boldness. It is such a brilliant experience to see people that have been bound and vexed by a limitation experience joy, peace and righteousness for the first time. They come in contact with the Kingdom of God. No, it's not just to see miracles take place — although that's certainly cool — but the miracles initiate those encounters with God where the things of the spiritual realm are experienced here on earth.

The miraculous breaks the lure of the world off the people, in the Church or otherwise. The world has great tools in its possession of enchantment and seduction... *anything* to get the people's eyes off the true power of God. Anything to keep them down and anesthetized to the joy of heaven. They are tranquilized in every sense of the word into a false sense of security that is Average.

The apostles *must* have miracles to release responses — the whole key to *parrhesia* is the boldness of God coming upon the apostolic people to war against that religious spirit that doesn't want people to encounter God. It doesn't want the people in the Church to respond to what they're experiencing. Because if they do, boldness comes on them! And it starts to spread like wildfire.

Rise up! We've got to fight against this curse of limitation that says we cannot experience God! Further to our studies of Matthew 16:19, binding and loosing, we've got to seek a breaker anointing that looses the people of God from the bondage of religious *nothings*.

You know, one of the things I appreciate most about my religious upbringing is I never learned one thing.... And because I never learned one thing, I never had to *unlearn* anything. I've said it before, I was raised American heathen, Southern California-style!

I'm not making some blanket statement that says we're not to be encouraged to be reared up in a Spirit-filled, Bible-believing church. I am certainly a big proponent for that, but where I grew up in California at the time, there *wasn't* any church like that, so I never had to unlearn anything about the religious nothings that can pervade even the most well intentioned churches out there.

I'm very grateful that I was born again and Spirit-filled in the Jesus Movement. It was during those early years of the Charismatic Renewal that I went to a Bible school that was under amazing revival. I thought six-hour miracle services were the norm! That was average Christian living to me.

Boy, did I get a rude awakening later on....

The point is the expression of heaven's liberties here on earth brings us into true freedom, right? But we are intimidated by this spirit of limitation that doesn't want the Church to express itself in freedom and liberty as they are experiencing it in heaven.

So let me tell you about the boldness of Sister Alma and encourage your faith.

ALMA'S STORY

I have taken teams over to India for ministry outreach to the tribal people w-a-y out in the secluded jungles. I mean, places so remote they've not seen white folks before. Those kinds of places. Anyway, on one of these excursions, a precious sister in the Lord from a Lutheran background was part of the team. Her name was Alma. This is what happened to her:

We were somewhere (who knows exactly — I don't think I can find it on a map) in northern-central India. People were coming in from many tiny villages to hear about this Jesus that we preached, and the Lord graciously revealed Himself to these people, whom most had never heard the plan of salvation. We were seeing some tremendous miracles and salvations. Night after night of these crusades, the crowds were swelling.

One night in particular, I was going down a line of Indians spread out before me, praying for nearly every conceivable type of sickness, disease or infirmity. I was seeing intense miracles, to the Lord's glory and honor: crippling conditions healed, crooked bones made straight, blind eyes and deaf ears opened. It was a blast to see the Lord touch these people.

A man stood before me. It didn't take a gift of discernment to see what was wrong with him. I didn't even need the interpreter. This guy had no arm. Now, by "no arm" I mean "no arm." Not a shriveled arm, not a crippled, mangled arm. It just wasn't there. No arm. I foolishly looked behind him to see if the arm was on the wrong side. Nope. No arm at all. There was his shoulder, and sticking out of the armpit was a hand. Just a hand, waving at me. Did I mention he did *not* have an arm? I'm persuaded it had never been created. Pretty easy deduction, I suppose, 'cause there was the hand, waving hi, but no arm.

Now, Alma was overwhelmed because there was just no way I could pray for the hundreds of Indians that were coming out, so I had gathered the whole team together and sent them amongst the people. I figured what better way to ease them into power evangelism than toss them all in the midst of a whole lot of folks with AIDS, cancer and worse.

But dear sweet, poor Alma. The first night a person with leprosy stood up in front of her. So she was a little freaked out, to say the least. Her confidence level was hovering around zero. When that service was over, she came up to me and said, "Now, Brother Jim," — please don't call me Jim — "I didn't know it was going to be this way. I thought I was coming to India to sing some songs and encourage the pastors. I can't handle this. So tomorrow night, when you call the sick up, I'll just go over there, behind the pulpit stand and intercede for you. Don't call me up to lay hands on people."

Of course, I didn't want anyone ministering among the people who didn't have the faith or confidence to pray for them, so I just nodded and said, "Sure, Alma. No problem."

Now before you cast me dark glances, dear readers, in my heart of hearts I *had* planned on honoring her request not to make her pray for anybody....

But here was this man that had no arm. Remember, he was armless. I had just gotten through telling all these people that there was only one true and wise God, and His name was Jesus, and to prove it to them, bring up all the sick and they'll be healed. So far I'd seen great success, until this guy with no arm stood before me.

I did everything I knew what to do. I prayed for this man in English, in tongues; I cast off, I spoke in. Every scripture I knew on healing poured from my lips. I jerked on the man's waving hand, nothing happened. He was still oh, so very armless. All eyes were upon me. The kingdoms of light and darkness were clashing — the pressure was astounding.

Finally after a few minutes, I gained enough spiritual sense to stop wearing myself out and prayed, *Lord, why isn't he getting healed?*

The Lord spoke to me. He said: "You give him... to Alma...."

Right-o!

"Oh, Alma? Alma, darling? Come here please...."

Alma was behind the podium, intensely praying in tongues, her eyes shut tight. You could hear her fervency. I guess she thought the Lord was calling her, 'cause she jerked her head toward the heavens, "Yes?"

"Look, Alma," I said, drawing her attention more earthbound. "I know last night you said you didn't want to pray for anyone, but I want you to pray for this guy here."

Her eyes alighted on the man. And he was armless, by the way. Boy, oh boy, talk about looking daggers at someone! She fixed me with this seething gaze as if to say, *I told you I didn't want to pray for anyone, and you give me this man? Oh, I'll deal with you later, Jim!* (Please don't call me

Jim; I prefer James.) But she went up to the armless man, miserable, but she went up nonetheless.

Now in case you didn't know, it's very *hot* in India. Like about 200 degrees, or something. Nine o'clock at night, 90% humidity. There were close to 500 mothers and their children who would hike, sometimes as much as two or three days, to get out to these meetings. And they'd stay the length of the crusade, some two, three, four days. We had to shelter them from the heat, so the crusade coordinators — indigenous pastors — constructed a makeshift pavilion out of rafters and put straw on the top.

Someone thought it was a smart idea to string light bulbs all the way across the rafters, because the gatherings went on well after dark. Problem was, most Indians are relatively short people, and I'm six-five. So the light bulbs were right at nose level to me, usually my head would hit the rafters on the stage.

Can you imagine the bugs that congregated around these light bulbs? I learned to talk through clenched teeth the whole time because if the heat is unbearable in India... the bugs are worse. Funky lookin' bugs, man! I mean little human faces on 'em, like that *Outer Limits* episode. Book of Revelation stuff, my friends! Fangs, fur, whatever. God only knows what I swallowed during the sermon! Strangely, I didn't go hungry....

The bugs were one thing, but we fed the children and the mothers there, under the pavilion, on the dirt floor. And where little kids drop food in India, there are rats. Now, the rats in India kill the cats. You think I'm joking, but I'm not. They're mongrels. They're Mutant Ninja Rats. I think the government created them as biological weapons. And periodically they dropped from the rafters to land on the food the kids were eating. We had guys beating them away all day, much to their own physical peril, 'cause the rats were notoriously foul-tempered. Demonized little monsters.

Anyway, I digress. So there's this pavilion with rafters and straw. And here's Alma and the armless man — who you'll recall did not have an arm — standing under the pavilion.

She approached him, boring holes into me with her eyes, and miserably flopped her hand on the one shoulder of the man that was perfectly normal, not daring to look at his waving hand on the other shoulder. She squeezed her eyes shut, shook her head, and muttered, "J-J-Jesus...."

At the first or second "J-J" — I mean, she didn't even get the word "Jesus" all the way out — wouldn't you know, that hand that was attached to the man's shoulder shook violently and *launched* out of the socket like a jet-fuel-powered cannonball, flying through the air. Thank God an arm was attached to it. Otherwise, that would've just been gross....

Keep in mind, Alma's eyes were shut tight, otherwise it's not as funny. But the man's hand, attached to his new arm, landed on top of poor, sweet Alma's head.

"AAAAAHHHHHH!!!!" She screamed and *knocked* that hand off her head. She'd thought a rat — dead serious here — had jumped out of the rafters and landed on her. She's screaming, dancing on tiptoes and brushing her hair vehemently, while the man's new arm swung like an ape's at his side. (He hadn't yet learned to control the muscles.) Luckily, the guy was too astonished at his new arm to be offended.

Alma recovered her composure and opened her eyes to see this man standing before her with this perfectly whole, swinging arm. She looked up at me, shocked, looked back down at the man's arm, looked back up at me and shouted:

"Brother Maloney! Oh my Lord! It works! It really works!"

From that moment forward, we couldn't control Alma....

Every time we gave an altar call on that trip, she'd tap me on the shoulder and say, "Excuse me, Brother Maloney...." And she'd cut in front of me to start wading out into the crowds, finding anybody with a crippled or maimed limb. No interpreter needed.

She'd point to each one. "You. And you. And, yes, you. And you...." Twenty or thirty every night.

To the best of my knowledge, she saw 100% success. I often thought, *What hath God wrought?!*

The point of this testimony is to show the importance of being released from a curse of limitation, a curse of religiosity, as we'll see in the next segment. In fact this curse of limitation is parallel to a curse of divination. The Spirit in His *parrhesia* is calling for the apostles to release a breaker anointing of **boldness** to see this curse reversed.

THE CURSE OF DIVINATION

Recall that spirit of divination that possessed the slave girl in Acts 16:16. Remember the python spirit? It's the same thing here: a curse of divination. It's a spirit that tries to squeeze out anything that pertains to life, something that restricts us. It is a hissing statement that the python spits out at us, a prognosis, or a sentence of limited expression in Christ.

A big problem facing us today is the enemy attempting to seduce us into shallowness, wallowing around in the fleshly realm, imitating the divine. This is why the apostles have to rise up in character as well as charisma, because as dangerous as the spirit of limitation and divination is, it's simply feeding off our greatest weakness: the flesh. It's not just the demonic — I wish it were, because then we could cast it out, problem solved. Really, in truth, our greatest enemy is our flesh. It's not just sin; it's religious vanity.

We run the risk of not experiencing God Spirit-to-spirit. As I've stated before, the apostles must teach the people of God the difference between the holy and the profane. Otherwise we all attempt to minister out of our own shallowness and vanity, and we're not touching the people's spirits. It will establish low-level living. It will limit and intimidate the people in the Church.

You know when the python was cast out of the slave girl, Paul and Silas were thrown in prison for it.

Gee, thanks for all your help....

But it's neat to notice that in Acts 16:25 Paul and Silas are found singing praises in the midnight hours. Here they'd just been beaten for delivering the girl, and they're praising God! I believe they entered into heaven's choir. See, what was happening in heaven, they entered into on earth, and their praises broke that spirit of intimidation. It created a great earthquake, so that they walked right out of jail. How awesome is that?

In Acts 3:8, after the lame man was healed, he went walking, leaping and praising God, just like the man at the bus depot earlier. It wasn't just the miracle that was so cool, but his response to being loosed from limitation: he was free to express himself to God! Except, note the reaction of the religious people in Acts 4: the priests were like, "Quiet these men down. Hey, don't share this stuff! Don't take it any further!" Typical religious vanity.

What was God's response to the intimidation of the religious men? After they had been warned to "Shut up!," Peter, John and the believers lifted up their voices in one accord, and the whole place was shaken and filled with the Holy Ghost. Their release into boldness produced a corporate impact, not just the miracle itself taking place, but a divine reaction and response to the curse of divination! You want us to be quiet? We'll show ya quiet! How 'bout this!

I am convinced there is a deeper purpose for signs, wonders and miracles. In and of themselves, they're awesome – people are set free! But moreover, the release of the miraculous releases *parrhesia*. The people become emboldened to rejoice and celebrate the power of God. The curse of limitation and divination is broken!

Check out Matthew 21:10-17. Here we see that the whole city of Jerusalem was moved when Jesus, the prophet from Nazareth, comes to town. What was the first thing He did? Well, the Prophet marches right up to the temple and drives out the thieves... with a whip.... Now *there's* a message right there!

But once the thieves were driven out, what happened? The blind and the lame were healed.

I don't think we're going to see greater miracles until we have deliverance in the house of the Lord and the thieves are driven out. After that, the children will begin to cry out, "Hosanna to the Son of David!"

Again the chief priests and scribes wanted the children to clam up. There it is: their reaction predicated on their religious *nothings* tried to dictate to the people, "Hey, let's keep our expression limited here, folks!" They were possessed of a spirit of limitation and divination. They endeavored to keep the people down, to keep them under. It's a curse! I believe their response was founded in the occult, my friends, in a curse of augury. They attempted to place an omen of intimidation on the people. In the freedom of the people, they would lose their authority of religious manipulation and control. How can we say that religiosity doesn't matter?

Remember Numbers 23:23 — if there is no enchantment, no divination, the people will rise up like young lions! Lions are pretty bold! But the world doesn't want the people to be blessed. It doesn't want them to roar.

Yet Deuteronomy 28:13, 47 shows that if we serve the Lord joyfully, gladly, with a singleness of heart, He will make us above and not beneath. We roar in boldness, His blessings pouring out of our lives. Fight against the limitation! Fight against the divination, apostolic people!

The curse of divination is an enchantment that attempts to get its victims to stay down, to stay under, to be impressed by the outward, by a personality that lures one away from a position of conviction in God's Word to following the person instead. It attempts to seduce one into a lie, to change one's heart motivation.

In short, it wants us to change our worship from God to something else....

It sentences us to experience limitation, intimidation, binding. We are not able to experience life in all its fullness. Again, it is a prognosis, a hissing statement that constricts. It attempts to cast a veiling of dullness over us. It wants us to accept a counterfeit, a substitute for the power of God. It's not just demonic counterfeit. We also deal with substituting the power of God with natural knowledge and wisdom. (Not that I'm against natural wisdom, mind you; but the knowledge from above, the knowledge of God, should be paramount in our lives. See 1 Corinthians 8:7.)

Under the veiling of divination, we can substitute the power of God, the healing virtue, with the natural remedies found in medical science. Now, don't get me wrong: I'm all for doctors and nurses. I love them! They do the best they can with the natural realm to help people. But sometimes, we substitute their knowledge for that which is greater: that is, divine healing and divine health.

Here's another example that'll probably ruffle some religious feathers. It seems we have an entire generation of leaders that are exercising their faith for release of finances only. I'm not saying there isn't a place for that; we could all do with more money to get things done. But it's almost like they exert *so* much time and energy believing for the miraculous, supernatural intervention for their financial needs, that if they would just put the same level of energy into seeing the sick and afflicted healed, I believe we would be experiencing more of the power of God in the miraculous. Remember, these kinds of issues can create a low level of living and experience in God.

Sometimes even the *blessings* can be a substitute for what is really needed.

The apostles have got to touch humanity where humanity is at. The apostolic people are gonna clear this whole thing up, I'm convinced. The apostles, prophets and ministers who have this settled in their hearts: to see God touch the people in a supernatural way. Men and women who are not in the ministry for the purpose of seeing their own needs met. Again, keep balance here, my friends — nothing wrong with having our own needs met; I'm all for prosperity. God wants us to be blessed, but not at the expense of people who are desperate for a tangible touch of His power.

But more importantly, if I had to choose between financial prosperity and the miraculous (and I *don't* believe we have to choose; I think we can have both, the miracles and believing God to meet financial needs supernaturally.) But if I had to choose what I'm going to put my concentration and energy into, I'd want to see the sick and afflicted healed! Wouldn't you?

We need to have our eyes opened to discern what God in heaven wants released at that time to touch humanity, that which has *lasting* rewards and eternal worth throughout time without end. We need to have our eyes opened!

THE BLIND MAN IN INDIA

I recall one instance where I had a line of about fifteen to twenty Indians standing in front of me with all manner of afflictions. Going down the line, I was seeing tremendous success to the glory of God. One man stood before me, blind as blind can be. I mean, no color, no pupils, just white eyeballs. He had not seen a shaft of light in his life of over thirty-five years. It's one thing to see someone healed who used to have their eyesight but lost it; it's another thing to see someone healed who has never had sight in their life. The outcome, once those eyes pop open, is often humorous — usually because *I'm* the first thing those poor people see....

Anyway, the Holy Spirit brought to my remembrance the statement of Jesus in Luke's Gospel, wherein He was quoting Isaiah. You know the one.

"The Spirit of the Lord is upon Me, because He has anointed Me to preach the gospel to the poor; He has sent Me to heal the brokenhearted, to proclaim liberty to the captives and recovery of sight to the blind...." (Luke 4:18)

That one. I love how David Alsobrook taught it: there is no reference of any blind person in the Old Testament being healed. Isaiah's prophetic word was stating that there would come a time when a Messiah, a Messenger, would come to open the blinded eye. (Isaiah 35:5) Of course, we know he was prophesying the forthcoming Sun of Righteousness with healing in His wings. But, to the best of our knowledge, it was at the first advent of Jesus that healing and deliverance for the blind came into being. So every time a blind eye is opened, it is proof that the Light of the world has come! It gives glory to the Lord, therefore, for the blind to see!

And what else was so amazing, as the above thought came to me, the Holy Spirit brought to my remembrance one of the Hebraic covenant names for God: Jehovah Rapha. That name translates as "I AM the Lord God that mends your life by stitch work." (Strong's #7495)

Sure enough, marvelous as it was to watch, the Lord began to stitch this man's eyes. It took several minutes, and it was like watching a needle "poke" color into the whites of those eyeballs. Line after line, his eyes were stitched into place! There were the colored irises, there were the pupils. Finally, his eyes looked normal, except for one small detail. They were covered with a filmy glaze and he still couldn't see.

The miraculous stitch work in and of itself boggled my mind, but I thought, *Well, God can't be finished because the man still can't see!* So I prayed a second time, and that film melted off his eyes and ran down his cheeks. The man had been following the sound of my voice, but suddenly he found he was staring at me... and he screamed!

Hurt my feelings a bit.... Oh, well, honestly I guess I'd scream to if *I* was the first thing somebody ever saw....

Interestingly enough, after he calmed down a bit, I noticed he began to act like me. See, we had the man come out over the next few nights of meetings to give his testimony. And he'd watch me, my mannerisms, my inflection (he spoke a different language, obviously), my gestures. When he came up to testify, sure enough, he'd move his hands in the same way I did, watching me for approval out of the corner of his brand-new eyes. He'd shout like I shouted, except only in his native tongue. He'd pray for people exactly how I prayed for them, this hand on their shoulder, this hand on their forehead, this leg a little behind the other. It was quite hilarious. I suddenly had a parrot, and he was such a dear parrot to watch.

The principle here, other than it's a powerful miracle to recount, is that this man identified with me because God operating in my life was the first thing he saw. So he just mimicked what I did. He'd found freedom in God, not only in the natural (his eyesight being restored) but also in the spiritual (his desire to reproduce what he'd "seen.") It's a startling revelation of apostolic grace when you see the people around you begin acting in total liberty, responding to the God they've just met.

The calling of the apostles and apostolic people is to establish a spirit of faith, reproducing others that have an understanding of their dominion in God the Father. To create a group of similar ilk who are *aware* — who just know that they know that God is capable of healing any manner of affliction. It takes an apostolic anointing to be able to create in people an ability to hear the true sound of heaven, to have their spiritual eyes opened much in the same way that dear man had his physical eyes opened. And the first thing these people see, after meeting that apostolic anointing, they will often begin to duplicate. They repent from dead works and have a faith toward God.

The apostles call people to repent in order that they might *see*. Dead works. That's all that we've been talking about here, these hindrances to the flow of the miraculous. Fruitless, unnecessary works that don't really change people. Things that stifle freedom. They keep things covered up and it hinders the flow of God's anointing. It takes a revelation, an unveiling, that without faith it is impossible to please God; whoever comes to Him must first believe that He is, and that He is a rewarder of those who diligently seek Him. (Hebrews 11:6) So we might say apostles bring faith into our understanding of just who we are in Christ, the new creations with limitless possibilities in the new realities of His authority and grace. People have got to get a better opinion of themselves and who they are in Christ!

Apostles must turn people's attention to the realm of the invisible, or eternal, realm. The secret to the supernatural is to walk as Jesus walked, doing that which only we see the Father doing, saying that which only we see the Father saying. The power of Jesus' actions was rooted in His ability to see and hear. (John 5:19) The Father is very committed to teaching us how to experience Him, to see Him, to hear Him. He is intent on seeing us loosed from the spirit of limitation so that He might open up the heavens to us.

HAVE YOU BEEN BEWITCHED?

We struggle with an imitation of the divine. Sometimes it can bind us to other people in the soulish realm, getting our focus and attention off God and His power to set people free. We become bewitched. Remember way, way back I talked about that, the Evil Eye of Bewitchment?

"O foolish Galatians! Who has bewitched you...?" (Galatians 3:1)

The curse of divination is a bewitchment. It limits an expression of God based on religious *nothings*. Remember, a glazing, dullness over the eyes, substitution for the divine. See, the Galatians were trying to heap *nothings*, vanities, on the naked truth of God's Word and power. Was it the works of the law that saved them? No. Of course not. But they had come under that bewitchment that said, "Hey, yeah, you gotta get saved. But you also gotta get circumcised. And you gotta meet on a specific day and eat specific things." It was an imitation of the divine. It caused them to be *indifferent* to the presence of God.

So what breaks the enchantment, the bewitchment, the curse of divination and limitation?

The Bible says it's the hearing of faith. (Galatians 3:2)

Paul was saying, "Therefore, He who supplies the Spirit to you and works miracles among you, does He do it by the works of the law, or by the hearing of faith...?" (Galatians 3:5) Incidentally, that word "supplies" (Strong's #2023) means "in an exceedingly bountiful measure, above and beyond the normal." It contains the Greek preposition *epi* (Strong's #1909), "above, beyond, fully." That kind of Spirit is ministered out by the hearing of faith, not by the law.

To be bewitched is to be smitten with an evil, dull eye. It means to experience a mirage. To experience a fake. Legalism, ultimately the curse of limitation and divination, yields a forgery of the bountiful measure of the Spirit. The Galatians, as many Christians today, were experiencing a glazing of indifference based on their religious *nothings*.

Paul was saying, "Hey, you began in the Spirit. Why are you trying to perfect your relationship with the flesh?" He was addressing false teachers, people who wanted to follow the old Judaic law and mix it in with the New Testament brought by Paul and the apostles. These people were creeping into the church at Galatia, trying to bring the people under the yoke of the law. I daresay we have people similar to that in the Church today.

But we have got to approach God the Father in the Spirit, through our spirits, and then let it trickle out into our souls and bodies. The hearing of faith, above the workings of law, shatters the bewitchment off the people. The apostles are called to let people "hear faith."

This apostolic unction is two-fold in operation. Firstly, the apostles bring a supernatural experience before the people that breaks the curse of bewitchment. This is the apostolic breaker anointing that exhibits some kind of miraculous manifestation, signs, wonders and mighty deeds in great perseverance. (2 Corinthians 12:12) This is why apostles *must* understand the principle of *parrhesia*. Boldness to roar, boldness to call down the miraculous, boldness to step out and shake people awake from the curses of limitation and divination. This is one of the signs of the apostles that are... indeed... "mighty deeds."

People experience a manifestation of the truth, something felt in their minds and bodies and spirits. Something tangible, truth manifested on the earthly plane. That means miracles, signs and wonders. Second Corinthians 4:2, you'll recall, speaks about this "manifestation of the truth." Quite simply, it's truth manifested to a person that exhibits a virtue, a touch of the power of God. The people *experience* the Spirit of God (Truth) *behind* the truth. The apostles tell of their bold faith, and the people "hear" the Spirit upholding the truth. This is part one of what the apostles are declaring in the "hearing of faith." You find many examples in the Book of Acts where the apostles shared of their encounters with the supernatural to bolster the faith of the people and bring them into their own encounters.

Secondly, the people "hear faith" through the teaching of the apostles, as they experience the truth by the breathings of God upon His Word. The Spirit exposes *rhemas* (Strong's #4487) within the written Word (Strong's #3056) to the people as the apostles share with boldness and anointing. The Holy Spirit causes the written Word to become alive to the bewitched, and the enchantment is broken. This also applies to the *rhemas* of the prophetic word.

You know, oftentimes, there have been a whole lot of prophetic words that have gone forth, but there's not been a whole lot of anointing going out with them. If you've been in a Charismatic circle for any length of time, chances are you've all heard tons of prophetic words, but many of them, it's sad to say, might just be so many "heady" words, lacking in actual, tangible power. I'm not being critical, but I am pointing out a lack. The apostolic, prophetic unction has got to be emboldened to "step it up" a notch. We've got to ensure that our prophetic words have got *power* underneath them, the Spirit breathing upon them to "hear faith."

The breath of God behind the prophetic word, that's *rhema*: that which has been "breathed upon" by the Holy Spirit. It manifests a virtue, a tangible power that people experience in their spirits and feel in their five senses. It's that "hearing of faith" that will shock them out of their bewitchment, out of their limitation, severing any connection to divination. The *rhema* lifts off the spiritual death caused by the betrayal of the enemy, the lies of limitation. The people experience the confirmation of God's Word through the spoken word. The prophetic must be backed by the breaker anointing.

Hebrews 2:3-4 shows that God confirms what He has spoken with a manifestation of His presence. God bears witness to what He said with signs, wonders, miracles and gifts of the Holy Spirit. How can we neglect so great a salvation as that? Do not be bewitched!

The apostolic anointing uses miracles and deliverance from demonic oppression — that is, "words of freedom" — to release the sound of heaven, to counteract the prognosis of limitation, to reverse the curse. So whose report are you going to believe? That of the Lord's which says there is no enchantment, no divination, no limitation, only *parrhesia*, so BE BOLD AS LIONS.

Or there's the other report.... The one of indifference, substitution, death.

You have to ask yourself: Have I been cursed with limitation? Have I been cursed with divination? Am I bewitched?

If so, pray these words with me (and mean them):

"Dear Father, in the name of Jesus, I pray for boldness. I pray for the *parrhesia* of Your Word to come upon me and shake me from any curse of limitation, any curse of divination. I separate myself from any bewitchment that has come upon me. I expect, in boldness, to see Your Word confirmed through an apostolic anointing. I expect the curses to be broken and reversed. I expect to see the signs, wonders and miracles that testify of Your truth through the hearing of faith."

Pray these things in the name of Jesus, begin to war against the spirit of limitation and divination, cast off bewitchment. A lot of it has to do with really, truly, deeply believing in the Lord, expecting Him to back up His Word.

Apostolic people — that's you and I, my friends — have got to war against nominalization and religiosity, those things that attempt to veil the glory of God in manifestation. We stand against the glazing of indifference toward the moving of God, we "hear faith" and come against that curse of limitation and divination. We expect, in all boldness, under the direction of the Holy Spirit, to be awakened, to encounter the Father, to have those spiritual scales removed from our eyes. Let nothing veil your mind! God is bringing His apostles to combat against this lack of confidence to see Him move in a mighty, tangible, explosive, *experiential* way!

THE TEENAGER WITH NO TOES

If we do not move apostolically to break this spirit of limitation, dullness, bewitchment — whatever term we want to use — we run the risk of totally missing the moving of the Spirit. I've seen it happen dozens, possibly even hundreds of times. A miracle will take place before everyone's eyes, and some people will *still* explain it away. How thick can you get? It takes the apostolic breaker anointing to cast off the indifference of a religious spirit.

I was once in a Charismatic church in the Midwest where the presence of the Lord was present to heal. Approximately two hundred people were in attendance, and there was a teenage girl sitting in that service whose toes had never been created. She had little stubs or bumps sticking out of her feet. No toes at all.

I instructed her to take off her shoes and socks and put her feet up on a chair for everyone to see. God as my witness (my wife was there as well), inside of forty-five minutes her toes were completely recreated!

You'd've thought pandemonium would've broken out in that church, right? I mean, here was this girl, who they'd all seen just three quarters of an hour earlier with no toes, wagging these perfectly whole digits for everyone to see.

But here's what the spirit of dullness does: even though the girl was healed, I went back to that church a year later, talking to the people about that tremendous miracle God did for the teenager. You know, the one where she didn't have toes and God recreated them in front of everybody's eyes.

What? Some looked at me puzzled. What are you talking about? We don't remember that miracle....

I was bowled over. I found myself thinking, *Then where in the world were* you?

Some of those people in that service were so brought under a spirit of dullness, a bondage of indifference, they couldn't even recognize or remember what had happened. They were totally clueless to what had taken place. Oh, sure, some remembered, but many were completely at a loss. Was it possible they were so self-centered they weren't even conscious of a miracle taking place?

It's a sad testimony, but I've had it happen loads of times where miracles have taken place in front of people's eyes, and if you were to ask them later — even *leaders* of a church on rare occasions — they were totally oblivious to what was taking place.

This is a real problem in the Body of Christ. We need to have an apostolic breaker anointing to wake the Church up. It's these powerful moves of God that will break off the bewitching spirit and lead people to a higher level of freedom in the Father.

THE LITTLE BOY FROM CENTRAL TEXAS

For you that are church history buffs, the late Brother Seymour, the famed Azusa Street revivalist, and Brother Parham established one of the oldest classical Pentecostal churches in North America in a central Texas town.

My wife, Joy, and I had been invited to this historical church for a series of meetings that were to last from Sunday to Sunday. At the time, I found it pretty humorous because prior to the start of the first Sunday morning meeting, some of the more elderly brethren came up to give me a few words of advice.

I'm always open to listening to what older people have to say, but I've got to admit that initially their advice didn't sit well with me because they kept calling me "Sonny." Many of these people were quite old and had been members of the church when over fifty years ago revival broke out. They told me that had been the last time God had moved... fifty years ago.

"Sonny!" One of them said to me. "Now, listen, you can't do nothin' we ain't already seen or heard! It's all old hat to us. But we're believin' God that the next eight days is gonna undo the fifty years of deadness we've had in this here church...." (OK, now maybe I'm overdoing the Texas twang a little bit, but this is what *was* told to me by the elders — literally and spiritually — of the congregation.)

Oh, Lord Jesus... Fifty years of religious nothing going on to overcome in eight days? Yeah, sure, no problem. I'll get right on that....

Back in those early days of ministry, one had to take basically whatever ministry opportunities came one's way. And one just had to believe God was gonna meet them there.

"So, Sonny," — nails on a chalkboard — "Sonny, we're expectin' somethin', but we ain't gonna be surprised by nothin'."

I smiled and got up to lead praise and worship. Yes, believe it or not, way back when, I used to have a pretty nice singing voice. (You couldn't tell now after 8,000 sermons....) But when we first started traveling ministry, my wife (who is quite a talented pianist) and I would lead praise and worship. We did a lot of it because we usually went to small, remote churches, and this was in the days when worship tapes were just starting to come out. So Joy would learn the new songs on piano, and I'd learn how to sing them. We'd teach the new songs to those tiny churches.

So there I am in a rousing number, some new song of supernatural power, and *nobody* was responding. Hey, I'm not *that* bad of a singer. What, am I off-key or something? No one followed us, no one raised their hands; they just sat there belligerently with their hands folded in their laps. *Great*, I thought, *a whole week of this? What am I gonna do?*

When I started to preach, every word I spoke seemed to fall to the ground. Oh, brother, what had I got myself into? I didn't even attempt to pray for anyone that first service.

So that Sunday afternoon, I was pacing the floor, concerned about how I was going to be able to pray for the sick. How could I prophesy and minister in the miraculous when these people were not open to it?

I felt the Holy Spirit speak to me suddenly. He said, "Don't pray for a single person till Thursday night...."

What? Why, Lord?

"It's going to take that long to break the spirit of bondage. Just preach and teach on revival, war against the legalism!"

Yeah, OK. So I did — never let it be said I'm disobedient. Monday, Tuesday, Wednesday, *nothing* happened at all. I stood up, preached, sat down. Might as well have been preaching to sawdust. I was dreading Thursday because I'd advertised to the congregation that was going to be the day for the miracle service. But I hadn't felt the Spirit move all week. What was going to happen? Oh, God, You'd better show up Thursday! How are we going to have a breakthrough?

Wednesday evening I get a phone call from a sister in the church. Thankfully, she didn't call me "Sonny."

"Brother Maloney," she said, "I wanted to let you know there's a group of about thirty born-again, Spirit-filled Methodists who've been prayin' and fastin' for three days and three nights."

It was like a lump of coal dumped in my stomach. "Uh-huh," I mumbled.

"Yep. And they're believin' that when they come to the miracle service tomorrow night this little boy they've been fastin' and prayin' for's gonna get healed."

Oh, boy. This was going from bad to worse.

"Uh-huh," I mumbled again.

"Now I ain't gonna tell you what's wrong with him.... But I sure hope you're prayed up, Brother Maloney!"

And she hung up the phone on me!

All day Thursday I envisioned this boy with three heads and twenty toes. Every little child that came into the service that night I studied, trying to see what might be wrong with them.

I was on the platform, leading praise and worship, everyone still resisting, no move of the Spirit at all, and the Methodists walked in.

They had come a little late because they thought the service started half an hour later. And there was the boy! You could immediately tell what was wrong with him. Here he was, approximately four-years-old, but he looked like an eighteen-month-old. I found out later the doctors said his growth was stunted; he had some sort of genetic dwarfism and he would never grow to normal size. They estimated he'd be about three feet, ten inches, maybe four feet at most. Further, he was and would always be sick and weakly because of the genetic deformity.

I watched that boy out of the corner of my eye the whole service. I tried preaching and teaching, but I was distracted. There was absolutely no presence of God whatsoever. Finally I sighed as I noticed people drifting off to sleep. I closed my Bible.

"Look, guys," I said. "You know, the Holy Spirit's not been free to manifest this whole week. I'm tired of wasting time. I'm not going to go through the motions. I'm going to sit down and wait on Him for just a few minutes, and if He's not going to show up, we might as well all go on home...."

So I sat down. And waited.

Now the parents of this little boy, thinking their opportunity for healing was passing them by, spontaneously got up out of their seats without waiting for permission, brought the child to the front of the church and stood there, looking at me. They'd been fasting and praying, along with the others, for three days and three nights. This was their chance for a miracle from God!

After a few seconds of them staring at me, I started feeling uncomfortable, so I stood and walked over to the platform.

"Can I help you?" I mumbled. Like I was some teller at a bank or a fry cook at McDonald's. Boy, God's gracious, isn't He?

"Brother Maloney...." — at least it wasn't Sonny — "We've been praying and fasting for three days, believing God that when you lay hands on our little boy, he's going to be healed."

Oh, Lord, Lord! I thought miserably. *Do I have the faith for this?* Now, those of you reading this, don't get all super-spiritual on me. You've probably been there before, too! You should hear some of the prayers of these mighty men and women of God: "Oh, Jesus, just bail me outta this one! If You answer this one prayer, I'll never ask for anything again...."

And so I resorted to an old standby that traveling ministers fall back to when they don't have the faith to minister to someone. They get out of it by saying, "According to *your* faith, be it unto you...!"

That's what I said. I flopped my miserly right hand on the boy's head, praying to God for mercy —

It was like someone exploded a cherry bomb in a trashcan. There was a loud *bang!* that everyone in the church heard. They all screamed, looking around. *What was that?*

The first thing that happened after the explosion was a third of the Methodist group fell under the power in their seats. The rest of the Methodists impulsively leapt out into the middle of the aisle and started dancing around, twirling, shouting and leaping.

"He's healed!" someone bellowed, Jericho-marching around the church.

The boy looked exactly the same to me, but the Spirit of God flooded those Methodists, and my wife and I found ourselves joining into the celebration. It was a wonderful time in the Lord.

Unfortunately, a vast majority of the Pentecostals did not join in. The Spirit seemed mainly to be moving among the Methodist group. The regular church attendees just frowned and folded their arms over their chests. You could tell what they were thinking, *Well, there's no change to the boy at all in the natural...* but you couldn't convince the Methodists of that! We partied the rest of the evening.

The series of meetings ended without so much as whisper from the Spirit for the Pentecostals. I left, feeling slightly dejected by the poor response, but also eager to hear about the boy.

It was five months later that I got a phone call. It was the lady who had called me the first time. Now I don't know how people always seem to get my phone number, no matter where I'm at in the United States, but if it's happened once, it's happened a dozen times. I get a random phone call from some person who's traced me down at three in the morning. Don't you people sleep?

It's always the same. "Brother Maloney! Hey, it's So-and-So from Somewhere! We're in an all night prayer meeting, and we feel you've got a word for us!"

At three in the morning? Yeah, I gotta word for ya! Dunno if it's from God or not, but I gotta word! I see the Lord saying, "Go to sleep, dude!"

Anyway, it's like three in the morning or whatever. I don't remember where I was at, but the phone rings, and the lady's hyperventilating on the other end. She didn't even say who she was.

"Brother Maloney! Oh, you're the *hardest* person to get a hold of!"

"Wh — ? Who is this?" I was rubbing sleep out of my eye, yawning.

"*How do you turn this stuff off?!?*"

"Huh? What are you talking about? Who *is* this?" I was thinking, *Is she talking about turning off her stove, or what?*

She huffed, taking a deep breath. The next thing out of her mouth came in a rush. "Do-you-remember-the-little-boy-you-prayed-for-five-months-ago-in-Texas?"

I scratched my head, tossing back my thick, luxurious hair.... (Bear with me, I'm sensitive.) "Uh, yeah," I managed to say.

"Well, the parents want me to ask how you turn this stuff off! They buy him a pair of trousers, he grows out of them in four days! A pair of shoes lasts a week. Shirts in three days! He's a head and shoulders taller than the other kids in his Pre-K class! He's eating them outta house and home! *How do you turn this stuff off?*"

How very cool is that?

What happened to that little boy? He was lifed! The *zoe*-life of God quickened him and it gave those Methodists an unveiling of the freedom of God. It showed the legalistic bondage of unbelief that was permeating the Pentecostals. It pointed out the spirit of dullness, and some broke free.

That boy certainly did!

THE BOBBY-PIN LADY

A by-product of confidence in the Lord is freedom. We've mentioned before *freedom*. Freedom to express ourselves to God, to express ourselves to others and freedom for God to express Himself back to us. It takes a certain level of supernatural confidence to be unafraid of what the Lord wants to do. A problem in the Body of Christ is a seemingly significant amount of trepidation when it comes to the moving of the Spirit. We're not so different from the Israelites all those years ago who wanted Moses to go up to the mountain instead of themselves. (See Deuteronomy 5.) We want the *leaders* to experience God and then let it trickle down to us.

But I believe an unveiling of the confidence of God will generate a level of freedom in apostolic circles that has yet to be seen on a grand scale. I believe whole churches, under the influence of the apostolic breaker anointing, will move up into greater levels of freedom. It takes the miraculous, once again, to shock people into the awareness that the movings of God are not all that scary. And, yes, while we've got to be careful not to cater to the flesh, we cannot in the name of "holiness" squelch vibrant expressions of the Father from awakening the people in His confidence and freedom. The apostles will have an understanding of the freedom of God that comes from boldness.

Let me tell you about a lady who had a startling revelation of the freedom of God.

I was hosting a miracle service in Southern California when the Lord gave me a word of knowledge. "There's a woman in this service with an incurable blood disease. The doctors have given you ninety days to live. Step forward, the Lord wants to heal you."

Now, how many know, a word like that is either right or wrong? Not much room for error there, like, "I think God wants to heal some people with back pain." Of course, there's nothing wrong with back-pain words of knowledge — we all gotta start somewhere. I'm happy if anyone receives something from God, but here once again, I'm jumping out on the ledge without a rope.

No one came up. Ooops. Maybe I'd missed it. But I didn't think so. I noticed this woman way in the back. She slipped into the service after it had started. She was wearing about a $10,000 outfit, complete with mink coat and diamonds. I saw her get in her car later — I think it was a Rolls Royce. Safe to say the lady was rich. Anyway, what was so weird was, I saw this immaculately dressed lady slink *under* the chair in front of her. I mean, she did *not* want to be called out.

So I figured it was her with the blood disease — because I'm smart like that when it's obvious — and being the tactful, mellow, eloquent, unassuming man that I am (don't you dare laugh!) I walked to the back and smiled down at her, "Sister, I think the Lord means you. Come on out." She shook her head and gave me *the look*. You know, *the look*. If it could kill, I'd be dead and buried.

But since looks can't kill, I said, "Hey, I know He can heal you right where you are, but I think He wants you to come forward. It's OK."

Her friend kicked her and threw her out into the center of the aisle, God bless her. So I walked back to the front, and the lady followed me, glowering. She stood in front of me, hand belligerently placed on her hip, and pointed her finger up under my nose.

Picture this. Her hair was flawlessly coiffed, every strand perfectly in place. You could tell she'd just been to the beauty salon. I mean, Marge Simpson would've been proud of this head of hair! I bet there were at least three dozen bobby pins holding that mane together. Her makeup was perfect; she was dressed to the nines, and she's got this soured look on her face, hand on hip, wagging this finger under my nose.

"Now, look here, preacher! I wanna be healed, but I don't wanna fall!"

My, my, that sounded so familiar.... Oh, the arrogance! Where had I heard that before?

Oh, yeah. Me. I said that once and ended up under the baby grand piano.... And here was this religious demon challenging me to the same thing. Ah, will they never learn? Little word to the wise, you should not challenge *moi*. I tend to get feisty, especially if the same dumb thing's happened to *me* before! Ya live and ya learn.

Now, I'm not saying this was from God, but I think He honored it, 'cause I just looked down at her with a sweet, innocent smile and said, "Oh, *sic* her, Holy Ghost."

Poor lady didn't just fall under the power of God. He jerked her feet out from underneath her (I'm not exaggerating), and I've got this horrifying picture in my mind to this day of her going *headfirst* toward the carpet, legs flailing up in the air. I remember a split-second thinking, *Well, I'm gonna get sued....*

Only thing that saved her from a massive concussion was that head of hair. It absorbed the shock nicely, and she kind of bounced on it — *wonga! wonga! wonga!* I mean out cold, slain in the Spirit.

She ruined the service for the next forty-five minutes (I timed it), gakking, sputtering, sobbing, makeup smeared all over the place. She was an absolute mess.

I tried to have the ushers pick her up and take her to a side room, but they fell under the power, too. So I thought I'd better go move her, but I couldn't pick her hand up off the ground. I'm a strong dude, but she was super-glued to the carpet or something. I finally stopped trying and just thought, *Gee, I guess God's doing something. Best to leave her alone.* I can be smart like that when it's obvious.

And... I don't know if it was the power of God... or if it was static electricity from the carpet and her hair, or what, that caused all those bobby pins to become electrical conduits. I don't know what it was. But every few minutes you'd hear this *ping!* and a bobby pin would launch into the air. I thought it might be lice jumping at first, but she looked like such a clean person. Then I saw the lice were metallic, and they made that noise when they reached critical mass. *Ping!* These things caught some serious *hang time!* It was just one of the funniest things I've ever seen. We all just sat there, dumbfounded, watching these projectiles fly into the air. *Ping!*

I counted, like, seventeen bobby pins on the floor by the time she came to.

Can you imagine what she must've looked like after forty-five minutes of this snot and coughing? I mean, makeup smeared everywhere, her hair flying out in a thousand different directions, designer clothes all rumpled, mink coat askew. About the only thing that looked normal on her was her manicured nails. She was totaled, drunk in the Holy Ghost, slimy. She fell over four people staggering back to her chair. Looked like the Bride of Frankenstein....

Her friend was just aghast, mortified. She pulled a compact out of her purse and stuck in the lady's face.

"AAAAAAHHHHHHHHH!" She screamed when she saw herself in the pocket mirror, and I finally understood the concept of holy-roller laughter. I mean, we just died, everybody out in the aisles, clutching their sides. It was so funny, I was tearing up, trying to catch my breath. We were laughing for the next hour.

See, we always want the anointing to be respectable, but many times it's at the expense of it! The freedom of God to move will crash into our preconceived notions of His solemnity. The moving of God's Spirit is not grim! And by the way, yes, that lady was *totally* embarrassed....

But she was totally healed.

Chapter Four Outline
"Unveiling the Confidence of God"

THE PARRHESIA PRINCIPLE

- *Parrhesia* (Strong's #3954) — "boldness" (Acts 4:31) — "confidence, freedom of speech, to be outspoken, the opposite of fear, cowardice and intimidation"
- The apostles of today, like the apostles of the early Church, are called to equip the apostolic people with boldness, through the power of the Holy Spirit
- Boldness only comes from relationship with the Holy Spirit; it is one of the greatest pieces of evidence that one is baptized in the Holy Spirit
- The breaker anointing casts off dullness, showing the people the aggressive side of the Holy Spirit
- The Spirit must be allowed to move in a powerful, aggressive way to break off the spirit of intimidation and unbelief that says if a person gets engaged in the acts of God, he or she will only be disappointed again and again

THE CURSE OF LIMITATION

- One of the greatest callings of the apostles is **to reverse the curse that limits the expression of God through His Holy Spirit.** The apostles are filled with a boldness to act with authority in signs, wonders and miracles to establish the Kingdom of God in the hearts of people here on earth

- The whole key to *parrhesia* is the boldness of God coming upon the apostolic people to war against that religious spirit that doesn't want people to encounter God

THE CURSE OF DIVINATION

- A curse of divination is a spirit that tries to squeeze out anything that pertains to life, something that restricts us, a statement, a prognosis, or a sentence of limited expression in Christ
- A release into boldness produces a corporate impact, not just the miracle itself taking place, but a divine reaction and response to the curse of divination
- The release of the miraculous releases *parrhesia* — people become emboldened to rejoice and celebrate the power of God, and the curses of limitation and divination are broken
- The curse of divination is an enchantment that attempts to get its victims to stay down, to stay under, to be impressed by the outward, by a personality that lures one from a position of conviction in God's Word to following the person instead

HAVE YOU BEEN BEWITCHED?

- "O foolish Galatians! Who has bewitched you...?" (Galatians 3:1)
- The curse of divination is a bewitchment; it limits an expression of God based on religious *nothings*

- "Therefore, He who supplies the Spirit to you and works miracles among you, does He do it by the works of the law, or by the hearing of faith...?" (Galatians 3:5)
- The hearing of faith, above the workings of law, shatters the bewitchment off the people. The apostles are called to let people "hear faith"
- The apostles bring a supernatural experience before the people that breaks the curse of bewitchment. This is the apostolic breaker anointing that exhibits some kind of miraculous manifestation, signs, wonders and mighty deeds in great perseverance. (2 Corinthians 12:12)
- The people "hear faith" through the teaching of the apostles, as they experience the truth by the breathings of God upon His Word

5

Unveiling the Power of God

VISITATION IN GERMANY

A few years back I was privileged to speak at a Bible school in Germany, a satellite of Christ for the Nations, that boasted some very fine students of the Word. And since my birth mother was pure German, I have a strong desire to find good German sausages and eat them. Ah, some of us have to rough it for Jesus with nothing but a plate of bratwurst and sauerkraut to fill our bellies. Poor me!

Now, the school was great, the students were great, and my accommodations were OK, but ultimately left something to be desired, to put it mildly. I was shown a tiny room upstairs above the school with a dingy bed kind of like a cot, and I thought to myself, *Yeah, I'm not fitting on that little thing!* I thought for sure I'd break it! It might have been five feet long and about three feet wide. I knew I was in for a rough night. It had a footboard! Now, dear readers, let me share with you a profound revelation: footboards and I do *not* get along.... I'm a tall guy, six foot five, and I don't slouch. (No, you're not getting my weight from me, so drop it!)

I stood there negotiating an engineering feat of genius to build up a little ramp made of pillows over the footboard so I could hang my size thirteens off the edge. Apparently I have no aptitude for building pillow ramps, and my genius failed me. So I tossed and turned for what seemed like the better part of the night, still suffering a little jet lag (I was living full-time in the States back then), when finally with a huff, I commando-rolled off the cot, snatched that flimsy, lumpy beast they called a mattress and tossed it on the floor. I took authority over all zee little, creepy crawlies that might have been waiting for a nibble and tried to get some rest there on the floor before my classes in the morning. Warm thoughts of a full German breakfast danced through my head, and I finally dozed off into a fitful sleep.

Friends, German potatoes may not seem like a spiritual mind-set for a visitation from the Spirit, but I was awakened in the pre-dawn light to the sound of a powerful wind coursing through the room. Like it had banged through the door and came rushing into the room. It was shockingly loud, tousling my thick, luxurious hair (that's a joke) and I thought to myself, this has *got* to be waking up the whole school! The noise it was making was deafening!

It sounded like I was in a tunnel, this rushing, mighty wind whistling through my room, vibrating everything around me, but what was so very strange about this wind was that it seemed to be flowing *just above* me. I could feel its force just above my delicate German nose, and I thought it was so weird that it wasn't going *through* me. So, intelligent person that I am, I asked the Lord what did this mean.

I have heard some theologians teach — and while I don't know if you can be doctrinal about this, it tends to make sense to me — that in Exodus 14 when God blew the waters of the Red Sea to one side so that the Israelites might cross over on dry land, if they would have just stuck their hands up in that divine, supernatural wind (a foreshadow of the Holy Spirit to come), it would have dealt with any issues the people were struggling with. And their trip into Canaan would have gone much more smoothly. They would've reached their inheritance without the trials, and ultimate death, of the wilderness wanderings. It's a neat concept, I think.

So while this wind was roaring overhead, I asked the Lord why it wasn't going through me, and the thought came to me that maybe I should just stick my hands up in the wind if it wasn't coming down to me. Makes sense. So often the supernatural acts of God require *us* to come up higher, instead of Him always coming down to our level.

I don't want to miss this experience! I said to myself and thrust my hands up into that mighty wind. Dear readers, let me tell you it was like sticking my hands into a thunderstorm. It felt like ten thousand volts of electricity arced through my body, igniting every inch of me. I had to struggle to push my hands against this wind as electric boldness (that's the only way I can describe it) coursed through me. The sense of power in that wind was mind-blowing! The thought came to me that this must have been what it felt like when the Holy Spirit blew through the faithful in Acts 2.

The wind blew for several minutes, and I just lay on that uncomfortable bedroll on the floor, soaking in this awesome, divine power, my arms struggling to maintain their position in this invisible force. My spirit became electrified, my body felt like it was humming, and I knew this experience was going to change my life from that moment on.

A little later on, I'll share with you what happened to me after this remarkable occurrence, but for now let's study a little bit about the power of the baptism in the Holy Spirit.

BAPTISM IN THE HOLY SPIRIT

If you haven't guessed by this point in the book, I'll just go ahead and let you know I believe in the baptism of the Holy Spirit with the evidence of speaking in tongues. Shocking, huh? No, seriously though, so often the supernatural is tied into your direct relationship with the

Holy Spirit, so I thought it would benefit you fine readers to share a little on what exactly the Holy Spirit's role is in the daily life of the Spirit-baptized believer. I believe it is in the power of tongues that the apostolic spirit is birthed, and we as apostolic people need to press into a deeper level of tongues release (that is, power release.)

If you are not Charismatic, I want to thank you for reading this book anyway, and I hope I can shed a little light on what we believe occurs when a born-again person speaks in tongues.

"Likewise the Spirit also helps our weaknesses. For we do not know what we should pray for as we ought, but the Spirit Himself makes intercession for us with groanings which cannot be uttered. Now He who searches the hearts knows what the mind of the Spirit is, because He makes intercession for the saints according to the will of God. And we know that all things work together for good to those who love God, to those who are the called according to His purpose." (Romans 8:26-28)

That word "weaknesses" (*astheneia*, Strong's #769), I think, is poorly translated. The stronger word is "infirmities," and it speaks to personal, inward infirmities and outward problems, physical and moral. The word "helps" is a really long Greek word (Strong's #4878) that could be translated "to take hold of together opposite" or "heaves with us" (Matthew Henry's *Commentary*.) We might modernize that and say "stands up against with," so that we might read the verse as "Likewise the Spirit also stands up with us against our infirmities."

There, I did your homework for you!

"Makes intercession" is the Greek word *huperentugchano* (Strong's #5241, #1793.) And I've heard, according to Dr. Chuck Flynn, it relates to a legal term in olden days, it connotes the Holy Spirit throwing Himself into the midst of our situation. He pleads our case before the Father. It means to intervene on the behalf of another, to interfere with the problems that men face. The word is also used in Hebrew 7:25, "Therefore He is also able to save to the uttermost those who come to God through Him, since He always lives to make intercession for them."

So the groanings of the Holy Spirit are prayers that intervene or interfere with the inward and outward problems we are struggling with. But in order for that to happen, the spirit man inside each of us must be *activated*: that is, the baptism in the Holy Spirit. If you are not familiar with the indwelling of the Holy Spirit in the life of a believer, take a moment to read Acts 2:1-4, 11.

Verse 2 says, "And suddenly there came a sound from heaven, as of a rushing mighty wind, and it filled the whole house where they were sitting." The author of Acts is historically considered to be Luke, who was a physician. In his writings, he tended to use medical terms in describing supernatural encounters. Here, he uses a medical term for "rushing"; it is the Greek word *phero*. (Strong's #5342) Specifically *phero* is a maternity term that could be translated "to bear" — as in giving birth. It was the singular moment when the baby came forth and took its first breath. That shock of life, that sharp inhale of oxygen that sets the baby crying.

Do it with me, inhale sharply. Careful not to swallow your gum!

See? That's *phero*, like a mother giving birth and the shock of the baby's first breath: it is the breath of God which gives life. It is the breath of God that raises up a church into life. The purpose of the Father is to bring forth a people who have experienced *phero*, to bring forth a generation of spiritual giants in the breath of God.

We have talked about Romans 8:26-28 in Chapter Nine. We know that for many Christians not all things are working together for good, right? But part of the problem is that they misrepresent the promise by leaving off Verses 26 and 27. That's why there's that little word "and" at the beginning of Verse 28 — see, something was supposed to go before it.

So in its context, we find that "all things" only work together for good when we experience the *phero* of the Holy Spirit. So to say, "that which has been breathed on by the *rhema* word of God"! Only *then* will all things work together for good. It takes the supernatural breathing of the Spirit to make things turn out all right.

"...Knowing this first, that no prophecy of Scripture is of any private interpretation, for prophecy never came by the will of man, but holy men of God spoke as they were moved by the Holy Spirit." (2 Peter 1:20-21)

There it is again. "Moved" is *phero*. Sorry, dear friends, you just can't get away from the Holy Spirit. You need Him to *phero* your understanding of the Father. If you are struggling with issues in your life, it is the Holy Spirit who can throw Himself into the midst of your case and breathe upon that scripture, so all things can begin to work toward the good.

"For you can all prophesy one by one, that all may learn and all may be encouraged. And the spirits of the prophets are subject to the prophets." (1 Corinthians 14:31-32)

What this is saying is that prophecy is a *good thing* — it is further revelation breathed on by the Holy Spirit, and by doing so, all can come to further knowledge and are encouraged. As the Holy Spirit moves upon you and you give utterance to what you perceive, you are built up in the knowledge of God. He is breathing life into you. And these divine utterances are within your control, and therefore become your responsibility to act upon them as the Holy Spirit moves. That's what it means by "the spirits of the prophets are subject to the prophets."

So come on, you say it with me: "I'll come to understanding as I'm moved on by the Holy Spirit!"

I'm trying, and probably failing, to be lighthearted here because I want to show you this whole concept of being baptized in the Spirit is not freaky. It isn't scary. It is a vital part of the believer's walk. We need to be moved on by the Holy Spirit for further revelation – we call this *rhema*. People often want to be spiritual giants, but they don't want to exercise their spirits! A lot of revelation is lost by beloved members of the Body of Christ because of their staunch denial of a need for the Holy Spirit.

Wow, that was pretty good....

Did you know the Holy Spirit was present at the time you were born again? Yeah, it's true.

"...'But whoever drinks of the water that I shall give him will never thirst. But the water that I shall give him will become in him a fountain of water springing up into everlasting life.'" (John 4:14)

The Holy Spirit is often represented by water. Here He is represented as well water, a personal storehouse of refreshment for the believer that gives eternal life.

"On the last day, that great day of the feast, Jesus stood and cried out, saying, 'If anyone thirsts, let him come to Me and drink. He who believes in Me, as the Scripture has said, out of his heart will flow rivers of living water.' But this He spoke concerning the Spirit, whom those believing in Him would receive; for the Holy Spirit was not yet given, because Jesus was not yet glorified." (John 7:37-39)

Here the Holy Spirit is represented as flowing rivers, streams of blessing that pour out of the in-filled person into the lives of others.

"And... He breathed on them, and said to them, 'Receive the Holy Spirit.'" (John 20:22) It was at this moment the disciples received the life of Jesus. They were born again. So the Spirit is present, and indeed a vital part, of the salvation experience. But notice, while these disciples had received the Holy Spirit unto salvation, it is the same disciples in Acts 2:4 that received the Holy Spirit further unto greater understanding. "And they were all filled with the Holy Spirit and began to speak with other tongues, as the Spirit gave them utterance."

I have heard Evangelicals say, "I am filled with the Spirit because I am born again." And they're not wrong. The Holy Spirit *is* present at salvation. But the Bible shows a further indwelling of the Spirit, a second dose, we might say, that brought about a *phero* which changed the disciples from followers of Christ into apostles working mighty miracles.

When one is saved, he or she is given the Holy Spirit as a personal well of refreshing. We might say the Holy Spirit is represented as a *cup* of water, yes indeed, a cup that never goes dry, but a cup nonetheless. When one is baptized in the Holy Spirit, we might picture that cup of water now being submerged into a *river* of water — without measure. There is *excess* water, that is the supernatural acts of a Spirit-filled believer; in short, the Holy Spirit intervening on the behalf of another in signs, wonders and miracles.

So if you are born again, yes, you have the Holy Spirit. But the question to ask is does the Holy Spirit have all of you?

The power of the Holy Spirit can be transferred from one to another, as shown in Acts 8:17, "Then they laid hands on them, and they received the Holy Spirit." The apostles were giving the Water away.

Now the thing to note here is the next verse concerning Simon the Sorcerer — whose infamy I have already alluded to in a previous chapter. Verse 18 says that he "saw" something when the Holy Spirit was given through the laying on of hands. What did he "see"? Well, doesn't this lead the reader to believe that he saw them speaking in tongues? What else would he have seen? If it was just some internal blessing happening in their lives, he wouldn't have seen it; there must have been a physical manifestation of the Spirit being received.

And when Peter attacks Simon's sin, he says in Verse 21, "'You have neither part nor portion in this matter for your heart is not right in the sight of God.'" What "matter" was he talking about? Wouldn't it lead the reader to believe it was the *speech* that Paul was talking about, i.e., speaking in tongues?

So then, it seems, we can believe that the baptism in the Holy Spirit within the life of the believer produces a physical manifestation, that is, speaking in tongues, evidence of the cup of water being submerged in the river.

"For they heard them speak with tongues and magnify God...." (Acts 10:46)

"And Ananias went his way and entered the house; and laying his hands on him he said, 'Brother Saul, the Lord Jesus, who appeared to you on the road as you came, has sent me that you may receive your sight and be filled with the Holy Spirit.'" (Acts 9:13)

Paul, then called Saul, received the Holy Spirit. We know this because he said, "I thank my God that I speak with tongues more than you all...." (1 Corinthians 14:18)

Further, he was able to impart the Spirit to others, for "...he said to them, 'Did you receive the Holy Spirit when you believed?' So they said to him, 'We have not so much as heard whether there is a Holy Spirit....' And when Paul had laid hands on them, the Holy Spirit came upon them, and they spoke with tongues and prophesied." (Acts 19:2, 6)

With all of these scriptures presented, can you not see the importance of being filled with the Spirit with the evidence of speaking in tongues, for "...'By the mouth of two or three witnesses every word [that is "doctrine, teaching"] shall be established.'" (2 Corinthians 13:1)

Therefore, receive the Holy Spirit!

In recent years, I seem to have noticed an alarming minimization of the importance of tongues within some Charismatic leadership circles.

I think this is incredibly sad and disquieting. We cannot overlook the magnitude of speaking in tongues as apostolic people, dear readers!

I want to thank Chuck Flynn and Kenneth Hagin for their insights into the doctrine of being baptized in the Spirit — their teachings really solidified the importance of tongues for me. I hope to do the same for you!

THE IMPORTANCE OF TONGUES

The initial sign (notice I didn't say the "only sign") of being filled with the Spirit is speaking in tongues. This is supernatural evidence of the Spirit's indwelling. Tongues are of great importance to the well-being of a believer, as God is a Spirit and, therefore, must be contacted in the spirit. Tongues are for spiritual edification.

"He who speaks in a tongue edifies himself, but he who prophesies edifies the church." (1 Corinthians 14:4)

Verse 2, just above, says, "...He who speaks in a tongue does not speak to men but to God, for no one understands him; however, in the spirit he speaks mysteries." That word "mysteries" implies "divine secrets and truths." (Strong's #3466)

In the Amplified Bible, Paul says, "For if I pray in a tongue, my spirit by the Holy Spirit within me prays...." (1 Corinthians 14:14)

Tongues remind us of the Spirit's indwelling presence, lest we forget.

"'And I will pray the Father, and He will give you another Helper, that He may abide with you forever — the Spirit of truth, whom the world cannot receive, because it neither sees Him nor knows Him; but you know Him, for He dwells with you and will be in you.'" (John 14:16-17) We are conscious of "another Helper" when we speak with tongues.

Praying in tongues will keep our prayers in accordance with God's Word and will. "But God has revealed them to us through His Spirit. For the Spirit searches all things, yes, the deep things of God." (1 Corinthians 2:10) Through the exercise of tongues, we begin to perceive the ways of the Spirit, how to pray and when to pray.

The heavenly language released through tongues releases and increases faith, for faith must be exercised to speak in tongues. "But you, beloved, building yourselves upon your most holy faith, praying in the Holy Spirit, keep yourselves in the love of God, looking for the mercy of our Lord Jesus Christ unto eternal life." (Jude 20-21)

Tongues keep us free from worldly vexations and secure in the love of God. We are insulated, kept apart, wholly (and holy) unto God. We are kept in constant communication with the Father through the exercise of tongues. In the context of speaking in tongues, Paul offers, "...Let him speak to himself and to God." (1 Corinthians 14:28)

Praying in tongues enables us to pray for the unknown, as shown in Romans 8:26 and 1 Corinthians 14:14. One of the facets of a prayer language is to pray always, continually, over a situation or problem until you have a note of praise, a release, which leads to victory. Literally pray *through* your problems. You may not know how to convey your problem to the Lord, but the Spirit knows, and by allowing Him to pray through you, you achieve the desired result.

"For with stammering lips and another tongue He will speak to this people, to whom He said, 'This is the rest with which You may cause the weary to rest,' and, 'This is the refreshing'; yet they would not hear." (Isaiah 28:11-12)

Spiritual thirst-quenching comes by way of speaking in tongues. It is a gift the Father gave to the Son, who in turn, utilizing the Spirit, conveys a means of rest and refreshing for a weary soul. How sad that so many Christians "would not hear" of the rest that the Father so willingly wants to give!

We also subjugate our tongue by speaking in tongues, for we know that according to James 3:8, the tongue is evil and poisonous, something no man can tame, but if your tongue is occupied singing the praises of Almighty God, it scarcely has time for evil, profaned sayings, right? Keep your tongue occupied!

Praying in tongues shows forth your appreciation to the Lord very well. "What is the conclusion then? I will pray with the spirit, and I will also pray with the understanding. I will sing with the spirit, and I will also sing with the understanding. Otherwise, if you bless with the spirit, how will he who occupies the place of the uninformed say 'Amen' at your giving of thanks, since he does not understand what you say? For you indeed give thanks well, but the other is not edified." (1 Corinthians 14:15-17)

I think Paul had it right here, ladies and gentlemen. He spoke in tongues, and he prayed in understanding. So many Christians, who are indeed true believers in Christ, neglect half of the equation and, therefore, only achieve half the answer. To recover the apostolic grace is to recover that which is on *both sides* of the equals sign. Otherwise the sum is unbalanced and left with variables. (See how I whipped a little algebraic illustration in there? I'm horrible at mathematics, but I thought that was pretty nifty, if I do say so myself!)

Tongues, for all intents and purposes, are the language of the Kingdom of God. Therefore, with our cooperation, the Holy Spirit incorporates a mechanism in our walk that builds up our knowledge of that Kingdom and reflects itself in a fruitful life, which is always to be an expression of the Kingdom to which we belong. So, to elucidate, tongues will lead us to a restoration of the supernatural demonstration of the Kingdom, which is the point of this entire book.

Our heavenly prayer language is the means in which our human spirit speaks to God in the Spirit. Tongues keep us in the love of God, looking forward to the fulfillment of His promises in scripture, including the release of the miraculous, among the others. The exercising of our spirit synergizes us to the Holy Spirit and assists in creating a personal habitation within our lives. When you pray in tongues, you build a home for the Spirit to dwell in, and the things in your life that were laid to ruin — your hurts, woundings, iniquities, veilings — begin to be restored.

The people who heard the disciples speaking in tongues in Acts 2 marveled at the "wonderful works of God" (Acts 2:11) they were hearing in their own languages. The Greek for "wonderful works" is *megaleios*. (Strong's #3167) By now, we know the prefix *mega*, and *leios* means "magnificent and sublime deeds."

In the song of Mary, found in Luke's Gospel, specifically 1:49, we find her saying, "For He who is mighty has done great things for me...." "Great things" is *megaleios*. Mary was speaking of birthing the Messiah, and it was as though those in the upper room were *birthing the Messiah* when they spoke in tongues of the wonderful works of God. The connotation, then, is that speaking in tongues births the mighty works of Jesus Christ Himself. That coincides with the word "groanings" — in the context of bringing forth life (giving birth) — found in Romans 8. So it is no great stretch to say that when we speak in tongues *we give birth to the Messiah* in every situation and experience we face!

By bearing the Christ, He crashes into our way of life and does His wonderful works! Speaking in tongues births Jesus on the scene and releases His anointing, so that it penetrates, surrounds and enlarges us, making our circumstances small in the wake of His great deeds.

Let's bring this around to the apostolic. What is all this information to show you as an apostolic person? What does this information have to do with the apostles and their breaker anointing?

The power of God is unveiled through the Holy Spirit – He is the Spark that sets off the dynamite residing within us. The apostles and apostolic people are here to remind everyone in the Body of Christ the importance and emphasis that is to be placed upon the third, and certainly not the least, part of the Godhead: the Holy Spirit. Apostles teach the people the importance of honoring the Holy Spirit – and that means *honoring His tongues...* a release of God's power. A veiling comes upon the people when they choose to ignore, or let's soften that and say "deemphasize," the importance of speaking in tongues.

Tongues release the breaker anointing, my friends, and that in turn creates a prophetic spirit upon the people.

The apostolic breaker anointing unveils this attribute of the Spirit for the people, and apostles themselves must learn to cultivate sensitivity and a love for the spiritual languages. Through recognizing the gift of the Holy Spirit, the apostles position themselves and the people of God to receive the Father's promises in their fullest measure.

RECEIVING THE FATHER'S PROMISE

"And being assembled together with them, He commanded them not to depart from Jerusalem, but to wait for the Promise of the Father... but you shall receive power when the Holy Spirit has come upon you...." (Acts 1:4, 8)

"'Therefore being exalted to the right hand of God, and having received from the Father the promise of the Holy Spirit, He poured out this which you now see and hear.... Repent and let every one of you be baptized in the name of Jesus Christ for the remission of sins; and you shall receive the gift of the Holy Spirit. For the promise is to you and to your children, and to all who are afar off, as many as the Lord our God will call.'" (Acts 2:33, 38-39)

"'But the Helper, the Holy Spirit, whom the Father will send in My name, He will teach you all things, and bring to your remembrance all things that I said to you.... But when the Helper comes, whom I shall send to you from the Father, the Spirit of truth who proceeds from the Father, He will testify of Me.... Nevertheless I tell you the truth. It is to your advantage that I go away; for if I do not go away, the Helper will not come to you; but if I depart, I will send Him to you.'" (John 14:26; 15:26; 16:7)

I know that's a lot of scripture, but I want to set a precedent that the Holy Spirit is a gift from the Father, and as with all gifts that come from Him, we must ask for them in order to receive. "Yet you do not have because you do not ask." (James 4:2)

To be an apostolic people, we must recognize the need for the gift of the Holy Spirit to be given, and knowing that a gift must be received, we then take it from the Father and apply it to our lives.

"'So I say to you, ask, and it will be given to you.... If you then, being evil, know how to give good gifts to your children, how much more will your heavenly Father give the Holy Spirit to those who ask Him!'" (Luke 11:9, 13) Jesus placed great emphasis on the action of *asking* the Father for the Spirit, rather than waiting on God to do something. I have heard many well meaning Christians say, "If God wanted me to speak in tongues, He would give the gift to me."

Oh, but allow me to retort, "Is that how you got saved? Waiting for the Father to give the gift to you sovereignly? Or did you ask for it?" Rhetorically speaking, we must then *ask* the Father for the gift of the Holy Spirit as well!

So then, after asking for the gift, we must receive it by faith — believe that you have received, then surrender your heart and tongue to the Holy Spirit. "'Men listened to me and waited, and kept silence for my counsel. After my words they did not speak again, and my speech settled on them as dew. They waited for me as for the rain, and they opened their mouth wide as for the spring rain.'" (Job 29:21-23)

If this seems like foolish action, remember that God takes the foolish things to confound the wise. (1 Corinthians 1:27) You have to cooperate with God as the Giver of the gift; you must accept it on His terms. God isn't going to do it for you because He always works through the human part of the equation, just as one must cooperate with God, on His terms, to receive salvation. It is the same for receiving the Father's promise of the Holy Spirit!

ANOTHER HELPER

And you desperately need to receive it! All apostolic anointings, all signs, wonders and miracles are provided through the help of the Holy Spirit. In order to be a complete believer in Christ, one must also believe He has sent the Helper to us. "'And these signs will follow those who believe [rather, "have believed" or "to those who are believing"]: In My name they will cast out demons; they will speak with new tongues; they will take up [rather, "cast away"] serpents; and if they drink anything deadly, it will by no means hurt them; they will lay hands on the sick, and they will recover.'" (Mark 16:17-18)

The Holy Spirit is an oasis in the desert: a God-given, life-giving Presence to bask in! He is given to wash away the spiritual poison, or toxic effect, of modern life.

The help of this hour, a poetic phrasing meaning our day-to-day lives, comes from the Spirit awakened within us. He lends a helping hand to aid us in our weaknesses and infirmities. The modern problems and pressures of this life can weaken us; we can become infirmed by the onslaughts of the enemy.

Permit me to define "Helper" as Jesus called the Spirit. Many of us are familiar with the Greek word *parakletos* (Strong's #3875), meaning "to be called alongside." Again this word has secular meaning, referencing an attorney, calling someone who is an expert in his field alongside to give aid to a needy person.

"Infirmities" as found in Romans 8:26-28 can speak of terminal diseases, muscular diseases, demonic vexations, plaguings (or plagues in the agrarian sense), or someone found to be invalid, comatose. One might literally render "infirmities" as "repeated whippings," that which consistently wears you down and beats your brow. The Holy Spirit offers deliverance at the whipping post, dear readers! There is help! So why choose to reject it? Why would *any* born-again Christian not want the help of the Holy Spirit?

According to 1 Corinthians 1:25-29, we might say there are three types of people in the world: the base, the weak and the foolish.

We might say "base" means "ugly." Some people — not you, of course, you're beautiful! — are just plain ugly. Can't do nothin' with 'em; they just a homely buncha folks, as we might say in Texan-speak! All the plastic surgery and makeup in the world doesn't help, you know? Sorry, that's kind of facetious, but that's how I take the meaning: *he be ugly!*

"Weak" we might put as "comatose." I bet you can all think of someone you know who's in an emotional, spiritual coma, barely "alive" in the fullest sense of the word, stumbling through life in a daze.

"Foolish" is where we get the word "moron" or "moronic." (Strong's #3474, *moros*) No, I'm serious here. Literally, a simpleton, a fool, either intellectually or physically, someone who is incapable of taking care of themselves.

In speaking of these kinds of people, it's as if Paul is saying, "We don't know what to do even in the smallest spiritual matter; we're like ugly, comatose morons!" It's as if the Holy Spirit is saying, "Without My help, you would all be spiritual basket cases!" How many know a spiritual basket case?

But not to worry! The Comforter is called alongside to help, if you'll ask for Him. He will stand up against your infirmities and weakness, making you beautiful, lively and fully capable. So, if you'll pardon my boldness, don't be a moron! Ask and receive the help of the Holy Spirit!

THE INSANITY OF THE HOLY SPIRIT

"Help" in Romans 8:26 has three parts in the Greek: *sun-anti-lambanomai* (Strong's #4878.) *Sun* is "with, together." *Anti* is "against," as in antifreeze or anticlimactic or anti-Christ. *Lambanomai* is "to take away." Respectively one might say these words correspond to "position" (*sun*), "attitude" (*anti*) and "desire" (*lambanomai*.)

The Holy Spirit is working with you against your infirmities to take them away. It's not necessarily passive; He is working with you, passionately, violently if need be, to seize and remove those infirmities. I have heard it taught that the help of the Holy Spirit is "revealing His lion-like nature." Let me explain to you what I mean.

We have always thought of the Holy Spirit as a "kind, sweet cosmic butler" as one of my preacher friends pointed out. The soft, gentle, loving touch of a Helper. And that's not wrong. There is a soft, sweet, wooing side to the Holy Spirit, to be sure. He gently convicts us, sits by our bedside, spoon-feeding us chicken soup until we get better, drawing us into hugs and kisses to bathe our wounds. There is spiritual and emotional therapeutic value in receiving a hug from the Holy Ghost. We love the Spirit!

But in the Greek, words can carry a passive, feminine connotation and an aggressive, masculine connotation. Hey, don't blame me; blame the Greeks!

Anyway, the word "help" is no exception. There is the soft, passive side — hugs from the Spirit — and the rough, aggressive side — the roaring lion.

The word corresponding to "position" is more passive; it means a "partnership," an invitation to cooperate with the Spirit and work together to achieve the desired result: freedom from repeated whippings.

However, the word corresponding to "attitude" is aggressive. Anti. The word "anti" conjures up a different word picture in our minds, doesn't it? Anti, against. Anti-war, anti-partisan, anti-anything. It can mean "violence, rage, anger, railing against an infirmity." Rick Renner, a powerful teacher in Russia, calls it the "insanity of the Holy Spirit." That means that the Holy Spirit, upon hearing of your sad plight, becomes so enraged that He enters into a blind fury, violently lashing out against that which repeatedly is beating you down.

Moreover, the word corresponding to "desire" also has a masculine, aggressive side. It is the Holy Spirit, rising up to fight, saying, "You have something that I want! If you don't give it to Me, I'll *take* it from you forcefully!"

This is what Jesus was talking about when He said, "'And from the days of John the Baptist until now the kingdom of heaven suffers violence, and the violent take it by force.'" (Matthew 11:12) In order to achieve victory over your infirmities, you need the Holy Spirit to become insanely angry at your weakness and take it from you by force! That is the "Helper" the Father sent to you through the Son!

But we combat against a religious spirit in the Church that honors God for what He has done in the past, but fights against what God is doing in the now. The Father is constantly progressive, always using His Spirit to bring fresh, new and exciting facets of His endless personality and expression. This is, in fact, the driving motivation behind the apostle's breaker anointing — to push against that religious spirit and usher in the fresh, new expression of the Holy Spirit.

So often we have no problem viewing the Spirit as a soft, meek, gentle floating cloud, bouncing around up in the heavens and occasionally flitting down to earth to speak some kind word of encouragement to us lowly types. But the Father has so much more to show us — yes, His kind, gentle side; but let us never forget He is the Creator of all emotion! So if you have the capability of becoming enraged at injustice, how much more so the Progenitor of holy rage? Yes, He is slow to anger, but that doesn't mean He never gets angry, right?

We are in a war against the nominal; our enemy is called "Average," who desires nothing more than to maintain the status quo of a mundane existence. This spirit wars against us constantly, messing with our lives to keep us from engaging in the Spirit. The Holy Spirit, if we will just simply allow Him, will intervene on our behalves and interfere with the works of the enemy. He will *throw* Himself aggressively into the midst of our cases; His prayers will meddle in the affairs of man, in a good way, discerning the spirit of infirmity and ripping it away from you. The enemy wants to sedate us; the Spirit wants to incite us!

We only come to greater revelation as we are moved on by the Holy Spirit. We need to be breathed on (*phero*) in a shocking way.

Did you know that Christ often referred to Himself as "the Son of Man"? (See Matthew 8:20 and 9:6, among others.) What does that mean, "Son of man"?

I'm glad you asked.

Christ was referencing Daniel 7:13. The prophet saw Him coming with the clouds of heaven. "Clouds" are nimbus clouds, thunderclouds. (Strong's #6051) We might convey the thought of a thunderstorm, or a whirlwind, as I have heard it given. Gives a different spin to "Son of Man" when we think of it as "He who comes like a storm," huh? Isn't that neat? The Anointed One moves about as in a whirlwind, stirring up that which is dormant, dust — that's us, that "man" part! — lounging languidly on the ground, comatose and of no special purpose. When the Whirlwind moves through us, He whips us into spiritual righteous, scriptural agitation, and the Holy Spirit is released to do His work, working all things for the good. Just food for thought.

DISCERNING THE SPIRIT OF INFIRMITY

When the Holy Spirit breathes upon us, and Christ is in His whirlwind-thrust maneuvers (I just made that up), we begin to perceive the spirit of infirmity that is upon us. A further thought on the spirit of infirmity yields us some interesting definitions I'd like to share now for your benefit.

A spirit of infirmity can also be connected to a spirit of familiarity. It brings out a *prognosis*, meaning "knowledge known beforehand." You'll recognize the word used in medical fields to this day, wherein a doctor gives a prognosis based on your symptoms. As in, "This rash indicates you have a skin inflammation." Or, "Since your mother had diabetes, you are likely to contract it yourself." Something to that extent. The doctor's experience with rashes and diabetes indicates to him or her that the root cause is an inflamed area of skin or a generational propensity toward a particular disease. He prognosticates your case based on your symptoms, something which he or she is familiar with.

Now don't misunderstand me here. I highly esteem the members of our medical fields. Doctors and nurses do the best they can based on scientific research, and their work is predicated on a general concern for your wellbeing. I thank doctors for their abilities, but sometimes the concern goes beyond the natural and into the supernatural.

A spirit of infirmity will "spit out" a prognosis — that gives a mental picture, huh? I believe the Lord gave me a revelation on this. It literally spits out a prediction about your life and circumstances. Prognosis means the spirit is able "to project an image (a word) based upon familiarity of something known from familial generations past." So, you might hear in your mind, "You know your daddy was a drunk. What makes you think you'll be any different?" Or maybe, "Your mommy died of cancer, and so will you!"

It is a lie that says the circumstances of the past will repeat themselves again and again. The point here is you need to be able to discern it for what it is: nothing more than a lie based on natural causes. The natural is always subject to the supernatural! And the Whirlwind can stir you up to greater heights than the mundane, so that you know that you know that you know these spirits of infirmity and familiarity are rooted in a false prognosis.

Further, a spirit of infirmity/familiarity will attempt to throw a veiling of hopelessness and inevitability on you. It will try to place a mental load, a yoke or weight, that doesn't permit you to rise up. Shake it off! The Holy Spirit will breathe upon you, giving greater revelation, so that you see your circumstances as God sees them — not inevitable, and just requiring a touch of favor to reverse the curse!

Based on the revelation I believe God gave me, the most literal description I can come up with for a spirit of infirmity is that which "tries to place upon you binding hands." It tries to reduce your mobility, as in the case of skeletal/muscular issues or fatigue. A spirit that chokes the life out of you, holds you down under the water until you drown. An apostolic anointing helps discern a spirit of infirmity. We must discern this spirit, speak against that prognosis, and forcibly jerk those hands off of us!

The spirit of infirmity attempts to get you to experience a weakness of intimidation. "I can't move like I used to, 'cause I don't want it to hurt!" It tries to bring you into agreement with that ailment. People actually become bonded to their infirmities, identifying with it so that it defines them. "There goes a crippled man!"

In short, your body begins to reject your spirit....

But the Holy Spirit knows the truth that is found in the Whirlwind, and He will aggressively make you see the lying spirit for what it is. Reject the prognosis! Rage against that which tries to bind you! It *has* to give in because your spirit is always stronger than your body!

AFTER THE GERMANY VISITATION

Let's go back to Germany now. You recall the powerful, rushing wind of the Holy Spirit that I had stuck my hands into? Well, the next time I ministered to people after that remarkable encounter, *something* was different. On some people that I laid hands on, I felt what I can only describe as a pulsation in my hand. This didn't happen with everyone I prayed for, but quite often this *hum* would begin in the palm of my right hand and spread out to my fingertips. It was a very unique feeling.

The Holy Spirit began to teach me that when I felt that quivering sensation, it was a sign (a gift of discernment) that I was dealing with a spirit of infirmity, a demonic veiling that was keeping the person down. Through the anointing of the Holy Spirit, I felt a release in my hand that "detected" – for lack of a better word – the infirmity that the people I was praying for were laboring under.

Now, I don't want to sound spooky or New Age-y here, but I feel it is important that I share with you these unique, supernatural encounters with God to bolster your faith in seeking encounters with Him on your own. I will just trust in the Holy Spirit to convince you of my honesty, and trust in Him to lead you on your own path as you draw into more intimacy with Jesus Christ. Do not get sidetracked here on the sensation – recognize that it is only a tool to draw a person closer to the Lord.

Anyway, it's not like the healing anointing or *dunamis* – it does not go into the person; it's a discernment of what is causing the ailment. If I sense the spirit of infirmity in their mind, I place my hand on their forehead, take authority over the spirit, and I can literally feel it lift, lift, lift off them until it hits the palm of my hand; and the veiling gets thrown off.

Sometimes I'm led to place my hands on their shoulders, and I can feel the impression of two hands that hold the person down; sometimes it feels like a cloak. Again, after taking authority over it, I can feel the hands lift off and back and fall down to the ground.

Most often, I just sense the gift of discernment sensation crawl up my hand, up my shoulder, until it hits my heart, and then it dissipates. Once it dissipates, I know the person is released. I take authority over the spirit and break it off them. Often, I then feel the healing anointing or the workings of miracles anointing flow out to them in a more powerful measure. To the glory of God, hundreds upon hundreds of people have been freed by His miraculous power from a demonic oppression that has plagued them, some for many, many years!

On the times that I would lay my hands on people and *not* feel the sensation, I began to understand there was no spirit of infirmity that was beating them down, and they simply needed a miraculous touch of God. The healing anointing would go out, and people would be blessed.

This gift of discernment made personal times of ministry easier for me, and I believe it helps people achieve greater results. Not that I have anything in myself, not that I am any more special for sensing this feeling; it just lets me know how I ought to pray.

Why do I share this with you? Not to puff myself up (it's not me anyway), but because I believe you can, as an apostolic person, press into a similar encounter with the Lord for yourself. I don't know if you'll start feeling a *hum* in your hand or not — that's not really the point. But you can expect to have your own kind of breaker encounter with the Holy Spirit that will energize your faith, break through any veiling that may be holding you down and allow you to translate that startling revelation to others. That's the point of this book: to show you that we can all have an apostolic unction, even though we are not all apostles, to see the miraculous power of God operate in our lives!

Apostles and apostolic people, in order to move into the greater miraculous power of God, have got to be able to tackle these more "difficult" issues in people's lives. We all know it isn't any more difficult for God, just in our own minds. But the Father, in these end times, is bestowing gifts upon His apostles, a greater discernment of the enemy's tactics — we deal with the demonic more often than many Christians recognize.

The Holy Spirit wants to help us in these different expressions of the apostolic, prophetic breaker anointing to set people free in a magnitude greater than has been seen in the world for a long time.

The apostolic person must strive for a discernment of spirits operation in their life.

The gift of discerning of spirits is not just something that is seen or heard, but it can also be felt. In Hebrews 5:14, it speaks of our spiritual senses being exercised to discern what is good and evil. Our spiritual faculties need to be developed. Our perception needs to be matured to discern what is of the soul and what is of the spirit.

In other words, there is a realm that *hears* in the spirit (this is the prophetic unction most Charismatics are familiar with, speaking forth what the Lord is saying); and there is a realm of the spirit that *sees* (we in prophetic circles call this the "seer anointing," aptly enough.) The seer unction speaks of perceiving, discerning, of *feeling* what is happening in the spirit. So this sensation in the palm of my hand is "feeling" the discernment of spirits.

THE SEER ANOINTING

The apostles must learn to cultivate all facets of discernment, hearing, seeing and feeling; and these types of discernment come only from a lifestyle of intimacy with Jesus. Then the apostles, in turn, can express these discernments through their own five senses, so people can encounter God. We find that God has many different ways of communicating, but I believe He wants people to encounter Him in a five-senses kind of way — not just a warm, fuzzy notion in one's tummy, some mystical force floating out there in the cosmic ether. The Lord is *real*; He can be touched and "seen" as well as heard.

In 1 Samuel 3, the passage shows that Samuel was learning to know the still, small voice of the Lord from a very young age. Verses 20-21 show that the word of the Lord came to him in Shiloh, and then the word of Samuel came to all Israel. (1 Samuel 4:1) See how it got translated to others?

But the phrase I want to point out here is: "revealed Himself to Samuel in Shiloh by the word of the Lord." When I researched "revealed" and "appeared," it means to me that Samuel was able "to discern, to have an experience with, to look upon, to enjoy, to see, to know" the Lord. It was a seer unction that Samuel cultivated, not just a hearing, prophetic operation. Seers experience or encounter the presence of God, rather than just hear from Him. My point in sharing this, other than it's a cool thought, is that apostolic, prophetic people need to cultivate this seer expression.

Flip to 1 Samuel 9:9, and if you have a handy, dandy *Strong's Exhaustive Concordance* available look up the word "seer" and then look up the word "prophet" (that's from 1 Samuel 3:20, remember.) They are two different words detailing two different expressions of prophecy (*nabiy* for "prophet," *raah* for "seer.") *Nabiy* (Strong's #5030) is the more commonly used word and connotes one hearing from God and speaking forth; *raah* (Strong's #7200) is a little rarer. See 2 Samuel 24:11 and 2 Chronicles 29:30 for more references of "seer." Gad and Asaph were "seers." Second Samuel 7:2 shows Nathan was a "prophet."

I know some people maintain the two words are completely interchangeable, and I can understand that thinking; they both connote a "prophet." But they really *are* two different words describing two different experiences: seeing and hearing. Take a look at 1 Chronicles 29:29, Samuel, Nathan and Gad are all listed in the same verse as a seer, a prophet and a seer respectively.

It's not that the seer anointing is "better" than the prophetic anointing; both are vitally important. But the seer anointing can give a more tangible expression of God to the people, manifesting His presence where it can be felt in the five senses. And I think apostles and prophets should cultivate both types of expression, hearing *and* seeing. But we have a lot of influence on the hearing of God's word, yet not as much influence on the "seeing," or experiencing, God's word.

See, I believe there is a new authority that is arising in the midst of God's people to decree that what we are seeing — and hearing — in heaven will be seen and heard in the now, on this earth. This is why we need to seek God for those greater signs, wonders and miracles of the apostolic and prophetic people, because that is *seeing* what is happening in heaven on earth. I am convinced we are on the verge of seeing a colossal manifestation and a blending of the seer, prophetic and apostolic anointings working together to present the Father in a tangible way, on a greater level than what has been in modern times.

People will be able to sense His presence, not just take it on blind faith that He is there — which of course, we as Christians *know* He is there, whether we feel anything or not. I know people are blessed who believe and have not seen. (John 20:29) But it stands to reason that God is a big enough God, secure enough in Himself, to manifest His presence tangibly to people. I don't think God ever intended the whole of humanity to worship Him without ever feeling Him in their five senses. If all of creation is His desire, why would He desire to give humanity the ability to feel and not expect them to feel Him? It just doesn't make sense.

So, by operating in that discernment of spirits where I *feel* something in my hand, it increases my faith to see the person delivered. Obviously if God is taking the time to show me the spirit of infirmity, that necessitates He wants them delivered of it, right? Inevitably, as the Lord has begun to show me the spirit of infirmity and I sense that manifestation, He has also begun to convey an evident token to the person I am ministering to; they actually *sense* something very powerful and unusual. They *know* they have encountered the Lord, and if they *know* He's capable of making them feel Him in the natural realm, they *know* He is capable of setting them free. It increases their faith, as well as mine, and our prayers of faith are energized to exercise power over the falsities of the infirmity.

THE PRAYER OF FAITH

I don't apologize for it. I'm a faith man. I believe in the word of faith, not in a "blab it, grab it" mentality, but to actualize that which Christ fought so hard to procure on our behalves, including freedom from a spirit of infirmity. I put full stock in the prayer of faith to save the sick, because I've seen the Lord confirm it time and time again. Sorry, folks, I'm already ruined; you can't convince me otherwise. I know in myself I have nothing that can help you, but the Spirit breathing upon us both will cause us to rise up and make our case known to the Lord, who is always eager to listen and judge rightly on our behalves.

The resting of the Father's reputation — remember, that's His "glory" — upon us conveys attributes of Himself in our midst. The apostolic anointing unveils the misconception that things must stay the way they are. The spirit of faith that is on a corporate Body brings great grace (remember that?) and strategies to loose the Body into the Kingdom of wholeness.

What does the Word of God say? "Is anyone among you suffering? Let him pray. Is anyone cheerful? Let him sing psalms. Is anyone among you sick? Let him call for the elders of the church, and let them pray over him, anointing him with oil in the name of the Lord. And the prayer of faith will save the sick, and the Lord will raise him up. And if he has committed sins, he will be forgiven." (James 5:13-15)

How can we argue with that? Obviously, James, being breathed on by the Holy Spirit, knew what he was talking about. The prayer of faith *will* save the sick. Period. Not maybe. Not, well, if the temperature in the room is *just* right. Not if the weather outside is nice and sunny.

So why doesn't it always work, then? You all can probably think of someone who called the elders, they prayed over the person, and the person still died. What's the cause? It can't be on the fault of the Word, or of God — that much is obvious. Perhaps one of the reasons is that not all prayers are prayers of faith! Our prayers must be energized prayers of faith — those which are breathed on by the Holy Spirit. Makes sense.

There are many different types of prayers. In Acts 4:23-31, we find they offered a *prayer of petition*, asking of the Lord for boldness, which was granted. (That term "prayer of petition" comes, I believe, from the late John Wimber, who also coined the "Dancing Hand of God.")

The prayer of faith is of a different caliber than the prayer of petition. We must understand the different styles of prayer. We must expect God to give us wisdom on how we should pray. (James 1:5) So often, we pray a prayer of petition: "Oh, Lord, if it's Your will, please heal me." That's not active faith; that's a prayer petitioning the sovereignty of God to move in spite of us. And, yes, that works sometimes, for God is a big God. But we should know, if we've been walking with Him for any length of time, that He requires more out of us than simply relying on His good nature to procure the blessings of the cross. We must actualize the workings of the cross and make them our own.

So take care to analyze your prayers. Are they loud? Are they soft? Are they strong, with crying and tears, or anger and fear? Perhaps you have not been praying the prayer of faith. Maybe that's a hindrance to receiving freedom from infirmity. I'm not giving a blanket answer here — some mystical formula for divine healing, but I am saying there *are* reasons we don't see the manifest glory of God in specific incidents, and since the prayer of faith *will* save the sick, the fault must lie with us. We must identify and rectify our style of praying.

Let's take a moment to study the prayer of faith that will save the sick, according to James 5. The word "save" is the Greek word *sozo*. (Strong's #4982) It is an action word, not a passive word. It conveys movement, activity, faith walking. Jesus activated His faith when He prayed. Even if the sick person's faith was not perfected, He demanded that they take a step with Him, working with Him to the best of their ability to achieve the healing. *Jesus had to get the people to believe He was capable of healing them.* Now, Jesus never condemned them for having a faulty, incomplete faith, but He did expect their faith — at whatever level it was — to be activated. He did admonish His followers to grow in faith.

It's important to note that Jesus did not work healings out of sovereignty. He was just as reliant upon His faith while on this earth as we are. Christ never healed anyone as God but as the Son of Man, otherwise how could we be expected to do similar works? (Of course, we know He was still completely God during His earthly ministry, but He chose to empty Himself, become as man, and rely on the gifts of the Holy Spirit to flow through Him. See Philippians 2:5-11.)

There is a difference between evangelistic anointings, where God is reaching out to the lost, and a faith expectation on behalf of people who are already in covenant with Him. In the case of power evangelism (that's the gospel presented and backed up by the miraculous), those are sovereign moves of love on the behalf of God. He doesn't expect the people out there in the world to have expectant faith — how can they? So He'll take whatever level of faith they possess and work with that, but as they come to know Him, God expects them to grow in expectant faith and activate it to receive the procurements of the cross.

See, when people took that step with Jesus, activating their faith as He healed, the Father met them halfway (or three-quarters, or whatever) and "downloaded," for lack of a better word, a measure of His faith (which is perfect faith, because *He* knows He can heal), mixing it with their imperfect expectation, and the result was achieved.

Have you ever been praying for something and suddenly it's like this special level of faith is just *dumped* into your spirit, and you felt you could accomplish anything? That is the Father's gift of faith being given to you. Once the desired effect is achieved, then that gift of faith lifts off, and the believer is left with his or her own measure of faith.

The idea behind it is that when God's faith is infused with yours, you begin to see that all things are possible, and the next time you need faith, your own personal faith is that much more increased to *believe* you have received when you pray. Your prayer of faith has become energized.

The word "sick" in James 5 refers, reasonably enough, to "the one being sick" or "exhausted." The Greek word for "raise" is *egeiro-autos* (Strong's #1453 and #846), and it means reflexively, "I raise or lift *myself* up from physical illness." The action is on your behalf; God is just empowering you "behind the scenes," we might say. It is the same word used in Mark 1:31: "So He came and took her by the hand and lifted her up, and immediately the fever left her. And she served them." Yes, He took her hand, but she activated her faith and "lifted up" (*egeiro-autos*.) It was then the fever left her. See, it was her action coupled with the action of the Lord that brought about the healing. To me, the word *egeiro-autos* implies that if one doesn't make the effort to raise themselves up, they would be left laying down. Yes, God will hold your hand, but He's only there for support, not as a crutch upon which you are totally reliant, implying you have nothing to do in the matter.

(Don't misunderstand what I'm saying here. I know we are all *totally reliant* upon the Lord, for without Him we would have no knowledge of faith at all; but as we grow, He expects us to know our reliance upon Him is based on *our* response to His gifts. Does this make sense?)

Notice that the people James is talking about in Chapter 5 are *church people*, folks that are already saved. These people are different than people out there in the world who know no better. God moves more sovereignly among them, because they are not yet *His* people. But people who are saved should know they are *covenant people*, and because of this, they have covenant rights that God expects them to take advantage of.

The word "call" (Strong's #4341, referencing #2753) in James 5 is a command. It means "I call or summon you." It is not just a request; it means, "Come!" The problem is *most Christians never obey* the command, or they issue the command in a wimpy way. "Pretty please, with sugar on top...." That's not active faith; that's passive faith.

We must exercise *expectant faith*. "When I call the elders, we will pray the prayer of expectant faith, and the Lord *will* heal me!" The problem is most prayers are not offered with an expectant faith, but rather a passive faith, which in actuality is merely *trust*. This is on the side of both the *elders* and the *sick person*. If the elders pray with passive faith, there is only a measured anointing given. If the sick person prays with passive faith, only measured results are given. So there might be an initial deposit of anointing that the elders and the sick person feel, which should encourage the faith and cause an expectation for the finished result. But often, both parties take that as a sign that it is all completed, and the faith is never energized. See, an energizing *has* to come to the covenant people's faith for the works to be established.

The apostles must have a firm understanding of this situation and allow the anointing to come upon them that will *break open* the veiling, and faith will then be energized. One of the great weapons of an apostle's arsenal is to energize people's faith.

In light of all this teaching, the importance of the Holy Spirit, His tongues, the operation of discerning the spirits of infirmity, the seer anointing coupling with the apostolic breaker anointing... I believe we begin to see certain keys and gifts the Father has placed within the hands of apostles and apostolic people to see a deeper level of His power released in their lives, to see our prayers changed into prayers of faith that see that power move miraculously in people's lives. Dear friends, we have *got* to press into that level of power; and the apostolic gifting is here today to help us, with the Holy Spirit working alongside us, to further unveil the power of the Father.

Chapter Five Outline
"Unveiling the Power of God"

BAPTISM IN THE HOLY SPIRIT

- "Likewise the Spirit also helps our weaknesses. For we do not know what we should pray for as we ought, but the Spirit Himself makes intercession for us with groanings which cannot be uttered. Now He who searches the hearts knows what the mind of the Spirit is, because He makes intercession for the saints according to the will of God. And we know that all things work together for good to those who love God, to those who are the called according to His purpose." (Romans 8:26-28)

- "Weaknesses" — (*astheneia*, Strong's #769) — "infirmities," personal, inward infirmities and outward infirmities toward others, physical and moral

- "Helps" — (Strong's #4878) — "to take hold of together opposite" or "heaves with us" — "stands up against with"

- "Likewise the Spirit also stands up with us against our infirmities"

- "Makes intercession" — (*huperentugchano*, Strong's #5241, #1793) — the Holy Spirit throws Himself into the midst of our situation, pleads our case before the Father, intervening on the behalf of another, interfering with the problems that men face

- "Therefore He is also able to save to the uttermost those who come to God through Him, since He always lives to make intercession for them." (Hebrews 7:25)
- "And suddenly there came a sound from heaven, as of a rushing mighty wind, and it filled the whole house where they were sitting." (Acts 2:2)
- "Rushing" — (*phero*, Strong's #5342) — a maternity term that could be translated "to bear" — as in giving birth, the breath of God which gives life
- "...Knowing this first, that no prophecy of Scripture is of any private interpretation, for prophecy never came by the will of man, but holy men of God spoke as they were moved by the Holy Spirit." (2 Peter 1:20-21)
- "Moved" is *phero*
- "And... He breathed on them, and said to them, 'Receive the Holy Spirit.'" (John 20:22)

The Importance of Tongues

- "He who speaks in a tongue edifies himself, but he who prophesies edifies the church." (1 Corinthians 14:4)
- "For if I pray in a tongue, my spirit by the Holy Spirit within me prays...." (1 Corinthians 14:14, Amplified)
- "'And I will pray the Father, and He will give you another Helper, that He may abide with you forever — the Spirit of truth, whom the world cannot receive, because it neither sees Him nor knows Him; but you know Him, for He dwells with you and will be in you.'" (John 14:16-17)

- "But God has revealed them to us through His Spirit. For the Spirit searches all things, yes, the deep things of God." (1 Corinthians 2:10)

- "But you, beloved, building yourselves up on your most holy faith, praying in the Holy Spirit, keep yourselves in the love of God, looking for the mercy of our Lord Jesus Christ unto eternal life." (Jude 20-21)

- "For with stammering lips and another tongue He will speak to this people, to whom He said, 'This is the rest with which You may cause the weary to rest,' and, 'This is the refreshing;' yet they would not hear." (Isaiah 28:11-12)

- "What is the conclusion then? I will pray with the spirit, and I will also pray with the understanding. I will sing with the spirit, and I will also sing with the understanding. Otherwise, if you bless with the spirit, how will he who occupies the place of the uninformed say 'Amen' at your giving of thanks, since he does not understand what you say? For you indeed give thanks well, but the other is not edified." (1 Corinthians 14:15-17)

- So many Christians, who are indeed true believers in Christ, neglect half of the equation and, therefore, only achieve half the answer. To recover the apostolic grace is to recover that which is on *both sides* of the equals sign. Otherwise the sum is unbalanced and left with variables

- Tongues, for all intents and purposes, are the language of the Kingdom of God. Therefore, with our cooperation, the

Holy Spirit incorporates a mechanism in our walk that builds up our knowledge of that Kingdom and reflects itself in a fruitful life, which is always to be an expression of the Kingdom to which we belong. So, to elucidate, tongues will lead us to a restoration of the supernatural demonstration of the Kingdom, that is the release of the power of God

- Speaking in tongues births the mighty works of Jesus Christ Himself
- The power of God is unveiled through the Holy Spirit — the apostles and apostolic people are here to remind everyone in the Body of Christ the importance and emphasis that is to be placed upon the third, and certainly not the least, part of the Godhead: the Holy Spirit
- Apostles teach the people the importance of honoring the Holy Spirit — and that means *honoring His tongues*

RECEIVING THE FATHER'S PROMISE

- "And being assembled together with them, He commanded them not to depart from Jerusalem, but to wait for the Promise of the Father... but you shall receive power when the Holy Spirit has come upon you...." (Acts 1:4, 8)
- "'Therefore being exalted to the right hand of God, and having received from the Father the promise of the Holy Spirit, He poured out this which you now see and hear.... Repent and let every one of you be baptized in the name of Jesus Christ for the remission of sins; and you shall receive

the gift of the Holy Spirit. For the promise is to you and to your children, and to all who are afar off, as many as the Lord our God will call.'" (Acts 2:33, 38-39)

- "'But the Helper, the Holy Spirit, whom the Father will send in My name, He will teach you all things, and bring to your remembrance all things that I said to you.... But when the Helper comes, whom I shall send to you from the Father, the Spirit of truth who proceeds from the Father, He will testify of Me.... Nevertheless I tell you the truth. It is to your advantage that I go away; for if I do not go away, the Helper will not come to you; but if I depart, I will send Him to you.'" (John 14:26; 15:26; 16:7)

- "Yet you do not have because you do not ask." (James 4:2)

- To be an apostolic people, we must recognize the need for the gift of the Holy Spirit to be given, and knowing that a gift must be received, we then take it from the Father and apply it to our lives

- "'So I say to you, ask, and it will be given to you.... If you then, being evil, know how to give good gifts to your children, how much more will your heavenly Father give the Holy Spirit to those who ask Him!'" (Luke 11:9, 13)

- "'Men listened to me and waited, and kept silence for my counsel. After my words they did not speak again, and my speech settled on them as dew. They waited for me as for the rain, and they opened their mouth wide as for the spring rain.'" (Job 29:21-23)

ANOTHER HELPER

- All apostolic anointings, all signs, wonders and miracles are provided through the help of the Holy Spirit
- "'And these signs will follow those who believe [rather, "have believed" or "to those who are believing"]: In My name they will cast out demons; they will speak with new tongues; they will take up [rather, "cast away"] serpents; and if they drink anything deadly, it will by no means hurt them; they will lay hands on the sick, and they will recover.'" (Mark 16:17-18)

THE INSANITY OF THE HOLY SPIRIT

- "Help" — (Romans 8:26, *sunantilambanomai*, Strong's #4878) — *sun*, "with, together" — *anti*, "against" — *lambanomai*, "to take away"
- The Holy Spirit is working with you against your infirmities to take them away. It's not necessarily passive; He is working with you, passionately, violently if need be, to seize and remove those infirmities
- The Holy Spirit, upon hearing of your sad plight, becomes so enraged that He enters into a blind fury, violently lashing out against that which repeatedly is beating you down
- "'And from the days of John the Baptist until now the kingdom of heaven suffers violence, and the violent take it by force.'" (Matthew 11:12)

The Seer Anointing

- The apostles must learn to cultivate all facets of discernment, hearing, seeing and feeling; and these types of discernment come only from a lifestyle of intimacy with Jesus
- Then the apostles, in turn, can express these discernments through their own five senses, so people can encounter God
- Seers experience or encounter the presence of God, rather than just hear from Him
- Apostles should cultivate both types of expressions, hearing *and* seeing

The Prayer of Faith

- "Is anyone among you suffering? Let him pray. Is anyone cheerful? Let him sing psalms. Is anyone among you sick? Let him call for the elders of the church, and let them pray over him, anointing him with oil in the name of the Lord. And the prayer of faith will save the sick, and the Lord will raise him up. And if he has committed sins, he will be forgiven." (James 5:13-15)
- In Acts 4:23-31, they offered a *prayer of petition*, asking of the Lord for boldness, which was granted
- The prayer of faith is of a different caliber than the prayer of petition
- Jesus activated His faith when He prayed. Even if the sick person's faith was not perfected, He demanded that they take

a step with Him, working with Him to the best of their ability to achieve the healing. *Jesus had to get the people to believe He was capable of healing them.* Now, Jesus never condemned them for having a faulty, incomplete faith, but He did expect their faith — at whatever level it was — to be activated. He did admonish His followers to grow in faith

6

Unveiling the Blessings of God

SIGNS, WONDERS AND MIRACLES: THE BLESSINGS OF GOD

So once again, I found myself in Madras/Chennai, India, leading a team of evangelists in a series of crusades. The magnitude of the needs of the people was totally overwhelming, to put it mildly. Sprawled out before us was a sea of humanity whose infirmities read like a chapter out of the Gospels or the Book of Acts. I kept looking for a boat to climb into so I wouldn't get crushed, but there wasn't a body of water anywhere near us. There was, however, every kind of sickness and disease imaginable represented in the vast crowd that thronged to hear every word being preached.

Still, the message of hope rang clear: eternal security was at their possession! Longing to hear the words of life that offered comfort to weary souls, the multitudes hungrily devoured the engrafted Word. (Reference James 1:21.) Thousands responded as the call was given to receive Jesus as Savior and Lord of their lives. They rushed forward with tears of anticipation.

In India, people don't just *walk* up to the altar — they *clamber* over people to get there! It was amazing to see the response of these precious souls receiving the greatest miracle of all: the born again experience! It warms the heart when I think of it.

However, at that moment of heart-warminess, a gnawing question rose up within my spirit. I immediately recognized it as coming from the Lord, and it shook me to the very core of my being. It carried a sense of tender compassion mixed with an intense desire. I heard these words resonate from within, "When will I be presented to the multitudes *today* as I was presented *yesterday*? Have I changed in two thousand years? Is it not still My desire to heal the sick and set the captives free?" My mind leapt to Luke 4:18-19 as these words reverberated through me. (Look the verses up, please.)

You don't have to look very far to see the vastness of desperation among people straining under the vexation of life's struggles. So often, bodies and souls are laden with torments, seemingly without any answer. Yet a clarion message is coming forth in these days that is restoring faith to the needy — Jesus Christ: the same yesterday, and today, and forever. (Hebrews 13:8)

With so many voices screaming to be heard today in the Church, we must ask ourselves the questions: "Is what I'm hearing in accordance with the example and teaching of Jesus? Would Jesus have functioned in the manner being presented to me? Am I seeing a clear representation of His present day ministry?" Those WWJD? bracelets carried a more poignant question than we give them credit for!

The apostles, with their breaker anointing, create an apostolic people who have an understanding of the eternalness of Jesus Christ. They know He has *not* changed one iota in twenty centuries — never in the history of mankind. It takes something a little more than the average, that breaker anointing, to create in people an attitude that Jesus Christ is desperately desirous of blessing the people of His Church and of the world. The apostles, while operating in the signs, wonders and miracles of Jesus Christ, show that He aches for the people. He is passionate about blessing us!

Since Christ is absolutely incapable of change, His attitude toward sickness must, therefore, remain the same: "He healed all manner of sickness and disease among the people." (See Matthew 4:23, 24; 8:16, 17.) We read in Acts 1:1, 2 and 17 of what "Jesus began to do and to teach." The Gospels display the marvelous deeds the Lord *began*, and the Book of Acts tells of what *continued* through His Body in signs, wonders and miracles after His ascension. History has recorded incalculable examples of God's continuing love and powerful interventions. Today, the apostles and apostolic people are writing the history of tomorrow!

Christ has not changed! He is still *Jehovah Rapha*. (Exodus 15:26; Isaiah 53:3-5) Our understanding of His personage and the attributes of His existence establish us in a greater faith, yielding confidence for the supernatural. In other words, the apostolic miracles breed *more miracles*. The blessings of God, represented by the apostolic, yield more blessings.

So I ask a question: Whatever happened to signs, wonders and miracles, dear readers?

This question, loaded though it is, should lead us to a focus from God's viewpoint. We come to realize the importance He places upon confirming His Word with miraculous demonstrations of His love. (See Hebrews 2:1-4; 1 Corinthians 12:7.) I am one hundred percent convinced those demonstrations continue to remain utterly important in His eyes. The whole point of this book has been to attempt to show you that we need the Dancing Hand of God.

Every manifestation of knowledge, wisdom and power – the miraculous – is a declaration from the Father that Jesus is, indeed, alive! As I've said before, Acts 4:33 shows that, "God gave the apostles witness of the resurrection of the Lord Jesus, and great grace was upon them all." It is not His intention that people just simply hear the story of the resurrection, but that they experience the living proof of it! We owe people an encounter with the living expression of Jesus on earth, releasing the *zoe*-kind of life that many have never experienced. (Check out Romans 8:2.)

God wants the opportunity to reverse impossible circumstances, to bring forth a greater reality of His love, acceptance and nearness. I'll say it again: everywhere Jesus went in His earthly ministry He manifested the reputation of God the Father into reality. (Hebrews 1:3; John 14:8-11) It's the Father's intense desire that His people express that same reality to a lost and dying world. To do otherwise is contrary to God's will.

Again, the scriptural purpose of every sign, wonder and miracle is to reveal the greatness of the Godhead. The glory of God is manifested by the miraculous demonstration of the Spirit. John 2:11 states, "This beginning of signs Jesus did in Cana of Galilee, and manifested His glory, and His disciples believed in Him." In the pursuit for the recovery of the fullness of the testimony of Jesus comes a tremendous awakening to God's purposes in demonstrating and revealing Himself. (1 Corinthians 1:4-9) With that unveiling of His awesomeness comes the quelling of so many voices of unbelief and confusion. It brings a sense of clarity and direction. (Reference John 3:2.)

Another scriptural purpose of God's miraculous intervention is the confrontation it can bring. We've talked about how signs, wonders and miracles can be used to force people to make a decision about God. Hebrews 2:1-4 — which you should have already read if you're looking up these scripture references — speaks of our great salvation that is to have the witness of the Godhead with signs, wonders, miracles and gifts of the Spirit. The demonstration of such divine authority (by that I mean the marked imprint of God upon a person) can produce many kinds of responses.

In short, signs solicit a reaction. Here finally I'll give the definition for "signs."

"Sign" is the Greek word *semeion* (Strong's #4592), and it means (drum roll...) "a sign."

All right, that was kind of obvious, I admit it. Here's something better: a sign is a miraculous display that can be used as a signpost or a turning point in our lives. Literally, a sign is a supernatural occurrence that points us to God. Better?

As we believe in the sign given by God, it serves to help us find direction, pointing us back to the right path of fulfilling God's destiny for our lives. It provokes a response.

An intervention of God exposes the motives of our hearts. His supernatural expression can be used to bring us to Him, or it can cause our hearts to become hardened. (See Luke 2:34-35; Isaiah 8:14,15.) Sometimes our offensive reaction to the moving of the Spirit can show us where we are lacking in our walk with God.

Since the Lord often (of course, not always) has a habit of placing an offence in front of a blessing, we should all purpose not to be offended by anything the Holy Spirit wishes to do. (Habakkuk 1:5) This should motivate all of us to come to repentance and a faith toward God. (That's Hebrews 6:1.) Martin Luther said, "The same sun that melts snow hardens soil." God offends the mind to reveal the heart.

And now, the definition of "wonder." Sometimes it is translated from *semeion* (Revelation 12:3, as an example.) So, "sign" and "wonder" are kind of interchangeable. But there is another Greek word that is translated "wonder." So no hoopla, I'll just let you know. This is the Greek word *thambos* (Strong's #2285), and it means (ta-dum-da-dum!), "a sign that makes you wonder."

These are kind of a letdown, huh? I've built them up several times over the course of the book, and they turn out to be more common sense than one realizes.

Nevertheless, *thambos* is to marvel at what God has done. To be shocked and awed, to be amazed and stunned into silence. Check out Mark 1:22, where it says the people were "astonished" at Christ's doctrine. That word "astonished" is, I think, rather weakly translated. It is the Greek word *ekplesso* (Strong's #1605, from #1537, #4141), and it literally means "to strike with astonishment." As in, to smite, to cudgel, to buffet. To be astonished, like smacked across the face. It implies a shocked reaction. *Robertson's Word Pictures* in quoting Gould says, "meaning strictly to strike a person out of his senses by some strong feeling...." That's a "wonder" – to astonish someone. Wonders have caused many to come to Christ, but they have also led others to question and scoff. Still, wonders elicit a reaction.

To be even more anti-climatic, you already know the Greek definition for "miracle." Yep, you guessed it – it's the word *dunamis* (Strong's #1411.) That explosive, reproducing power of God manifested on the earthly plane. Dy-no-mite!

Forgive me, dear readers, I'm having a bit of fun at your expense. But it doesn't negate the importance of signs, wonders and miracles. *Dunamis* can be used to release a greater faith in the heart of the recipient to be used by the Lord to bring salvation and healing to others. Again, it generates a response, a reaction.

As we begin to ponder the unchanging greatness of the Lord in a world that is constantly changing amidst intense turmoil, we need an astonishing revelation of who He is. Honestly, we must admit that the Lord is not presented in the powerful, tangible way as He would like. This has got to change!

The Lord Jesus is looking for opportunity to unveil the goodness of His heart to people in need of the *demonstration* of His compassion and not merely the *declaration* of it. (Go to Matthew 9:35-36.)

There are times in our pursuit for the supernatural intervention of God that we feel if we only had enough faith we would be able to experience a miracle, yet at times we see in scripture that God moved sovereignly. There are miracles performed without much cooperation or activation of a person's faith. (An example is found in John 18:10-11.)

At other times, Jesus required a more cooperative faith on the part of the person being healed, wrought by the working together of the divine and human to achieve the desired result. (An example is Luke 6:6-10.)

The Holy Spirit, who is our great Teacher, will guide and teach us in our quest for His miraculous touch, coupled with the apostolic, breaker anointing. Even with our faulty, incomplete faith the Lord will teach us how to operate in His faith, for He is the author and finisher of our faith. (Hebrews 12:2) It has been stated before, our wonderful Lord never refused anyone who came to Him in faith, even if their faith was not perfect. He did, however, desire that they would grow in faith through His Word. (Luke 17:5-6; Romans 10:17) We are therefore admonished to call upon Him in expectant faith, believing that His ear is open to our prayer. (1 John 5:14-15)

Further, we are also taught to increase our faith through the help of the Holy Spirit in His wonderful ministry of breathing His *rhema* influence within our hearts. (John 15:7) As we study and meditate upon the scriptures and experience His intimate, manifest presence, God's faith that had originally come from Him as a gift will be returned back to Him. That's important to understand. The result will be a supernatural work of grace within our hearts that will set in motion an operation of His miraculous power.

At the risk of beating a dead horse, I'll say again we must be careful that in our pursuit to see God do the *spectacular* — we don't miss the *supernatural*. The Lord wants to intervene in the everyday practicalities of life. Those personal words of encouragement from Him, His renewing presence — these, too, are signs of His enduring love toward us. They are all supernatural in content and reality.

We are living in a day when the Holy Spirit is in the process of restoring to the Church everything that pertains to life and godliness. (Acts 3:19-21; 2 Peter 1:3) The Lord in His infinite wisdom has purposed in His heart to anoint His people, chosen of Him, to have signs following their testimonies. (Mark 16:20) In this process of restoration, the establishing of the miraculous is of paramount importance in the Church's witness to the world. This is why we desperately need apostles in our churches — to bring that unveiling anointing we are to move into!

As we are living in a world with increasing demonic demonstration (just flip on your television), it behooves the Church to press in for the dominion faith that has been promised. (Luke 10:19) As we honor the Lord and His Word, a release of benevolent, supernatural power will accompany our compassionate desire to minister to humanity's needs.

The spiritual vacuum that has been created in many hearts will be filled, and the reality of the truth will be expressed in a way that may convince the most hardened, unbelieving person.

People today deserve as clear a picture of Jesus as was presented 2,000 years ago. Jesus worked miracles then, thereby captivating the complete attention of His audience. His brand of evangelism arrested the hearts of His listeners quite successfully. Two millennia ago, His hands were never extended in vain; and today as the Body of Christ, we are His hands reaching forth to this world.

So, apostolic people, I'll ask one more time: just whatever happened to signs, wonders and miracles?

A Bulldog Demon of Rage

During one of my overseas mission trips to India, I found myself preaching to a few thousand Indians in this pavilion of sorts that weakly attempted to block out the oppressive heat. I was standing on a stage about eight feet in the air above the people. In front of me on the ground were about one thousand children that the attendees had pushed up to the front. These children were sitting in piles looking up at me as I began to share the plan of salvation through an interpreter. I was eager to see Jesus release blessing upon them and call them unto Himself.

All of a sudden, from way in the back I saw the entrance gate flung open from the outside — it made an audible *crack!* as it hit the post and shuddered violently. There wasn't anyone outside that I could see, but I had entered into the realm of discerning of spirits. And then, out of nowhere, one of the ugliest demons I've ever had the displeasure of seeing came charging into the pavilion. I can only describe it as a bulldog — all jowls and snarls. I can't estimate the size correctly, but it was massively huge — much, much larger than your average bulldog. Maybe about the size of a small elephant, I'd say.

This demon huffed and snarled and started charging toward the stage I was preaching from, weaving in and among the people. I stepped back in shock as it reached the children in front of me. As it made a pass between the thousand or so kids, in instantaneous unison they all leapt up and began fist fighting each other. Screams and squeals assaulted me as blood began to pour. These dear children, as the demon roared pass, became exceedingly violent, for no reason that they could detect. It was just pandemonium. Total chaos and rage. I feared they would begin seriously injuring each other.

The bulldog demon had circled around and was coming through them again for another pass. I realized that I was losing control of this crusade, and I would not be able to continue with the altar call. Suddenly the brute made a beeline for me, straight through the crowd of fighting, screaming children, as if to leap upon me and devour me.

Just before he reached the stage, bellowing in frenzy, I saw from above me a flash of fire streak down to the ground in front of the stage like lightning. It struck the ground just as the demon lunged for me, and God as my witness, the beast slammed headfirst into the bared chest of a warring angel!

Now, I'm standing on a platform about eight feet in the air, and I'm six feet, five inches tall. (No, I won't tell you how much I weigh — stop asking!) When the demon hit the chest of this angel, directly in front of me, I saw the form of the angel's broad, muscular shoulders at my eye-level, acting as a shield between me and the demon. That would make the angel about fourteen feet tall. These shoulders can only be feebly described as "huge."

The creature hit the angel's chest and collapsed to the ground in a whelping heap. His form left a physical indentation in the dirt. He flopped around for a second, stunned, shaking his enormous, bulldog head and then staggered back to his feet. He looked at me with a growl, turned and fled out the gate from where he had entered. Instantly the fighting subsided and the children began looking around, confused and scared, some bleeding. They had no idea why they just started fighting and slowly began to settle back down in a daze.

See, the enemy will always attempt to destroy the next generation, to prohibit an encounter with God in the miraculous. He hates that imprint of the finger of God that wants to mark the next generation with His zeal. He doesn't want them to respond to God's call, for them to *know* God is real. That bulldog attempted to thwart the transfiguration that would occur when those kids, and adults, encountered Jesus. But rage and chaos are no match for the power of Jesus' call!

After the demon ran out, the power of God fell and people began to respond to His call for salvation and restoration. To the Lord's glory and honor, we saw some startling miracles, some true signs and wonders that pointed to the ultimate power of the King Jesus Christ. I am convinced God permitted me to witness this startling sign as a demonstration of His overwhelming desire to move miraculously among hurting people. God desires to bless every man, woman and child who will just simply come to Him, completely and totally.

Without signs and wonders, the blessings of God, without that dynamic intervention of Jesus in the earthly realm, the people are fodder for the bedlam and anger that displays the incapability of man to overcome his weaknesses. The demonic simply preys on that inability. It takes a breaker anointing, a release of the miraculous, to stop that demonic onslaught in its tracks. Those signs and wonders, that apostolic breaker anointing you and are I pressing into, are resounding calls that the Father is eager to bless His children, and that He is all-powerful against an enemy that breeds malice and confusion. The devil really hates it when God shows up.

Let me share with you another testimony that hallmarks the release of the blessing of God, and how we as apostolic people are commissioned to release that blessing through signs, wonders and miracles.

THE PUTTY-FACED GIRL

As one of the instructors at Christ for the Nations Institute, I used to hold healing services in my class, The Theology of Healings and Miracles. Makes sense, right? Seemed like a good place to have a healing service....

I can recall one of these services where we had about two hundred students show up. A wonderful pastor friend of mine named Tommy had come up from Louisiana to minister with me. My son and my faithful assistant, Carol, were there as well, working with me.

This particular service, the Lord spoke to me and said there were about thirty students in need of healing due to deformity in their bodies, so I gave a call for those with deformities, and sure enough, about thirty students came forward. I just love it when a plan comes together!

The first young man had a clubfoot. We prayed for him; the foot shook visibly and flipped right into place, filling out to its proper shape. Pastor Tommy prayed for a man whose sternum was twisted and turned at an odd angle. When he placed his hands on his sides, the whole chest moved straight into place. We were excited, to say the least.... God's Dancing Hand was moving!

At the very end of the line stood a young lady, and I felt an unusually strong presence resting over her. When you looked at her, you immediately knew what was wrong. The left side of her face was deformed. It was hard to describe. It was twisted looking, mangled. My heart went out to her as the compassion of the Lord poured forth, and I raised my hand to place it on the left side of her face.

She pulled away.

I knew then there was something more that needed to be healed, more than just her physical deformity. Rejection. Years of hurt and wounding because of verbal taunting, condemnation, teasing. She needed inward healing as well as outward. Hesitantly she permitted me to place my hand on the side of her face as I went to touch it a second time.

When I did, I felt Someone reach over my right shoulder. What I mean is I could feel the physical sensation of Someone's hand reach over me and place Their hand on the back of my hand, pressing it to her face. I knew it was the hand of Jesus.

I had the sensation that the bone structure of that area of her face became soft. My fingers pressed into her face, the muscles slackened, the bones became like putty, and the Holy Spirit rose up within me, sharing that passage of scripture in Jeremiah 18, concerning the potter and the marred piece of clay, and how it was molded after his design and purpose. (Jeremiah 18:1-6)

For the next five minutes, I stood in front of this lady, feeling the hand of God move with mine. It was like we were blended as one, working together, co-laborers, molding her face. The awesomeness of the miracle wasn't just that Jesus was healing this lady, as amazing as that is. But I was sharing in this experience with Him. Participating with Him. We massaged the side of her face like a piece of clay, pushing into the skeletal structure, one finger moving this part of her face, another finger moving another part.

She gave a shocked intake of breath as I felt the Lord remove His hand from mine. I felt her face harden into place and removed my hand. When I looked at her, the face was perfectly whole. The Lord removed *all trace* of deformity!

The young lady put her hand up to face, felt the newly formed bone structure and skin. Her whole body shook and she fell to her knees, sobbing. As I was standing there, I had the unique sensation that Jesus was standing over her, looking down at her, ministering to her. It was beautifully intimate. She began to release her heart's cry, and I felt that I shouldn't have been eavesdropping.

"Oh, thank you, Lord Jesus!" She wept. "Thank you so much! I've been believing that You would heal me since I was five years old. And You have! You love me! You really do love me!" She repeated that over and over again.

The Lord not only restored to her a tremendous sense of inward beauty to go alongside her physical healing, but He gave her a testimony so she could fulfill her purpose and destiny to bring the blessings of God to the next generation. How remarkable!

See, apostolic people, the release of the miraculous, the demonstration of signs and wonders, is a breaker anointing that shatters people's inward and outward woundings. The apostles of the Lord are anointed to release the power of the blessing. That blessing in turn creates a sense of purpose and destiny in a person's life; they find themselves more fruitful in the Lord. We *must* release the blessing!

Testimony of a Blessing

First Peter 3:9 warns us not to "[return] evil for evil or reviling for reviling, but on the contrary, blessing, knowing that you were called to this, that you may inherit a blessing."

That's a rather strange phrase, "inherit a blessing." We are possessors of an unfulfilled prophecy – something God has spoken to us of His faithfulness in ministering grace and favor, so that we might have a testimony of His blessing. You should already know that a testament required the death of the testator for the inheritance to take place (recall the teaching of the "Covenant Makers.") In this case, the death and resurrection of Jesus (the New Testament) provides for you a testimony and inheritance of blessing. Everyone has a testimony they should share. Everyone has a blessing to inherit. One of the keys found in the apostolic anointing is to unveil the blessing of God and show that you have a part to play in inheriting that blessing. You must make actual what Christ already provided for you.

Job 22:28 says, "'You will also declare a thing, and it will be established for you; so light will shine on your ways.'" I think "a thing" is speaking of blessing (light shining on our way.) So one could say your role, upon being released in the apostolic, is to declare a blessing and testify of favor. There is power in a blessing, and it is power we desperately need to tap into!

To define "blessing," we will say it is "to invite divine favor, to confer favor or talent, to confer prosperity (which you'll recall is "well-being throughout your walk of life.")" Further, a blessing means "to pronounce favor, to impart a spiritual quality, to call into life from things that are dead, to release God's creative power, to seal and protect." Now that we are on the same page regarding what exactly a blessing is, let's continue.

Grace is what I am writing about here. Grace, for this purpose, may be defined as "God's riches at Christ's expense, God's mercy granted to the undeserving (or ill-deserving.)" You'll recall it is "unmerited favor and God's persistent power manifested in the life of a person." To have favor is to obtain grace in the eyes of someone, in this case, God the Father. It speaks of beauty, attractiveness, for the people, for the Church, for the city found in the grace of God.

Paul conferred, "Grace to you and peace from God our Father and the Lord Jesus Christ." (Ephesians 1:2) In Verse 6 of the same chapter, he writes of "...the praise of the glory of His grace, by which He made us accepted in the Beloved." Verses 7 and 8 speak of "...the riches of His grace which He made to abound toward us in all wisdom and prudence." Further on in Chapter 2, Verse 7, Paul speaks of "...the ages to come [that] He might show the exceeding riches of His grace in His kindness toward us in Christ Jesus."

There are exceeding riches to be recovered in His grace!

"...Indeed you have heard of the dispensation of the grace of God which was given to me for you...." (Ephesians 3:2) We live in a dispensation, an age, of grace — literally that word (Strong's #3622) means to be "stewards" of God's grace. And we all want to be good stewards, right? Further, it is a gift that is to be ministered to others, which is why Paul admonishes the Ephesians, "Let no corrupt word proceed out of your mouth, but what is good for necessary edification, that it may impart grace to the hearers." (Ephesians 4:29)

You'll recall from previous chapters how the apostolic church in Acts was found with "great power" and "great grace." (Again, Acts 4:33.) The *mega* grace they harbored meant that all aspects of their lives were enriched and energized — they were fruitful people. And we all want to be fruitful, right?

So, all of that leads us to this: we have the power to inherit a blessing. We are designed by God in Christ to give a testimony of blessing out there to the world, and for this reason I am convinced we are coming into a season of great grace and blessing under the release of apostolic anointing. Jeremiah 5:24-25 quotes the Lord as saying, "'They do not say in their heart, "Let us now fear the Lord our God, who gives rain, both the former and the latter, in its season. He reserves for us the appointed weeks of the harvest." Your iniquities have turned these things away, and your sins have withheld good from you.'"

That tells me, as we are confessing our sins and breaking off iniquities, we will obviously be primed for a *kairos* moment wherein we have the power to birth a blessing. (Hopefully you remember that word from before — an appointed "season" in the flow of normal, calendar time, *chronos*.) A *kairos* hour is approaching us where the natural flow of time gives way for an opportunity of divine, foreordained purpose. It will be the very act of a special intervention. That time is coming quickly, I hope you believe!

For the mothers out there, I am speaking of a time, as in maternity, where something is brought to birth, something comes to full term and is brought to completion. Indeed, the birth pangs are getting closer!

And since these contractions are coming more quickly, it demands the intervention of God's purpose (the *kairos*) to be brought forth. In short, we give birth to a time of great grace and blessing. In the pre-ordained knowledge of God the Father, through Christ, we have the power to release a blessing! How wonderful is that? We are to have a testimony of purpose. Ponder on that.

"...You were enriched in everything by Him in all utterance and all knowledge, even as the testimony of Christ was confirmed in you, so that you come short in no gift, eagerly waiting for the revelation of our Lord Jesus Christ...." (1 Corinthians 1:5-7)

"Enriched," for us, means to be made "full, complete, strong" in everything by Him. My friend and colleague, Dr. Larry Hill, taught on this concept, and he outlined four characteristics of a fully enriched Church. Permit me to share these characteristics with you. One, we are to have strong, spiritual relationships with the other members of the Body — we are all to be valued and encouraged as one group. Two, we experience spiritual growth in the Body — we press on into deeper and deeper levels of knowledge (unveiling) in God. Three, we possess a spiritual vibrancy — lively, joyful, happy. And, four, we are spiritually transgenerational in our viewpoints — meaning, the blessing is passed on to the younger generation.

Which begs the question: are we really the "Last" Generation? I'm not so convinced we are. Whether or not Christ returns tomorrow or a hundred years from now, we have to look at life as the future being ours! When the elders claim *this* is the "Last Generation," it's like committing spiritual abortion to this upcoming generation's dreams and visions of furthering God's Kingdom and fulfilling their destinies! That's a strong statement, I know, but a fitting one. Look, if Christ comes back tomorrow, *no one* — young or old — will be found complaining. Poor us! We get to enter into the eternal blessings of heaven with God the Father.

But let's say He doesn't come back tomorrow, please don't kill the aspirations for each succeeding generation to bear more fruit than the last. Don't forget, God works through the generations, and to deny the next generation's dreams and visions is to slit our own throats, spiritually speaking.

I remember being a young pup *wayyyyyy* back when, and hearing someone give a prophetic word to us Jesus Freaks that, "Thus saith the Lord, Jesus Christ is going to return January 1, 1974!" We all whooped and hollered. *All right!* Christ was coming back! And sure enough, young as we were in the Lord, full of zeal and zippo knowledge, a whole group of us Hippies gathered on a mountaintop in Southern California, December 31, 1973. 11:59 struck, and we all hunkered down into our rapture positions – you think I'm kidding – and when that clock hand hit midnight, we jumped onto the balls of our feet. *God, here I come!*

But we didn't go anywhere. Except some of us to fall in the snow maybe.

So we boo-hooed and held one another, wondering what went wrong. Wasn't it a "Thus saith the Lord"? Finally after about fifteen minutes of crying on each other's shoulders, a voice from the back of the group cried out, "Thus saith the Lord, the previous person missed it!"

Well, *duh*…. Are you kidding?

"Yeah, he should've said, 'Thus saith the Lord, Jesus Christ is going to return January 1, 1975!'"

Ohhhh….

And did you know there were still some people who had the same audacity and ignorance to climb up that same mountain the next year? Thankfully, I wasn't one of them….

Guess what, it's currently 2008 while I'm writing this. And we're still here!

The point is, we have to instill in this next generation a mandate to pass what they have learned on to the next one, 'cause we may just not be the "Last Generation." God is looking for fathers who will raise their sons and daughters with a proper attitude toward future *kairos* moments. The apostolic anointing can be used to ignite a passion for our futures, whether Jesus returns tomorrow or not. Take a moment to study Psalm 78, especially Verses 1-8, intently.

To release a blessing, the Church must be a historical community. There is certainly supposed to be continuity with the old, but newness should always be infused with that continuity, otherwise we stagnate and potentially miss out on great opportunities to see what blessings God is releasing in *this* moment.

You know, in today's culture, a person's life is solely judged by what he is doing in the present; but, in truth, we can never fully judge a person's life until we see what his children and his grandchildren do with theirs.

"'I will bless those who bless you, and I will curse him who curses you; and in you all the families of the earth shall be blessed.'" (Genesis 12:3)

This promise was fulfilled only as succeeding generations appropriated the covenant of blessing. Notice how Abraham had the ability to pass the covenant onto his progeny. We, too, must take an active role in the futures of others, entering into their devotions, prayers, disciplines and destinies.

When God wants to establish a testimony in the earth, He starts with a person, but He doesn't end there because He is transgenerational in view, and so then, a *legacy* is born. He births a *movement*.

Apostolically minded people are transgenerational in their thinking, and they know that everything God is going to do will not be accomplished through one person, nor even one generation. They plan and act with great wisdom and strategy to prepare future generations to change entire nations.

"By faith Isaac blessed Jacob and Esau concerning things to come." (Hebrews 11:20)

THE BENJAMIN GATE

"Now it came to pass, when she [Rachel] was in hard labor, that the midwife said to her, 'Do not fear; you will have this son also.' And so it was, as her soul was departing (for she died), that she called his name Ben-Oni [Son of My Sorrow]; but his father [Jacob] called him Benjamin [Son of My Right Hand]." (Genesis 35:17-18)

Rebuilding the Wall around the City of David is recounted in Nehemiah, Chapter 3. In this passage are listed several gates around the City that were reconstructed. They are as follows: the Sheep Gate, the Fish Gate, the Old Gate, the Valley Gate, the Dung Gate (that'll preach! *Selah.*), the Fountain Gate, the House Gate and the Benjamin Gate.

What is a Gate? Obviously it is a place for ingress, simply a way in. People must pass through a Gate to enter into Jerusalem, the City of Promise. To be straightforward, I'm writing about spiritual paths to the new blessings the Father has promised.

The Father, through the prophet Jeremiah, preordained the rebuilding of the City. "For thus says the Lord: After seventy years are completed at Babylon, I will visit you and perform My good word toward you, and cause you to return to this place. For I know the thoughts that I think toward you, says the Lord, thoughts of peace and not of evil, to give you a future and a hope. Then you will call upon Me, and I will listen to you. And you will seek Me and find Me, when you search for Me with all your heart. I will be found by you, says the

Lord, and I will bring you back from your captivity; I will gather you from all the nations and from all the places where I have driven you, says the Lord, and I will bring you to the place from which I cause you to be carried away captive." (Jeremiah 29:10-14)

Psalm Two is a Messianic declaration, wherein the Lord, upon laughing at the kingdoms of the earth for their vanity in standing against Him, holds conversation with His Son, the King. "'I will declare the decree: The Lord has said to Me, "You are My Son, today I have begotten You. Ask of Me, and I will give You the nations for Your inheritance, and the ends of the earth for Your possession."'" (Verses 7-8)

Moreover, to an illuminated (read "born again") mind, we see that the Father is speaking of the nations, turned over from Christ to us, and that we are to inherit all the blessings associated with reigning alongside the Son. However, we must pass through the Gate — that is, spiritually enter in to what the Son has left for us.

This section of the book speaks more to a prophetic statement, rather than a teaching to be responded to. If you will take what I am about to share to heart, I am convinced that it will help prepare us for something that is coming; and, indeed, is beginning to break with the restoration of the apostolic anointing. We have a future and a hope, based on the good thoughts the Father has for us, that being rescued from captivity into the Kingdom of Jesus, we are to inherit untold riches (blessings) as co-rulers with Christ. The unveiling of the blessing of God lends the reader a deeper understanding of what it means to pass through the Benjamin Gate. Follow along with me for a few pages, please.

The restoration of the Gates, the Wall, the City, spoken about in Nehemiah 3 represents specific releases and moves of God, moving His people into spiritual restoration. Many of our spiritual gates have been closed or destroyed and are in need of repair, once we come out of captivity (veiled thinking.) I am firmly persuaded we are coming into the day of the Benjamin Gate.

"All the land shall be turned into a plain from Geba to Rimmon south of Jerusalem. Jerusalem shall be raised up and inhabited in her place from Benjamin's Gate to the place of the First Gate and the Corner Gate, and from the Tower of Hananel to the king's winepresses. The people shall dwell in it; and no longer shall there be utter destruction, but Jerusalem shall be safely inhabited." (Zechariah 14:10-11)

There is a connection between the release of the prophetic and the Benjamin Gate found in prophetic praise, worship and travail. Indeed, all the land shall be raised up in these actions! The new generation – the Benjamins – will host multitudes of young people crowding through the Benjamin Gate, entering into the City on the sounds of explosive praise, passionate worship and intense travail.

These will experience a birthing of new life – a new wave of promises!

But, in the process of new life coming, sometimes something has to die. Rachel died in order to bring forth Benjamin to birth. In spite of all our efforts, the Church (represented by Rachel) is having great difficulty in childbirth. Yes, we have had great successes in renewal expressions (let me call these "spiritual adoptions"), but we are still struggling to bring forth new babes and children of our own. Do you follow my meaning?

It's like this: with all these renewal expressions around various parts of the world, it seems that the spiritual sons and daughters – perhaps even the biological ones – are having difficulty translating these renewals into community-changing *revivals*. Don't misunderstand my intent here – I am so thankful of the renewal moves of God, but I believe these renewal expressions are *starting* points to an explosive national revival, the "Third Great Awakening" as some theologians are terming it. In some instances, it's as if we've adopted an expression instead of birthing a movement. And our children are having difficulty translating it to the rest of the world. (Again, not a blanket statement about *every* renewal expression, but I believe you would agree with me that *many* expressions affect the believers and not the disbelievers.)

Of course, there is nothing wrong with adoptions, but I want to point out a need for our own children metaphorically (revivals) and actually (our sons and daughters) as well.

We have struggled to have even our own children serve God with the zeal that their parents had. Some see these generations (the X-ers and the Millennium children) as "problem generations." So we dope them up on Ritalin, in the secular fields, and in the Christian fields we often do the same thing spiritually by pacifying them into a state of lethargy — "Don't worry, God is coming back, so just play Nintendo." Or something to that extent. (Not that there's anything wrong with a little Nintendo now and again, but you understand my intent.)

In fact, we have many future "rulers [who] take counsel together, against the Lord and His Anointed, saying, 'Let us break Their bonds in pieces and cast away Their cords from us.'" (Psalm 2:2-3)

In other words, these future leaders — that's the next generation, see — confer together to cast off what was foundationally taught by God's Word, through the spiritual fathers and mothers. Their connection to the past is a burden to them. The old is old. So they plot their own ways, most often contrary to what a generational God has established as law.

So "why do the nations rage and the people plot [imagine] a vain thing?" (Psalm 2:1)

Perhaps paternal authority is shrouded and veiled, the Father image in their spiritual upbringing is distorted, and it tears up the family of

God — as we see so prevalent in American society and other countries, for the natural reflects the spiritual. A lack of fruitfulness in a generation stems from a lack of conception (that is, bringing the children forth — spiritually.) We haven't properly shown them the Father, so they stay outside the Gate, and it affects future generations.

Benjamin represents to us a generation that God wants to bring forth out of the agony of the Church. See, there were two views held about Benjamin: Rachel saw him as "Sorrow"; Jacob saw him as his "Right Hand." Which was right? I believe Rachel's view was tainted by the "now" — the agony of labor she was undergoing, and I don't demean that agony; it cost her her life! But the father's view was long-term, tinted with a father's favor and blessing. How does *the* Father, then, see this generation?

A Time for Identity

I trust we are all familiar with the story of Esther. If not, take a few minutes to read it. It starts on page 697 of my Bible. Find Malachi and go left.

Anyway, I want to point out Mordecai's request for Esther to go to the king that he might spare the Jews. Her response is basically, "If I show up and I haven't been invited, the king'll kill me," as kings are often wont to do. Particularly note Mordecai's response:

"...Yet who knows whether you have come to the kingdom for such a time as this?" (Esther 4:14)

This statement was enough to convince Esther she should try and see the king. She was so emboldened that she said, "...So I will go to the king, which is against the law; and if I perish, I perish!" (Verse 16)

Wow! What a strong woman! She had found identity in these words; she began to realize that her being there was not a mistake. She was born for a purpose, even if it cost her life. This generation must have a similar awakening: you were born at just the right time! You are not a mistake!

The King has a demand *on* your life and *for* your life. He has produced something that can never be replaced: you! For as you know, there is only *one* of you. (I know some of you are thinking, "Thank God!" right now.) But this generation must have a revelation of just how important it is in the grand scheme of things — there is something that God intended for this generation to do that no other generation can! That is to arise in apostolic favor and power to release a blessing to the world!

"'You have seen what I did to the Egyptians, and how I bore you on eagles' wings and brought you to Myself.'" (Exodus 19:4) God is saying to this generation today: "I am going to bring you unto Myself!

He is pleased with all our strivings to find purpose, our determinations to be of intrinsic, irreplaceable value. Oh, I want to be brought unto Him — don't you? I want to hear Him say, "I will be found of you."

Many times, we think He's going to reward us with some tangible object of desire. But we need to understand that *He* is our reward. We are seeking Him! The Father sees this generation as a generation of great favor, and that favor is found in Him, and Him alone!

The reward is being able to hear Him clearly, in a manner not heard in this generation before. Just as Samuel, as a small child, could hear the Lord, in the Benjamin Gate, there will be youths who can hear Him likewise.

"Now the boy Samuel ministered to the Lord before Eli. And the word of the Lord was rare in those days; there was no widespread revelation... and while Samuel was lying down, that the Lord called Samuel. And he answered, 'Here I am!' Then the Lord appeared again in Shiloh. For the Lord revealed Himself to Samuel in Shiloh by the word of the Lord. And the word of Samuel came to all Israel." (1 Samuel 3:1, 4, 21; 4:1)

In the Benjamin Gate there will be magnetism, an allure, and a sufficiency that Christian youth have perhaps been lacking in the past. Others will be drawn to them because of their excellence and skill. Notice how David is anointed king in 1 Samuel 16. We know David was possessed of an excellent spirit; he knew how to play the harp, he was a brave man, a warrior and very fine looking. Truly the Lord was with him! It is the same with those of the Benjamin Gate: youth who are going to come forth with a spirit of faith. Recount the tale of David and Goliath in the next chapter of the same book. Just as David was, standing before the giant Philistine, this generation is as of yet untried in the arena of faith.

But just as David was suddenly possessed with a faith to win a great battle for his generation, so will this generation be possessed of an apostolic passion, a skill and equipment, to topple their giant and cut off his head.

In the Benjamin Gate, God is going to bring co-laborers together which defy our traditional approaches, just as we have looked at in 1 Samuel 18 concerning Jonathan and David, being knit together in the Spirit. This new generation of youths will find themselves able to be made vulnerable to one another, laying aside the marks of their warfare and prestige at the victory over the giant. I mean to say, they will have no problem working together, in spite of their personal talents.

Now here's an interesting thought. All new generations have their own expression in music right? Usually much to the annoyance of the older generation. Here in the Benjamin Gate there will also be a new musical expression that defines the generation. A different kind of music than what the previous generations' ears are attuned to. I'm speaking about praise and worship here – a fresh, new explosive twist to what we're used to. Just as the Beatles reshaped the secular music world, our new generation of Benjamins will reshape what we as the Church are used to in our approaching the Father through worship and praise. In history, there is always a musical communication that doesn't exist anywhere else in history. It is unique and defining for that moment in time, that generation. It is progressive, fresh and usually alarming to the older establishments, but it has within it the power to define an entire generation and to pacify the older ones. This new music can be a bridge between the old and the new.

"'Let our master now command your servants, who are before you, to seek out a man who is a skillful player on the harp. And it shall be that he will play it with his hand when the distressing [evil] spirit from God is upon you, and you shall be well.'" (1 Samuel 16:16)

This generation, upon passing through the Gate, will be made of an excellent, apostolic spirit. They will have reached the point of no return, having made a decision to pursue excellence, even that above their predecessors. They will set their foreheads as a flint, not being distracted, deflected or retracted. They will never turn and run. Everything is dust, but seeking Him and His will. Their hearts will be locked on His heart. Take a few moments to study Psalm 22, pondering the previous pages.

The signs, wonders and miracles of the apostle release the identity of this generation into the blessings of God. I remember once, while a teacher at CFNI, sitting on the platform and looking out upon those students. I felt the Lord spoke to me, saying, "This is your future! These are My leaders of tomorrow!" What a worthwhile endeavor – to speak into this generation! See, with the signs, wonders and miracles of the apostle prevalent in their lives, the next generation *itself* will become a sign and wonder to the world! (Isaiah 8:18)

The father apostles, through the eye of faith, must look upon the heart of this generation of Benjamins, not solely on the outward appearances. The apostles must help this generation identify the Gate they are to cross through, to find their purpose, their expression and release, by operating in the miraculous that unveils the objectives of the Father for these people. God wants to use His apostles to express Himself through their humanity, as having treasure in earthen vessels, so that this generation will reflect His great designs for their lives.

Apostles, raise up this new generation in the power and the blessings of the Father. Spiritual sons and daughters, be born in your identity as the new generation! Make use of the Gate before you!

Attributes of a Blessed Person

As this generation enters into an unveiling of the Father's blessing, we would do well to outline the apostolic attributes of a blessed people. We should define the spirit of excellence upon them, for clarity's sake and for goals to notice as we pass by them.

Dwayne Vanderclock, an awesome minister whom I went to Bible school with, offered some great thoughts in a teaching on leadership identification. I'd like to list a few of them here, pertaining to the attributes of a blessed person.

A blessed person is of a good reputation, not just what he or she does, but who he or she *is*. He or she is a finisher, looking at the end result, instead of focused on where they are now. He or she is willing to pay a price for those end results (the manifestations of blessings), always finding a way to improve.

The blessed generation will realign its motivations, giftings, talents and abilities. The people will begin to fit their personality profiles, instead of seeming fractured and disjointed, acting out of character —

something so prevalent in this generation currently. But they will be transformed (see Romans 12 again) into visionary leaders, apostolic men and women, who are directional; that is, being able to lay out clear plans of action to release the blessing. They will be strategists, devising how the process toward blessing is developed. Their people management skills (to borrow a secular term) will be motivational in execution, causing others to rally around their cause; that is, seeing the blessing manifested.

They will be team-builders, bringing everyone up to their fullest potentials. They will have great shepherding, counseling anointing that brings others to repentance, and they will be able to reproduce productive people. They will be quite entrepreneurial in motivation, cultivating their influence in new arenas of daily life. They will be engineers, problem-solvers, bridge-builders; that is, conflict managers and negotiators, for the business people out there. (Dwayne Vanderclock)

I know to some extent this has always been in place in the Church on some scale, but I see a greater development toward these attributes that invite the blessings of God to manifest in a way not previously seen since Early Church days. That apostolic spirit of excellence will create a revolution — a new strategy for church evangelism with power. In short, the breaker anointing we have been talking about throughout this book.

But every generation has a spirit over them that must be dealt with.

"...'O faithless [unbelieving] and perverse generation, how long shall I be with you?" (Matthew 17:17)

Every generation has an unbelieving, perverse spirit that must be broken off in order to enter into the time of blessing. My generation had to deal with the spirit of the '60s in order to enter into the Jesus Movement revolution.

"And with many other words he [Peter] testified and exhorted them, saying, 'Be saved from this perverse [crooked] generation.'" (Acts 2:40) Literally this generation must escape perversity, changing its direction, its outward image, which has become its curse.

Parents, your families must align themselves with the apostolic. Your kids will come through the Gate into blessing. Apostles must nurture these kids; they must live for the next generation and realize their rewards will continue into that generation. It is the only way to be saved from a crooked spirit.

So, take heart, new generation; this perverse spirit is dealt with when the people of God enter into the Gate laid open before them.

Proceed, then!

Chapter Six Outline
"Unveiling the Blessing of God"

SIGNS, WONDERS AND MIRACLES: THE BLESSINGS OF GOD

- The apostles, with their breaker anointing, create an apostolic people who have an understanding of the unchanging Jesus Christ
- It takes something a little more than the average, that breaker anointing, to create in people an attitude that Jesus Christ is desperately desirous of blessing the people of His Church and of the world
- The scriptural purpose of every sign, wonder and miracle is to reveal the greatness of the Godhead. The glory of God is manifested by the miraculous demonstration of the Spirit
- "This beginning of signs Jesus did in Cana of Galilee, and manifested His glory, and His disciples believed in Him." (John 2:11)
- Signs solicit a reaction
- A sign is a supernatural occurrence that points us to God (*semeion*, Strong's #4592)
- *Thambos* (Strong's #2285), "a sign that makes you wonder"
- Wonders have caused many to come to Christ, but they have also led others to question and scoff. Still, wonders elicit a reaction
- *Dunamis* (Strong's #1411), a "miracle" is an explosion of God's power

- *Dunamis* can be used to release a greater faith in the heart of the recipient to be used by the Lord to bring salvation and healing to others. Again, it generates a response, a reaction

TESTIMONY OF A BLESSING

- First Peter 3:9 warns us not to "[return] evil for evil or reviling for reviling, but on the contrary, blessing, knowing that you were called to this, that you may inherit a blessing."
- We are possessors of an unfulfilled prophecy — something God has spoken to us of His faithfulness in ministering grace and favor, so that we might have a testimony of His blessing
- One of the keys found in the apostolic anointing is to unveil the blessing of God and show that you have a part to play in inheriting that blessing. You must make actual what Christ already provided for you
- "Blessing" is "to invite divine favor, to confer favor or talent, to confer prosperity, to pronounce favor, to impart a spiritual quality, to call into life from things that are dead, to release God's creative power, to seal and protect"
- "...Indeed you have heard of the dispensation of the grace of God which was given to me for you...." (Ephesians 3:2)
- "...You were enriched in everything by Him in all utterance and all knowledge, even as the testimony of Christ was confirmed in you, so that you come short in no gift, eagerly waiting for the revelation of our Lord Jesus Christ...." (1 Corinthians 1:5-7)

- Apostolically-minded people are transgenerational in their thinking, and they know that everything God is going to do will not be accomplished through one person, nor even one generation
- "By faith Isaac blessed Jacob and Esau concerning things to come." (Hebrews 11:20)

THE BENJAMIN GATE

- "Now it came to pass, when she [Rachel] was in hard labor, that the midwife said to her, 'Do not fear; you will have this son also.' And so it was, as her soul was departing (for she died), that she called his name Ben-Oni [Son of My Sorrow]; but his father [Jacob] called him Benjamin [Son of My Right Hand]." (Genesis 35:17-18)
- "For thus says the Lord: After seventy years are completed at Babylon, I will visit you and perform My good word toward you, and cause you to return to this place. For I know the thoughts that I think toward you, says the Lord, thoughts of peace and not of evil, to give you a future and a hope. Then you will call upon Me, and I will listen to you. And you will seek Me and find Me, when you search for Me with all your heart. I will be found by you, says the Lord, and I will bring you back from your captivity; I will gather you from all the nations and from all the places where I have driven you, says the Lord, and I will bring you to the place from which I cause you to be carried away captive." (Jeremiah 29:10-14)

- "'I will declare the decree: The Lord has said to Me, "You are My Son, today I have begotten You. Ask of Me, and I will give You the nations for Your inheritance, and the ends of the earth for Your possession."'" (Psalm 2:7-8)

- The Father is speaking of the nations, turned over from Christ to us, and that we are to inherit all the blessings associated with reigning alongside the Son

- We have a future and a hope, based on the good thoughts the Father has for us, that being rescued from captivity into the Kingdom of Jesus, we are to inherit untold riches (blessings) as co-rulers with Christ

- Many of our spiritual gates have been closed or destroyed and are in need of repair, once we come out of captivity (veiled thinking)

- "All the land shall be turned into a plain from Geba to Rimmon south of Jerusalem. Jerusalem shall be raised up and inhabited in her place from Benjamin's Gate to the place of the First Gate and the Corner Gate, and from the Tower of Hananel to the king's winepresses. The people shall dwell in it; and no longer shall there be utter destruction, but Jerusalem shall be safely inhabited." (Zechariah 14:10-11)

- Benjamin represents to us a generation that God wants to bring forth out of the agony of the Church; there were two views held about Benjamin: Rachel saw him as "Sorrow"; Jacob saw him as his "Right Hand"

A TIME FOR IDENTITY

- "...Yet who knows whether you have come to the kingdom for such a time as this?" (Esther 4:14)

- This statement was enough to convince Esther she should try and see the king. She was so emboldened that she said, "...So I will go to the king, which is against the law; and if I perish, I perish!" (Verse 16)

- She had found identity in these words; she began to realize that her being there was not a mistake. She was born for a purpose, even if it cost her life. This generation must have a similar awakening: you were born at just the right time! You are not a mistake!

ATTRIBUTES OF A BLESSED PERSON

- A blessed person is of a good reputation, not just what he or she does, but who he or she *is*. He or she is a finisher, looking at the end result, instead of focused on where they are now. He or she is willing to pay a price for those end results (the manifestations of blessings), always finding a way to improve

- The blessed generation will realign its motivations, giftings, talents and abilities. The people will begin to fit their personality profiles, instead of seeming fractured and disjointed, acting out of character — something so prevalent in this generation currently. But they will be transformed into visionary leaders, apostolic men and women, who are directional; that is, being able to lay out clear plans

of action to release the blessing. They will be strategists, devising how the process toward blessing is developed. Their people management skills (to borrow a secular term) will be motivational in execution, causing others to rally around their cause; that is, seeing the blessing manifested

- They will be team-builders, bringing everyone up to their fullest potentials. They will have great shepherding, counseling anointing that brings others to repentance, and they will be able to reproduce productive people. They will be quite entrepreneurial in motivation, cultivating their influence in new arenas of daily life. They will be engineers, problem-solvers, bridge-builders; that is, conflict managers and negotiators, for the business people out there. (Dwayne Vanderclock)

7

Unveiling the Simplicity of God

BACK TO THE BASICS

Well, we've done it. We've managed to find ourselves at the last chapter of this book. I want to thank you for taking the time to read this. I pray to the Lord that He has encouraged your faith and increased an expectation within you to see Him move more fully in your life and ministry. I trust the Holy Spirit that I've presented the truths contained in this book in as concise and realistic a fashion as possible without "glossing" over what I feel are key components to the release of an apostolic spirit over the people of God.

There just remain a few points to bring out that sum up the gist of the book. One of the most vital components of releasing an apostolic spirit is to recognize the simplicity of God's plan for reviving the people of the Church to express so great a salvation to the people of the world.

I tend to agree with many of the detractors of the apostolic reformation when they say some revivalists have moved away from the basics of Christian foundation. That may sound like a cop-out in light of the encounters this book presents, but I beg to disagree. I think it is true that sometimes the Body of Christ tries to make things too difficult and loses sight of the importance of heart-felt, church-changing repentance, vibrant worship of God, personal, accountable relationships with the brethren and a deeper desire to study the black and white letters of God's written Word.

Way back in Chapter One of Volume 1 I stressed the preeminence of systematic study of the Bible as a vital key to the apostolic spirit. Without a true foundation based upon the sound fundamentals of our Christian theology, we are susceptible to fleshly fads that can lead to dangerous deception. We need to get back to the basics of the Church's foundation. Everything the apostles saw in the Book of Acts was centered and rooted in an expression of Christ's bodily ministry on the earth: they did what He did, they saw as He saw, they heard as He heard.

Now, I can't change a cessationist's mind. The bottom line is if you don't believe in miracles today, transcendent encounters, speaking in tongues and the gifts of the Spirit, you won't believe the contents of this book. You can't. Your beliefs and the testimonies contained herein are diametrically opposed to one another. The best you can say is I'm deceived — that these encounters didn't really happen as I say they did. The worst you can say is I'm a charlatan operating out of a fleshly desire to "hoodwink" well-meaning Christians to follow some bunny trail of esoteric experiences, to achieve some altered state of consciousness in an effort to dupe people in the name of God. These accusations are nothing new in my over thirty years of ministry; I've pretty much heard it all.

But you cannot shake my conviction that these encounters *did* happen, and that God is desirous to *continue* these encounters in the day-to-day lives of His people. I believe that *is* getting back to the basics, to the simplicity of God's desires to bless His people, the same today as He did in times past.

The apostolic reformation is a revival; a revival of the key components of the early Church. Yes, there has been flesh. Yes, there has been excess. There is no excuse, just shortcomings to work out. But I am convinced the majority of God's people are operating out of an intense desire to see His glory manifested in their lives and in their ministries.

This revival is a return to the basics; that sincere worship of God, that earnest relationship with Jesus, that pursuit of godly knowledge found in studying the Bible. All those things the apostles in the Book of Acts sought out, as well as the signs, wonders and miracles they saw, too.

Why can we not have both? Why can we not be balanced, well-studied Christians who have supernatural encounters wherein we see God cleanse the sick, heal the brokenhearted and sweep souls into His Kingdom?

I strive to find a balance between the move of God and the teaching of His Word. Look, I'm not saying we're supposed to bark at the moon here, dear readers. I don't harp on about holy laughter if it doesn't lead people to *see the miracles that Jesus saw*. I don't care if you get slain in the spirit in one of my meetings if it doesn't lead to *seeing the miracles that Jesus saw*. Getting drunk in the Holy Ghost is all fine and dandy, but if it doesn't allow me to *see the miracles that Jesus saw*, I'd rather stay sober, thank you very much.

My point here is this: a return to the basics, in my mind, is ... a return to the basics (chuckle.) That is, let's see what Jesus saw. Let's operate how He operated. Let's minister and pray and love and teach as He taught. Let's do it like the apostles of the old days did it. So many naysayers out there are nay saying (that's clever), "Hey, if one part of the reformation is goofy, the whole thing's goofy, so let's just do away with revival all together."

I think that's sad.

Yeah, sure, let's fix what's wrong, keep what works, and build on a greater experience of Christ, with a distinct fear of the Lord but also a passion to operate how He would like us to operate.

The restoration of the supernatural signs, wonders and miracles of the apostolic *is* a return to basics — the basics of the early Church. The simplicity of God's notion that the world is lost and hurting without Him, and we need His supernatural touch coupled with His authoritative Word centered in Christ working with the Holy Spirit to achieve the Trinity's desired results.

THE SIMPLE EXPRESSION OF THE APOSTOLIC

Let's itemize some of the simplistic operations of a person with an apostolic spirit. These are the "basic" day-to-day functions of an apostle. First and foremost, apostles have had such dynamic experiences in Christ that they are able to identify their motivation, their calling. Further, they are able to translate that motivation to other people, releasing them in their callings. The apostles prepare their hearts and prepare the hearts of the people to return to their first love, that is, the Lord Jesus Christ.

Apostles, through their glory encounters, cultivate sensitivity toward the anointing, and in turn they are able to encourage the people to foster a similar sensitivity. The apostle's faith is increased, teaching them to believe for the miraculous out of their very spirits — again, this, too, can be translated to the apostolic people. There comes a blending of the apostle's words with God's words to see His will fulfilled in the lives of people.

Apostles initiate people into the spiritual realm of God's power, elucidating the truth of the miraculous anointing that the Lord has given them. There is a discerning of spirits gift released over the people in these glory encounters that brings the manifest presence of God. In other words, there is power and authority behind the apostle's words and operation that can be converted into a revelation for the people.

Within these transcendent experiences, the apostles learn to proclaim God's purposes for the Church. They provide a sense of simplicity and clarity, demystifying the expression of God, creating precision encounters that change the hearts of the people. In short, apostles bring the Body toward further maturity in Christ.

The return to holiness is the hallmark of an apostle's supernatural expression. The signs, wonders and miracles present in an apostle's ministry call for supreme repentance, returning to the first love of the Christian faith. The apostles reveal the heart motives behind the people's actions. The apostles bring conviction, simplicity of methodology and a restoration of godly fear, purity and holiness in thought and deed.

The character of Christ, the fruit of the Spirit, is revealed in the purity and simplicity of the apostle's operation. As was written earlier, this character, this fruit, is an expression of the fatherhood anointing of God. In these expressions, the apostles are used to restitute the lacking thread of family that is pervading worldly culture. In other words, by their very expression of apostolic character, holiness, fathering/mothering spirits, keeping their families together, the apostles show how the supernatural anointing defines moral fiber and integrity.

With an apostolic slant, there is a supernatural release of strategy that outlines how the Church is to be presented to the community. This is where creative demonstrations of God's power are blended with outreach programs, social care and political initiatives. Imagine prison ministries and soup kitchens that heal the sick and restore the brokenhearted! The widows get more than financial relief and care; they get spiritual restoration as well! Orphanages present divine love that changes the spirits of the parentless, creating character and identity for children that would otherwise be lost!

The corporate apostolic church affects the political climate of the community, imparting godly power in the sorely needed areas of social justice and moral righteousness. Imagine words of knowledge and wisdom given in a timely manner to the city's leadership. How would that affect lawmaking decisions? It's something more than political pressure and caring for society's needs. It's the miraculous moving behind those motivations. It's a mixture of mercy and integrity coupled with a dynamic release of the breaker anointing. Lastly, true apostolic expression imbues the miraculous power of God into all facets of the administration of the church without the "rule of the iron fist" mentality, encouraging all congregants to achieve their fullest potential as co-laborers.

What about an apostolic influence on prophetic praise and worship? Imagine a supernatural breaker anointing that is released when the church is released in liberty to mimic the sounds of heaven, the spiritual warfare that is found in the praise and worship of the Father. With that kind of worship, the gifts of the Spirit are given free rein to touch God's people, and those souls who attend the service seeking a reality of the Father. I can't imagine a more exciting Sunday morning service to attend! Can you?

Let's take it a step further. Imagine prophetic intercession coupled with a release of the dynamic apostolic anointing. We'd find intercessors receiving a burden from God supercharged with supernatural strategy and unction to release that burden – perhaps on a citywide or even regional scale!

And some say the time of the apostle has passed?!?

It's simple to conceive of a need for the miraculous in the Body of Christ today. And while many people will disagree with the contents of this book, passing them off as superfluous, mystical "brain-washing," I beg to differ.

And I think many people out there would beg to differ with me. Those against the apostolic reformation might attack the importance of a book like this, but before you toss this finely crafted book (smile) in the trash:

ALLOW ME TO RESPOND

There's going to be a certain amount of controversy surrounding a book of this nature. I'm prepared to accept that. Some people will say I'm lying when I recount the testimony of Sister Mary in Southern California who came out to one of the meetings.

The Lord gave me a word of knowledge, and I pointed at her, saying, "You're scheduled for heart surgery in a couple of weeks because a portion of your heart is dying. God wants to heal it."

Sister Mary began to rejoice. I moved onto the next person God wanted to minister to, following the divine flow of love that aches to see people healed, saved and delivered. Fifteen minutes later, Sister Mary decides to disrupt my whole service by screaming out and running to the front, jumping up and down, hyperventilating as I was prophesying over another man.

She bounces up to me, knocks my hand off the other man's forehead, and I think, *How rude!* (Really, I don't mind God disrupting my services in *this* way.)

"Brother Maloney, God has healed my heart!"

"Uh, that's great, sister. Bless you."

"No, you don't understand.... God has *really* healed my heart."

So I give the tiniest of shrugs to the man I was praying for and turn to her. "Well, what do you mean?"

"I just had my third pacemaker put in. I can't find the pacemaker! And not only that, I can't find the scar!"

God not only healed her heart, He dissolved the pacemaker and made the scar disappear! Now, some will say I'm deceived. Some will say I imagined the encounter. Some will say it was a mental projection of some internal psychological desire for Sister Mary to be healed. Whatever that means. Some will even say I'm lying.

But you'll have a hard time convincing Sister Mary of that!

The truth is Jesus Christ hasn't changed. His Kingdom is established in the hearts of people as they're encouraged and edified, not only in the Word but also in the reality of His power made manifest in their mortal bodies.

The missing key ingredients, I believe, to this apostolic reformation are those life-changing, humbling supernatural encounters with God's authority and power. If the hecklers are blasting the renewal moves for the display of fleshly emotional outbursts, why not devote more time and energy to bringing balance by teaching what the Word of God shows that Jesus and the apostles did? I'm beginning to think there is some truth to that old quip, "Don't throw the baby out with the bath water."

If the critics and disbelievers are upset at the "weird" things going on in Charismatic services, why don't they seek out a revelation of an unchanging Christ who healed people in His day and wants to heal people in *this* day? Rather, they say all is false, all is wrong, all is excess. And people are still dying, unloved, untouched, unsaved. There must be *some* answer out there.

Why don't we all seek to have an encounter with the Father that not only drives us to worship Him in unity, enlightened by scripture, but also heals the poor souls with cancer and AIDS at the same time? How more evangelistic can you get? What's wrong with desiring something better for the people in *this* life than what Islam and Buddhism can offer? Why can't the Catholics, Baptists, Anglicans, Lutherans, Methodists, etc., see incontrovertible proof that God is not confined to their own human, denominational affiliation's definitions?

Why can't they be shown that Jesus is the only Way, Truth and Life ... and to prove it, your blind can see, your deaf can hear, your lame can walk? That's what *He* did when He was on the earth. That's what His apostles did when *they* were on the earth.

What's changed?

I find it strange that critics of the apostolic reformation harp on and on about all the "extra-scriptural" activities that are found in renewal, revival expressions. And, yes, mooing like a cow is extra-scriptural. But the basics of Christ's and His apostles' ministry — that is signs, wonders and miracles, visions, dreams, blind eyes opening, deaf ears hearing, lame people walking, dead people waking — is anything *but* extra-scriptural. It's because of the scriptures that we know how He and His operated. In fact, doesn't it seem extra-scriptural to say any of that activity ceased? I don't find that in my Bible, some verse that says, "And behold, this was the way things *were* done, but not anymore." Sure, cessationists can mold and warp a translation of scripture to support their hypothesis — something the Charismatics are incessantly accused of — but concerning the basics of supernatural activity (what Jesus and the apostles saw consistently in their ministries), it doesn't need superfluous interpretation. Jesus, Paul and Peter and a slew of others saw sick people healed, saved, delivered from demons and mental torment all the time. That was normal, not exceptionally esoteric experiences. And you find continuous, irrefutable proof of the supernatural's continuance throughout church history. It wasn't mystical to any of them, it was practical. It was the apostolic function in operation, under the motivation of God the Father.

This whole book has been about the *functionality* of the apostle. How is the apostle supposed to operate in ministry? My answer: by moving in the supernatural anointing just as the early-Church apostles did. We have many well-meaning bishops, prophets and pastors and church-planters catching the importance of apostolic *strategies* but losing the explosive power of apostolic *operation*; that is, signs, wonders and miracles *in* those strategies. Healing the sick, serving the brokenhearted with anointing that removes the hurt, evangelistic opportunity that is comprised of the tangible presence of God. Not just clever advertising, flashy websites and Twenty-First Century stratagems that incorporates splicing DVD clips of *The Passion of the Christ* with *The Lion, the Witch and the Wardrobe* into an ingenious thirty-minute (or less) sermon, complete with puppet show and full-color handouts.

Nothing wrong with any of that, I say, but how come we can't have the tangible presence of God with signs, wonders and miracles as well?

And, folks, I'm a measured man. I am not here saying I have obtained even a remote part of the fullness of supernatural expression that Christ and the apostles reached. If you were to come out to my ministry, please know that I don't see all that I'd like to see concerning this release of signs, wonders and miracles. We are all pressing toward that high standard, but it is my sincerest desire, as quantified as I am in ministry expression, that this book encourages and releases all of us to cooperate with the apostolic Spirit in faith so that we can enter into a greater demonstration of the apostle's anointing and functionality.

THE SIMPLE FUNCTIONALITY
OF THE APOSTOLIC

Apostles cannot be focused solely on strategy, but they must also be focused on functionality, operation, execution. They must have supernatural encounters *themselves*. Those kinds of encounters that *change* them into a whatever-it-takes-I-gotta-see-Jesus-move kind of person. Apostles must have encounters with Jesus that add the supernatural to their strategies. It's the missing ingredient that answers the critics' valid questions.

Without signs, wonders and miracles, divine healing, vibrant, prophetic heavenly worship and praise, the tangible anointing and complete inner-healing, deliverance and restoration, we are left with just another set of creative programs and philosophies that cannot impact the people with supernatural evidence that is found in the fullness and simplicity of God the Father's power. Critics will continue to criticize. People will leave churches unchanged, unmotivated and ultimately unfulfilled.

Here it is, all nicely wrapped up in one definitive sentence: *an apostle must have supernatural expression in his or her ministry to be truly apostolic.*

That's tough to swallow. Am I saying people who act apostolically are not called to be apostles because they don't have supernatural expression? No. I believe many people calling themselves apostles are truly called to be apostles, but it's possible they're lacking the central ingredient that will revolutionize their ministries: signs, wonders and miracles. The apostolic reformation is not just about renewal expressions. It's about renewal expressions that restore the miraculous in people's ministries — that's apostolic. Now, please note, these renewal expressions can be miraculous in nature, but only in a measure. Greater encounters in the Father, through relationship with Jesus, are what it takes truly to infuse a miraculous constitution in one's expression. That's what I hope this book aids: those greater encounters.

Our current definition of the apostolic has delivered some awesome aspects of the office of the apostle to the Body of Christ. But we need more. We need to be seeking those encounters with Jesus that incorporate the miraculous in our ministries on a regular, consistent basis. We need to have a physical manifestation in this realm, not just in the spirit. We need the Dancing Hand of God ... and the Word, and the character, and the relationships, and the strategy, and on and on. That's getting back to the basics. That is the simplicity of God's perfect plan for His people. All of Him. Not this part, excluding that part. The fullness of God. In spirit and in truth... and in demonstration.

Apostles must have transcendent experiences, or glory encounters, whatever you want to call them. Consistent moments in time where heaven invades this realm; the natural order of life is changed by the supernatural order of God's life. Apostles cannot release an apostolic breaker anointing without a revelation of the Father, the Son and the Holy Spirit in operation and manifestation that impacts them so much they're ruined. In a good way. Ruined on seeing the tangible Dancing Hand of God no matter what it costs, no matter what anyone says, no matter what strategies they have for making the Church "cutting-edge" in this day and age.

Maybe your apostolic expression is as a gatekeeper for your city. Maybe you're all about unity in the body. Maybe you're all about prophetic praise and worship. Maybe you've got an idea for mercy houses that take care of unwed mothers and AIDS victims. Maybe you want to reach the socially outcast with food lines and church planting and street mime. Great. You've got an apostolic heart. Now all that's needed is a supernatural expression that gets the AIDS victims healed, the unwed mothers restored, the socially outcast changed into the people of power God destined them to be.

It all comes from your own supernatural encounters. You would be so impacted by your experiences that you couldn't help *but* to translate those experiences to other people. Whether you're governmental, pastoral, evangelistic — incorporate the supernatural! Press in to your own experiences! That will advance the Kingdom of God! That will change the world! That will be apostolic....

In Acts 2 when Peter gave his famous sermon, revival broke out as he spoke under the influence of the Holy Ghost. Yes, that was a sovereign move of God, but when Peter was sharing what kind of encounter he'd just had, he was *expecting* the Spirit to come down on the people listening to him. He expected a manifestation of God. (Check out his statement in 1 Peter 1:12.) He provoked the people into the presence of God. The Lord honored his revelation by providing an encounter for the people gathered around him.

So press in!

Remember the statement from Pastor Bill Johnson I quoted way back in the beginning: "Wherever I have found the activity of God — that activity can also become my possession." People can inherit the manifest presence of God based on your experiences as the Holy Spirit wills and directs in wisdom! The Dancing Hand of God can be translated. The fullness of God's greatness, power and authority is there for the taking!

So, apostles and apostolic people, press in!

Chapter Seven Outline

"Unveiling the Simplicity of God"

BACK TO THE BASICS

- One of the most vital components of releasing an apostolic spirit is to recognize the simplicity of God's plan for reviving not only the people of the Church, but the people of the world as well

- Everything the apostles saw in the Book of Acts was centered and rooted in an expression of Christ's bodily ministry on the earth: they did what He did, they saw as He saw, they heard as He heard

- Without a true foundation based upon the sound fundamentals of our Christian theology, we are susceptible to fleshly fads that can lead to dangerous deception. We need to get back to the basics of the Church's foundation

- The restoration of the supernatural signs, wonders and miracles of the apostolic *is* a return to basics – the basics of the early Church. The simplicity of God's notion that the world is lost and hurting without Him, and we need His supernatural touch coupled with His authoritative Word centered in Christ working with the Holy Spirit to achieve the Trinity's desired results

THE SIMPLE EXPRESSION OF THE APOSTOLIC

- Apostles have had such dynamic experiences in Christ that they are able to identify their motivation, their calling. They are able to translate that motivation to other people, releasing them in their callings

- The apostles prepare their hearts and prepare the hearts of the people to return to their first love, Jesus Christ
- Apostles, through their glory encounters, cultivate sensitivity toward the anointing, and in turn they are able to encourage the people to foster a similar sensitivity. The apostle's faith is increased, teaching them to believe for the miraculous out of their very spirits — again, translated to the apostolic people
- Apostles initiate people into the spiritual realm of God's power, elucidating the truth of the miraculous anointing that the Lord has given them. There is a discerning of spirits gift released over the people in these glory encounters that brings the manifest presence of God
- Within these transcendent experiences, apostles proclaim God's purposes for the Church. They provide a sense of simplicity and clarity, demystifying the expression of God, creating precision encounters that change the hearts of the people
- The return to holiness is the hallmark of an apostle's supernatural expression. The signs, wonders and miracles present in an apostle's ministry call for supreme repentance, returning to the first love of the Christian faith. The apostles reveal the heart motives behind the people's actions. The apostles bring conviction, simplicity of methodology and a restoration of godly fear, purity and holiness in thought and deed

- The character of Christ, the fruit of the Spirit, is revealed in the purity and simplicity of the apostle's operation. This character, this fruit, is an expression of the fatherhood anointing of God. The apostles are used to restitute the lacking thread of family that is pervading worldly culture
- With an apostolic slant, there is a supernatural release of strategy that outlines how the Church is to be presented to the community
- The corporate apostolic church affects the political climate of the community, imparting godly power in the sorely needed areas of social justice and moral righteousness
- Apostolic expression imbues the miraculous power of God into all facets of the administration of the church, encouraging all congregants to achieve their fullest potential as co-laborers
- Apostolic influence on prophetic praise and worship creates a supernatural breaker anointing that is released where the church is at liberty to mimic the sounds of heaven, the spiritual warfare that is found in the praise and worship of the Father
- Prophetic intercession coupled with a release of the dynamic apostolic anointing creates intercessors who receive a burden from God supercharged with supernatural strategy and unction to release that burden

THE SIMPLE FUNCTIONALITY OF THE APOSTOLIC

- Apostles cannot be focused solely on strategy, but they must also be focused on functionality, operation, execution
- They must have supernatural encounters *themselves*
- Without signs, wonders and miracles, divine healing, vibrant, prophetic heavenly worship and praise, the tangible anointing and complete inner-healing, deliverance and restoration, we are left with just another set of creative programs and philosophies that cannot impact the people with supernatural evidence that is found in the fullness and simplicity of God the Father's power
- An apostle must have supernatural expression in his or her ministry to be truly apostolic

About the Author

James Maloney has been in full-time ministry for nearly forty years, traveling extensively across the United States and abroad in more than 40 countries, averaging 250-300 services yearly. In America, he speaks in healing and prophetic seminars, teaching the mechanics of ministry anointing release, and in leadership conferences, ministering to hundreds of pastors. He preaches in many local and regional church conferences, hosting schools of the supernatural, helping to equip the people of God in a release of the miraculous so they can extend the rule of His Kingdom in their own communities. He has made numerous media appearances on Christian television programs and radio shows.

As a revivalist, his work is marked with an apostolic/prophetic anointing for the release of God's power. In his revival conferences, one of his main messages is the release of the glory, drawing people into encounters with a mighty God. Ministering in a prophetic flow, he has spoken the personal word of the Lord to thousands individually, producing a greater sense of identity, motivation and clarity of direction. Operating in the revelation gifts of the Spirit, physical conditions are revealed, creating faith to receive healing.

He actively hosts international crusades and has preached to crowds of tens of thousands, evangelizing in extremely remote areas of the world, with heavy influence in closed countries of the Middle East and

Asia. He has worked with indigenous ministers in establishing many churches worldwide, licensing and ordaining hundreds of pastors.

James holds a D.D., a Th.D. and a Ph.D. He has taught for over twenty years in several Bible schools, including Christ for the Nations Institute in Dallas, Texas, and Kingdom Faith Training College in Horsham, England.

Dr. Maloney is the president of The ACTS Group International (AGI), an apostolic network that provides peer-level accountability and mentoring to this generation of ministers, and the next, who are eager to see a fuller release of the miraculous power of the Lord Jesus Christ by hosting teams in overseas crusades and conferences.

James and his wife, Joy, live in the Dallas-Fort Worth area.

For more information, please contact:

The ACTS Group International
P.O. Box 1166
Argyle, Texas 76226-1166
www.answeringthecry.com

Printed in the United States
By Bookmasters